MANAGEMENT RESET

Organizing for Sustainable Effectiveness

Edward E. Lawler III and Christopher G. Worley
with David Creelman

Foreword by Michael Crooke

JOSSEY-BASS
A Wiley Imprint
www.josseybass.com

Published by Jossey-Bass
A Wiley Imprint
989 Market Street, San Francisco, CA 94103-1741—www.josseybass.com

Readers should be aware that Internet Web sites offered as citations and/or sources for further information may have changed or disappeared between the time this was written and when it is read.

Limit of Liability/Disclaimer of Warranty: While the publisher and author have used their best efforts in preparing this book, they make no representations or warranties with respect to the accuracy or completeness of the contents of this book and specifically disclaim any implied warranties of merchantability or fitness for a particular purpose. No warranty may be created or extended by sales representatives or written sales materials. The advice and strategies contained herein may not be suitable for your situation. You should consult with a professional where appropriate. Neither the publisher nor author shall be liable for any loss of profit or any other commercial damages, including but not limited to special, incidental, consequential, or other damages.

Jossey-Bass books and products are available through most bookstores. To contact Jossey-Bass directly call our Customer Care Department within the U.S. at 800-956-7739, outside the U.S. at 317-572-3986, or fax 317-572-4002.

Jossey-Bass also publishes its books in a variety of electronic formats. Some content that appears in print may not be available in electronic books.

Library of Congress Cataloging-in-Publication Data
Lawler, Edward E.
    Management reset: organizing for sustainable effectiveness / Edward E. Lawler and Christopher G. Worley; foreword by Michael Crooke. —1st ed.
        p. cm.
    Includes bibliographical references and index.
    ISBN 978-0-470-63798-2 (hardback)
    ISBN 978-1-118-00842-3 (ebk)
    ISBN 978-1-118-00843-0 (ebk)
    ISBN 978-1-118-00844-7 (ebk)
        1. Organizational effectiveness.   2. Management.   3. Sustainable development.   I. Worley, Christopher G.   II. Title.
    HD58.9.L389   2011
    658.4'08—dc22

                                                                                                2010050246

Printed in the United States of America

FIRST EDITION
HB Printing   10 9 8 7 6 5 4 3 2 1

Contents

Foreword

When I was first introduced to integrating environmental concerns into a company's thinking, I was working for a private lumber company in Northern California. The company had been family owned for over a hundred years. Clear-cutting (removing all of the trees in one area) was not allowed. Instead, the company left the biggest, most prolific trees to seed the land after the other trees had been taken. The result of this century-old silviculture prescription was a business that worked in every way. The land produced a steady, sustainable volume of trees to keep the mill running near capacity. The small company town of Scotia was a robust center of commerce where the well-paid and motivated employees intertwined their lives with the company and the sacred land with which they coexisted. Hunting, fishing, hiking, and camping were all regular weekend activities.

The day that a large financial company purchased our lumber company was a sad one. Within a month of the purchase we were directed to write timber harvest plans to cut down the very trees that were giving life to the next generation of trees. Clear-cutting became the standard method of extracting as much, as fast as we could. In an instant a previously sustainable company began maximizing short-term growth and profits to pay off the leverage that was used to gain control of the hundred-year-old firm. We all know the rest of the story: a quick rise of wealth creation for the raiders and bankruptcy for the company.

Unfortunately, this story and many like it are all too common. I do not think that short-term financial engineering is what Milton Friedman had in mind when he wrote of management's goal to "maximize shareholders' wealth." I'm convinced Mr. Friedman would not have sanctioned the actions of the lumber company.

It is time for us to be clear that there are right and wrong ways to maximize shareholder value. It is time to embrace a new way of thinking, or, as Lawler and Worley posit, a *reset*, that brings social responsibility and environmental stewardship to the mission of the organization. The authors also argue that organizations are designed for stability, not change. This puts the focus on a different kind of sustainability—the ability of an organization to sustain itself in a tumultuous world. Put the need to see beyond short-term profit together with the need for organizational structures that are built to change and you are talking about the need for a complete management reset.

After my forestry experience I went to business school to find out what had happened and why. I wanted to understand leveraged buyouts and their value to society. Who, exactly, did this one-time wealth creation event enrich? It certainly was not the employees. It was not the company's suppliers, who also had a short-term spike in sales for a few years, after which the revenue stream ended. It was not the company's customers, who started getting inferior-quality product after the virgin trees were gone. Unsurprisingly, those who were enriched turned out to be a few financial engineers who "cracked the code" and optimized their personal financial situation to the detriment of society at large.

We are at the crossroads. Will we evolve Friedman's message to include a long-term perspective or will we fail to glean the wisdom of our recent history and continue to follow a path that is not sustainable? We need to accept business models that don't destroy the forest in an attempt to get more trees. We need business models in which being nimble and future-focused is coded into the organization's DNA so that change does not threaten the survival of firms. This book presents one that does just that.

In another chapter of my career I was the CEO of Patagonia, Inc. Patagonia, much like the lumber company in Northern California, is a private company that makes all of its strategic decisions with a long-term perspective. The founders, Yvon (YC) and Malinda Chouinard, handcrafted the corporate culture in a mirror image of themselves. They are the antithesis of the financial engineers who bankrupted the lumber company. YC is committed to "the best product possible" and to the product being made "with the least amount of harm to the environment."

Malinda is committed to social responsibility and understanding and preserving the wisdom of the past (architecture, indigenous cultures, customs, and so on). Together they synergistically developed a unique culture, which has propelled their company to the top echelons of successful organizations worldwide.

There was something at Patagonia that was "magic." Something about the value alignment between the stakeholders and the organization. Customers had a strong emotional connection to the brand. Internally, job satisfaction (happiness) was very high. We had over nine hundred applications for every job opening in the organization, and we were moving up *Fortune*'s "Best Companies to Work For" list on a regular basis.

I started referring to this "magic" as FLOW, as defined by Mihaly Csikszentmihalyi. I had read his ground-breaking book describing a condition in which an individual becomes so involved in an activity that nothing else matters; as the task becomes harder, the individual skill set increases and the feedback mechanism delivers motivation to keep the activity escalating. Often this state is described when paradigm-breaking creativity is launched.

Serendipitously, Mihaly came to Patagonia in 2000 to interview YC and me for a book he was writing, *Good Business*. When I got the chance to talk to him directly, I surmised that FLOW (and the motivation associated with it) could be a by-product of alignment around powerful values guiding shared goals and objectives. I had "come under its spell" at the lumber company pre-buyout and at Patagonia. I wondered out loud if this FLOW had anything to do with our high job satisfaction and overall success. Mihaly was intrigued. I entered the PhD program at Claremont Graduate University within months, and Mihaly and I started working on the IV Forces model.

The IV Forces (IVF) is a model of contemporary values. It is hoped that this model could be thought of as an "update" to Mr. Friedman's model. The IVF model captures the relevant "macro-values" of society today: environmental stewardship, corporate citizenship, product or service quality, and financial strength.

These four macro-values encompass the most pressing issues facing organizations today and were the bedrock beneath the lumber company and Patagonia. I refer to them as macro-values or forces because they are essentially broad categories that encircle numerous related values. For example, the macro-value of environmental stewardship refers to the need for organizations to recognize and mitigate their impact on the natural environment; it also represents the ultimate goal of integrating environmental concerns into product (and service) design in order to develop closed-loop manufacturing processes that eliminate waste. Corporate citizenship represents the social realm and the organization's relationships with stakeholders, ranging from employees to suppliers to neighbors in the local community to government entities. Product or service quality echoes Patagonia's mission to make the best product and relates to the need to excel at the organization's core competency. Finally, financial strength refers to the need for organizations to be financially sound; without this, the other values become irrelevant.

The main point of the IVF model is that none of the four forces can be ignored without massive degradation of the organization's output. The values do not operate in isolation; rather, they function as a system and feature many areas of overlap and interaction. Decision making is rarely, if ever, guided by one of the four forces individually. For example, product or service quality is defined as striving to achieve the best possible product with the least possible social and environmental harm. Financial strength is integrally related to the other three values, which cannot function without an economically viable organization.

Furthermore, the four forces are mutually reinforcing: each of the elements is important individually, but when leveraged as a collective group the relationships are synchronous. The power of environmental stewardship is amplified when financial strength is realized, and vice versa. The same can be said of any of the values. For example, when an organization is financially successful, it can invest in environmental innovations, such as new recycled and recyclable fabrics or not having to harvest trees close to a stream, which prevents erosion and increases biological activity in the stream; these are examples of activities that ultimately reduce long-term expenses and enhance long-term financial performance.

So how do we begin to develop an organization that wants to embed and integrate these values or forces into an organization? How do we create structures that not only respect those values, but are robust in the face of disruptive change? I believe that reading *Management Reset: Organizing for Sustainable Effectiveness* is a mandatory prerequisite. Edward E. Lawler III and Christopher G. Worley have, without question, developed the building blocks of executing an IV Forces model. The book not only captures the spirit of the moment but also interprets that spirit into a guide on how to design sustainably effective organizations. The authors outline exactly how a sustainably effective organization takes these principles and converts them into company initiatives.

Reading *Management Reset* was so refreshing. There are hundreds of "eco-groovy" business books that have very little real-world understanding of the complex conditions that organizations must face on a day-to-day basis. There are many "pure play" business books that do not deal with the complex conditions that organizations face. *Management Reset: Organizing for Sustainable Effectiveness* is a pragmatic, research-backed text that delivers a compelling message. In short, it has the right message at the right time.

So what would Milton Friedman say about companies that subscribe to the sustainable management approach? My guess, and hope, is that he would acknowledge that in order to "maximize shareholders' wealth" an organization must look at all the market forces and optimize for the long term.

I am an optimist, and as such I will continue to believe that we can turn the tide and build a society in which aligning one's personal values with those of their chosen work will not only increase the probability of FLOW, it will lead to sustainable effectiveness.

MICHAEL CROOKE, PhD
Visiting Distinguished Professor of Business
Graziadio School of Business and Management,
Pepperdine University
Former CEO, Patagonia

Preface:
From Change to
Sustainable Effectiveness

When we published *Built to Change* in mid-2006, the economy was still growing. Shortly thereafter, the signs of a deep financial crisis appeared, and soon there was a global recession. Not surprisingly, many corporations had difficulty adjusting to the dramatic changes the recession created. To our relief, organizations that had many of the agility features we described in *Built to Change* fared better than most other firms. Because they had routines for looking into the future, cultures and reputations that supported change, flexible human resource practices, and effective change capabilities, change was easier for them. Adapting to the economic crisis was just another change, not something that required new behavior.

Watching corporations struggling to adjust to the recession prompted us to do something we were considering doing anyway—write an updated version of *Built to Change*. *Built to Change* was a research-based vision of what an agile organization should look like. Our idea was to write a new book that was more results-based, that put more "meat on the bones," and that described how organizations were actually implementing our agility design ideas. We felt that because our research post–*Built to Change* had given us new insights into and ideas about how organizations can effectively respond to change, it was time to write a new book on agility. But our next book on agility will have to wait; *Management Reset* is not it.

In *Built to Change* we focused primarily on financial performance, in particular how to achieve consistently above-average financial performance. As we began to discuss our new book on change, we realized that this focus was seriously limited and out of date when viewed within the context of the dramatic changes that have taken place recently. It is now clear that financial sustainability is a necessary but insufficient organization objective.

Organizations must perform well financially, but they must also address at least two other kinds of performance in order to be viable in the long term. In today's global economy, organizations also need to focus on their social responsibility bottom line and their environmental bottom line. Simply stated, we no longer agree with Milton Friedman that organizations should be only concerned about their financial performance and that they should only do "good" when it leads to financial gains and the creation of shareholder value. What was once a compelling argument in the capitalist world is no longer valid, and as a result, organizations that follow it ultimately will be obsolete.

Because of our changing views on organizational effectiveness, we decided to write a book about how organizations can be designed and managed so that they are economically, socially, and environmentally sustainable—in our words, sustainably effective. *Management Reset* is not about convincing you that organizations need to be sustainably effective; it is a book about how organizations can be sustainably effective.

We feared that spending time on why organizations need to change would result in an overly judgmental tone and take up valuable space that is better dedicated to describing how to move toward sustainable effectiveness. It may also be unnecessary, as a recent UN global survey of CEOs found that 93 percent believe that sustainability issues are critical to the future success of their companies. We believe there is too much sensational and emotional rhetoric about why there is a need to change and not enough discussion about how to change. Thus we will leave to others the arguments about whether it is the right objective for organizations at this time.

What we won't leave to others is the writing of a useful guide to how organizations need to be managed and designed to deal with the complex issues involved in achieving sustainable effectiveness. Creating a sustainably effective organization is clearly a major challenge, greater than that of designing organizations that are built to change. Thus we begin the book by making the bold statement that what is needed is a major management reset, not merely an approach to organization design that allows for rapid change.

Just to be clear, we believe that being agile is an important part of being sustainably effective. We use and adapt many of the principles from *Built to Change* in this book. But being agile isn't enough. A sustainably effective organization must also adjust its strategy, organization design, and leadership practices to support goals that include social justice and environmental health.

We believe that the management reset we present is long overdue and should be the third major management reset since the beginning of the twentieth century. We realize this is a bold position and in some respects an arrogant one. For over a decade, management gurus have been calling for and trying to develop a new approach to management that deals more effectively with today's business environment. We don't claim to have all the details worked out on what that management approach should look like, but we do believe that in this book we identify the key design features that will support organizations in achieving sustainable effectiveness.

We wrote *Management Reset* with an eye toward three types of readers. We want it to be readable and read by managers who are interested in a new approach to management. We want it to be read by consultants whose business it is to advise organizations on strategy and organization change. Finally, we want it to be read by academics who are concerned with organization design, organization development, and strategy.

Writing a book that is credible and readable by managers, consultants, and academics proved to be a significant challenge. We decided to present rational, logical, and credible arguments that are based on research and consulting. But we didn't stop there. We decided to go beyond rational arguments and include a personal element and perspective. We also decided to put more emphasis on showing people what is possible than on telling them what they should do. In trying to balance good solid thinking about organization effectiveness with what is interesting to a diverse audience, there were times when in the early drafts of this book we slipped into an academic, preachy tone. We think we corrected this in later drafts, and hope that as a result our book is both helpful and compelling. That is the ultimate goal we set for ourselves.

Of course, *Management Reset* is grounded in good research and thinking, but we found ourselves needing to push beyond what researchers have studied. We also had to ignore some research that was interesting but simply was not useful because it focused solely on financial performance. We have included numerous examples and some personal experiences in order to make it clear that there is a reality to our ideas and suggestions, not just academic theorizing.

We think we can guarantee that what we have written will raise your awareness of the issues and the challenges that are involved in creating sustainably effective organizations. Even if you don't agree with us that organizations need to pay attention to sustainable effectiveness, we think you will find our arguments and suggestions about how organizations should be designed intriguing, thoughtful, and in some instances radical.

We don't believe anyone who has been a careful observer of today's business world can make the argument that current management approaches are effective and represent the best way to organize and manage complex organizations. All too often, an organization that has outstanding financial performance today ends up being a mess tomorrow. All too often, the best financial performers are the ones that have poor social and environmental records. There has to be a better way.

Our society needs approaches to organizing and managing complex organizations that produce consistently good financial performance and contribute to the well-being of the planet and those who live on it. The old ways of managing organizations simply are not good enough. We think we have made a strong case in this book for a management reset that changes the very essence of how organizations are managed and as a result positions them well to deal with a broader definition of effectiveness than we used in *Built to Change*.

As we wrote this book, we frequently paused and thought to ourselves, "Who are we to claim that we have the insights and expertise to develop a major management reset?" It was, and is, an audacious target. But we are more and more confident that most, if not all, of our shots are on target. We may not have all the pieces in place, and we certainly don't know all the details of how to make sustainable management work, but we believe that we have gone a long way toward identifying the major elements of an approach to management that will achieve sustainable effectiveness. We hope you agree and will share your comments—both affirmative and critical—with us. Sustainable effectiveness is something that everyone needs to learn more about and get better at. There is a lot riding on our being successful.

| Time for a Reset

The time for a management reset has come. A management reset is needed that is not simply a matter of making leaders more effective or adopting the latest twist on how to engage employees. It must be a seismic change, a complete rethinking of what an organization's objectives are and the way they are achieved, the kind of reset that has happened only twice in the past century.

What will this new world of management be like? Consider the following scenario. Your work week begins with you walking into a company meeting of 150 people. While many people are physically present, many are attending virtually. Everyone has gathered to design a new product or service solution to reduce water use in rural homes—an issue your futuring process has determined will soon become a huge environmental issue in Southeast Asia. Included in the meeting are company employees as well as members of nongovernmental organizations, governments, health officials, and potential customers.

For the next two-and-a-half days you work in a series of small groups, describing and designing a solution that everyone agrees will generate a reasonable profit, a positive impact on the natural environment, and an improvement in the quality of life in rural communities. At the end of the meeting you are exhausted but delighted by the outcome of the meeting. You wish you could go to "your office" to decompress and catch up on what has happened in the past two days, but like almost everyone else in your company, you do not have an office. Instead, you access your video mail via the link in your car and arrive home in time to spend an evening with your family.

Will environmental and social issues really be a front and center issue in the next management reset? Absolutely. The next reset will require companies to be as keenly tuned to a range of societal stakeholders as they are now to a range of investors. Just this orientation already exists at Patagonia, PepsiCo, and Unilever.

Will you really get a chance to think ahead and address issues before they become crises? Yes, and it won't be just you and a few key managers involved in futuring processes. It will include most members of your organization and key stakeholders. Such broad involvement in thinking about the future is the only way organizations will be able to keep up with the pace of change.

Will your job description call for you to participate in large-group design meetings? The answer is no because job descriptions lost their usefulness years ago, and the next management reset will acknowledge that jobs themselves are an obsolete notion. Instead, work will be defined by the projects and initiatives that drive current effectiveness and create future strategies. And don't count on your place in the hierarchy to give you power—there are many leaders in your organization because people rise to the occasion when leadership is needed.

Will offices be a thing of the past? Yes—to a large extent they already are. They are an expensive artifact of an era when the Internet did not exist and office size and location was a source of status and a valued reward. In the next reset, where you work will be determined by what you are doing and who you are doing it with. It is just as likely to be conducted in virtual space as it is in physical space.

A Brief History of Management

To understand the future of management, you first have to understand the past. We cannot successfully build the nimble, future-oriented, and socially savvy organization of tomorrow if we don't understand why new management approaches are created. Let's look at the first two resets so we will be able to drive the next one.

In the early 1900s, Western civilization had reached a developmental tipping point.[1] A shift in consumer demand was driven by population growth and an expanding number of social classes that multiplied the range of products and services that people wanted. At the same time, mass production technology burst onto the scene thanks to Henry Ford's development of the assembly line.

The first management reset occurred when the rational principles of bureaucracy—the only management framework available— were married with the scalable technology of mass production. It was a match made in heaven and led to the development of what we call *command and control organizations* (CCOs). Buoyed by the certainty of demand growth, the ability of CCOs to meet customer demand fostered an era of unprecedented economic growth.

Business and social changes also triggered the second management reset. The growing complexity of work, the rising education level of the workforce, and innovations in management practice led to the creation of organizations committed to employee involvement. In contrast to the assumptions embedded in CCOs, people were considered sources of creativity and innovation and not just mindless dolts needing autocratic supervision.[2]

The second reset led to the development of high involvement organizations (HIOs) and showed that people could be an important source of competitive advantage when they are managed in the "right way." Buoyed by the certainty of long-term productivity improvements, the high involvement approach to management garnered a lot of attention and generated significant increases in profitability. However, it did not replace command and control management as the dominant approach to managing large organizations.[3]

The economic success that accompanied both resets reinforced the management principles used by CCOs and HIOs. While GM and Exxon conjure up images of mechanistic bureaucracies, Whole Foods and Procter & Gamble are associated with visions of employee involvement. We are not going to debate whether the CCO and HIO management principles served us well; instead, we are going to argue that they are now obsolete for three reasons.

The first reason is the way social and business environments are changing. In the past, both the rate and complexity of environmental change were manageable using CCO and HIO principles. The luxury of growth in demand covered up mistakes in product and market development. Today, demand growth is much less certain, and most organizations are overwhelmed by the rapid changes that come from so many places and in so many different forms. Managers now find it nearly impossible to achieve the speed and agility required to keep up with, much less get ahead of, changes in the business environment.

There is an easily identified explanation for their confusion. CCOs and HIOs have trouble dealing with rapid change because they both wrongly assume that the business environment will be relatively stable. Buried deep in the managerial psyche is the belief that change is the enemy and that financial success can be achieved best by remaining stable.

We believe organizations must change the way they view change. To respond effectively to the type and rate of change they are experiencing, organizations must see change as inevitable and a chance to create a new source of competitive advantage. If they don't, they are going to go the way of the dodo bird and the dinosaur.

A second reason the CCO and HIO management principles are obsolete is the rapid pace of globalization. China is now the world's second-largest economy (and headed toward being the largest). Emerging markets will contribute more to economic growth than the U.S., European, or Japanese markets. Organizations that operate globally have no choice: they must operate within a variety of social, regulatory, and governmental contexts and with diverse workforces.

Unfortunately, the path to globalization is littered with cases in which organizations from developed countries have been fully or partially responsible for supporting sweatshop working conditions, child labor, environmentally damaging practices, or other unethical activities. Too many organizations, especially those from the United States and Western Europe, have exhibited patronizing attitudes—not every culture needs or wants a Swanson's Hungry Man dinner or a McDonald's drive-thru window.

We believe that organizations must see developing countries, emerging markets, and different cultures as sources of innovation and diversity, not something to be homogenized or conquered. The business models of CCOs and HIOs are not able to deal with today's complex, global business environment. They were designed for a world that no longer exists and should be relegated to history!

The third reason the CCO and HIO management principles are obsolete is environmental degradation. It is occurring at an ever-increasing rate. The more material wealth organizations create, the more the natural environment suffers. CCOs and HIOs have proven to be hauntingly shortsighted and complicit in doing harm to the planet's natural environment. As long as organizations operate without having to account for the damage they do to the environment, they will continue to destroy it.

We can no longer hope that technology will come to the rescue; the available evidence suggests that the damage being done to the planet exceeds any technology's ability to repair it. A management approach is required that maximizes value creation, not just shareholder return. Value creation must be judged by a proper accounting for an organization's impact on the planet and people as well as its profits.

A management approach is required that maximizes value creation, not just shareholder return. Value creation must be judged by a proper accounting for an organization's impact on the planet and people as well as its profits.

The failure of the existing management approaches to deal with today's world compels us to argue strongly for a third management reset. The management reset we will describe in this book involves more than just modifying how organizations handle globalization, the number of levels of management they have, how diversified they are, and how they treat their people. This is not a book about sustainability initiatives and being more "green," nor is it about corporate social responsibility programs. It is about designing and managing organizations to be sustainably effective. It is about a new coherent approach to managing large, complex organizations that fits today's and tomorrow's world.

Sustainable Management

What does a new management approach need to do in order to be effective? It must create organizations that value change and people and have the capability to implement strategies that generate profit, support social well-being, and improve the environment. Profitable organizations need to be built that are as interested in their community as they are in their debt, as concerned about their carbon footprint as they are about their cash flow.

We think the right name for the management approach that works best in today's world is *sustainable management*. Sustainable management organizations (SMOs) are much more agile and adaptable than CCOs, much more outward looking than HIOs, and much more effective at addressing the demands of multiple stakeholders than is either of the old management approaches.

Organization Effectiveness

For most of the twentieth century, it was accepted that organizations should primarily serve one stakeholder—the owners—and focus on one goal—maximizing profit. Corporate boards and the financial markets judged organization effectiveness only in terms of financial performance, including revenue and earnings growth, stock price, and profitability. There was little concern for other stakeholders or for the ability to innovate and change.

The logic and design of CCOs and HIOs makes them incapable of supporting both rapid change and multiple outcomes. They love stability and are optimized for financial performance.

We believe that organizations should pursue sustainable effectiveness. They should be agile enough to remain effective over time and perform effectively in three areas: people, planet, and profit. Organization effectiveness should be judged on two dimensions:

- *Does the organization generate sustainable outcomes and act responsibly toward all stakeholders?* This is often referred to as the triple-bottom line, but the broader principle is manifest in the day-to-day decisions that give social and environmental outcomes equal standing with economic concerns.[4] SMOs are designed to do consistently well in all three of these areas; they do not let the desire for profit squeeze out the others.

- *Can the organization sustain effectiveness?* This translates to questions about adaptability, innovation, risk management, and an appropriate identity. Whereas CCOs assume stability in their structures and processes, and HIOs assume stability in their workforce, SMOs assume little will be stable in the long term. To be truly sustainable, SMOs commit not only to triple-bottom-line goals but also to having execution, innovation, and implementation capabilities that support change.

The Way Organizations Are Managed

Four core issues determine the way organizations are managed. To be effective, SMOs must address each of them with principles and practices that fit the business environment and produce sustainable effectiveness. We will introduce them here, and we will return to them throughout the book.

- *The way value is created.* SMOs substitute robust strategies for competitive ones. A robust strategy is successful over a broad range of conditions over a long period of time and capable of changing to address short-term opportunities and threats. It is crafted to create a combination of social, environmental, and economic value. It looks for a series of momentary competitive advantages.
- *The way work is organized.* SMOs need a design that makes them adaptable, responsive to changing conditions, and responsive to multiple stakeholders. The structure, work processes, and management processes of SMOs need to facilitate innovation and execution, collaboration and efficiency. Achieving this requires high levels of contact between employees and the business environment; the development of innovative units; flexible, budget-less control systems; new ways of working; and value-creating networks.
- *The way people are treated.* Key to the success of organizations that create value based on their competencies and

capabilities is how they treat talent. It is critical that the right talent be attracted, retained, developed, and motivated. To do this, SMOs need reward systems that focus on skills, talent management systems that identify and retain the "right" employees, and performance management systems that are tied to the organization's strategy.

- *The way behavior is guided.* How employees behave is strongly influenced by the combination of their organization's leadership style and culture. SMOs need to be led with an approach that creates leaders throughout the organization and that rejects the imperial CEO model. They need a culture that loves change, innovation, and sustainable performance.

The sustainable management approach is being invented by organizations and researchers around the world. By looking at organizations that are breaking free from their CCO or HIO roots, it is possible to specify the major features of sustainable management. It is a management approach that may at times seem bizarre and at other times compelling. Consider for a moment a few common questions and the way some uncommon organizations answer them:

- Do you think that maximizing profits is the overriding reason for a corporation to exist? Certainly that is not what drives people to work for Patagonia, a company committed to environmental responsibility. Chick-fil-A closes on Sundays because religious values trump the profit motive. Even hard-driving GE devotes considerable attention to matters of integrity, as documented in its *Citizenship Report.*
- Do you think of your organization as a stand-alone entity rather than as part of a value network? Management at Eli Lilly used to think of it as a fully integrated pharmaceutical company, but now they think of it as an integrated pharmaceutical network. What difference does this make? It means options that formerly would not have been considered are now a natural way of operating.

When leaders at Lilly have tough chemical problems to tackle, they do not just assign them to their crack team of scientists, they reach out to a broad network of scientists by posting problems on the Internet and rewarding the best solutions. Lilly operates in terms of accessing the capabilities needed, wherever in the world they exist. Accessing capabilities is not a matter of whether or not they sit within the company's walls, it is a matter of where they exist.

- Do you define your market as a demographic segment to which you sell products and services? Management and staff at DaVita, a Fortune 500 health care services company, believe it is a "village first and a company second." One fifth of its customers—patients in final stages of kidney failure— die every year, and yet the company defines itself as a village. In every one of the thirteen hundred kidney dialysis centers throughout the United States, the Wall of Fame connects patients and teammates around pictures, stories, and facts about the people who work together. It's not simply a slogan: DaVita opens its quarterly earnings call with its clinical out- comes, because a village would worry about its own first, and then worry about "profit." (Oh, by the way, an investment in DaVita increased in value by over 1500 percent from 2000 to 2010.)

- Do you have job titles in your company? W. L. Gore, an organization that lives by many of the principles we discussed in our previous book *Built to Change*, does not. Is this just a gimmick? We do not think so. Job titles emphasize stability, and W. L. Gore believes the world is volatile and uncertain; its management practices reflect that. Gore has built fluidity into its organization so that change is natural; most organizations (without consciously thinking about it) build structures as if they will be permanent.

As we describe sustainable management in greater detail, you will see that it represents radical change. Many have called for a new approach to management, but few have appreciated just how much sustainable effectiveness requires deviating from the management approaches of the past. Even fewer have explored its implications for strategy, structure, decision-making practices, human resource management, and leadership.

Management: The Old

Command and control and high involvement organizations differ dramatically from sustainable management organizations and from each other in how they view people and value creation. As noted, command and control organizations are the oldest and most common type. Large global organizations are particularly likely to use command and control management. Although less common, high involvement organizations often get better results with respect to profit and people, but high involvement management is harder to implement. If we are to understand why sustainable management is superior to them, we need to take a brief look at both.

Many have called for a new approach to management, but few have appreciated just how much sustainable effectiveness requires deviating from the management approaches of the past.

Command and Control Management

Command and control management is based on an image of organizations as well-oiled machines. It has gone through a number of revisions and names, but all emphasize carefully defined jobs, hierarchical organization structures, rules, regulations, discipline, and control. We refer to it as command and control management because it employs top-down leadership approaches, clearly specified performance metrics, and rigid control processes. It is intended to support the reliable production of services and products at a low cost. At its core is the belief that top-down control and discipline will lead to profitability through efficiency and execution.

CCOs have evolved over the past century thanks to changes in information systems, process engineering, quality control, and organization design. The popularity of reengineering and total quality management in the 1980s gave CCOs a much-needed performance boost. More recently, enterprise resource planning (ERP) systems have made CCOs more effective at controlling material costs, labor costs, and other expenditures. These innovations were popular and quickly embraced by CCOs because they support the underlying assumption and beliefs that control is good, that predictability and stability lead to effectiveness, and that people need to be directed and controlled to optimize productivity.

For decades, management writers have argued that the command and control style is obsolete.[5] Despite its evolution, it still has a deep-seated faith in the power of top-down management, simple standardized jobs, and tight budget-driven controls. It continues to focus on producing profits and often does so at the expense of people and the environment. Ironically, it often fails to produce sustainable profits precisely because of the way it treats people and the environment as well as the risks it encourages executives to take in order to maximize profits.

CCOs were the best approach in the first half of the twentieth century because they fit the relatively stable local business environments, the nature of the workforce, and the type of products and services that were demanded in most developed countries. But in the decades since, the workforce has become more educated, involved, diverse, and informed. We have gone from producing Model Ts to space shuttles, from a cash society to a complex electronic world of consumer spending, and from a world in which a high school education was enough to a world in which a college degree is the bare minimum required for many jobs. Competition has become global and, increasingly, governments and the public are demanding that organizations reduce their destructive impact on the environment.

With all the changes that have taken place since command and control management was developed, it is hardly radical to argue that it is outdated. But it is a big mistake to underestimate how deeply CCO assumptions are embedded in our thinking. It is still the way most corporations, governments, nonprofits, and nongovernmental organizations (NGOs) are managed.

High Involvement Management

High involvement management is based on an image of organizations as a participative community. When Douglas McGregor wrote about Theory Y, he argued that when people are involved in making important decisions and given interesting work, they are highly motivated and committed to organization success. He championed the idea that the way CCOs are designed decreases the motivation of individuals and creates a dysfunctional adversarial relationship between employees and the organization. As a result, instead of leading to lower costs, CCOs actually create high costs, because they have high employee turnover, excessive absenteeism, adversarial union-management relations, worker health problems, and a poorly motivated workforce.

The high involvement approach assumes that investments in workforce development, work design, and participative decision making will result in high performance levels and low overall costs. It evolved rapidly during the 1980s and 1990s under the banner of employee involvement.[6] Advances in the design of self-managing teams and in the understanding of participative leadership have contributed greatly to its effectiveness and to our knowledge about how and where it should be implemented.

High involvement management fits well in businesses with complex production processes that are not facing rapid, technological change. Perhaps the most advanced and sophisticated versions of the high involvement approach are found in process production plants (such as for chemicals, food, and energy) and other complex workplaces. In them, employees actually run the operation and are so committed to the organization and its performance that there is little need for supervision. The high involvement style also fits well in companies that are in relatively "stable" businesses and are able to commit to building teams, offering people careers, and providing interesting work. HIOs are particularly good at attracting talent that wants to do work that is significant and challenging and wants an involved long-term relationship with a company.

Given its obvious appeal, many wonder why more organizations have not adopted high involvement management. The answer is that it is hard to implement, and it is easy to break. It is hard to implement because it challenges traditional notions of power and status and it involves a complex constellation of structures, beliefs, people, and practices that must be aligned. Getting all the pieces right is difficult. It also is easy to break because it depends heavily on trust, which can be destroyed in a moment, and on long-term investments in people, which can be difficult to maintain in a rapidly changing business world.

Given its obvious appeal, many wonder why more organizations have not adopted high involvement management. The answer is that it is hard to implement, and it is easy to break.

The major problem with HIOs, however, is not that they are hard to create and maintain. It is that high involvement management is not a good fit for organizations that need to change rapidly and frequently to keep up with an uncertain and unpredictable world. Technology, globalization, and workforce changes are forces to which the organization must adapt again and again. Because of this, HIOs are a poor fit for most of today's technology and knowledge work organizations. As appealing as high involvement management is, something as different from it as an HIO is from a CCO is needed.

Is a Reset Really Required?

But is a full reset really needed in management thought and practice? Can't CCOs and HIOs just make some adaptations so that they are more agile, more thoughtful about people, and more in tune with the natural environment? The mass media are full of reports describing how many large corporations are implementing a variety of sustainability initiatives, corporate social responsibility programs, and agility capabilities.

We think these sustainability, social responsibility, and agility programs will always fall short of producing an SMO because they do not fully acknowledge and address the forces demanding change. Technology and globalization are demanding that organizations be more agile. Societies, cultures, governments, and NGOs are challenging organizations to make their demands equal to those of owners. These demands are familiar, but to understand why a reset is necessary, we need to review them. It will show that trying to adapt the command and control approach or the high involvement approach to deal with agility and multiple stakeholders will not enable an organization to achieve sustainable effectiveness.

Agility Forces

An organization cannot be sustainably effective unless it is agile enough to handle the complexity and change that characterize today's world. The three familiar forces for change—technology, globalization, and workforce—have created a business context in which change is rapid, large in magnitude, and often unpredictable in direction. Together, they define the new normal: change—faster and faster change. It was these forces and their implications that led us to write about agile organizations in *Built to Change*.

There is little doubt that information technology and scientific knowledge are among the biggest changes that have occurred in the past three decades. ERP systems, mobile devices, the Internet, and Web 2.0 technologies provide access to information and people in ways that never existed before and that continue to expand at a dizzying pace. Virtual presence technology is proliferating, closing the distance between people and challenging our concept of time. In addition, the amount of research and knowledge produced increases every year, creates opportunities for new products, and fuels progress. As a result, organizations are constantly facing the need to change and innovate.

The impact of globalization is multifaceted and demanding.[7] Various countries and locations have the potential to exploit new sources of competitive advantage, including cheap raw materials and new types of technical expertise. India's software and information systems management expertise is on par with any other country in the world. Recognizing this, Cisco Corporation has created a co-corporate headquarters to take advantage of the talent that is available there. China now has supercomputers that are as fast and perform as well as any that are made in the West. The globalization of knowledge and technology has forced organizations to continually modify the services and products they offer as well as where and how they produce them.

Finally, the workforce of most organizations has become more diverse in terms of gender, national origin, race, and age and more central to success. With respect to age it is likely to become even more diverse. More and more individuals in developed countries lack the financial wherewithal to retire, cannot be forced to retire because of age discrimination laws, and want to work for most of their increasingly long lifetimes.

While physical and financial assets remain important, for many organizations their major assets are their talent, intellectual property, and brands. Talent, intellectual property, and brands are often virtually impossible to separate because they feed off of each other, are much more mobile and perishable than physical and financial assets, and are more challenging to utilize and manage.

In combination with technology changes and globalization, the nature of work itself is changing; simple well-defined jobs are being replaced by knowledge work that is much harder to direct, measure, and perform. Organizations in developed countries are increasingly doing complex work that requires highly skilled employees who cannot be closely supervised.

Clearly, surviving in this complex and unstable world requires high levels of strategic and organizational agility. CCOs and HIOs struggle to adapt because they are designed to be stable. They were born in a time when change was glacial compared to today's rates, and so their foundation is stable structures, jobs, and processes—stability is in their blood. HIOs may be a little more fluid in terms of structures and jobs, but they are committed to a stable workforce—it is in their soul. CCOs and HIOs are like buildings made of concrete—it's possible to modify them, but it doesn't come easily.

In *Built to Change*, we described how organizations could be more like Lego towers and have the capability to respond quickly to technological change, globalization, and workforce changes. However, even if we make CCOs and HIOs more agile, they will not be sustainably effective as we have defined it. They may be able to meet owners' goals over time, but are likely to do so at the expense of social and natural environment outcomes. Agility alone is insufficient to produce sustainable effectiveness, because agile organizations—as derivatives of CCOs and HIOs—still focus on only one stakeholder: investors.

Stakeholder Forces

An organization cannot be sustainably effective unless it produces outcomes of value to all its significant stakeholders. In today's connected world, even small stakeholders can directly or indirectly harm the organization if they feel betrayed. In the case of social and ecological stakeholders, these are not "new" forces. They have always been a part of the environmental scans organizations do during their traditional strategic planning processes. However, they are rarely viewed as important and certainly not relevant enough to be prioritized over economic forces. Today, social and environmental groups have become formal and well organized, and they are focusing their demands on organizations in meaningful and powerful ways.

The social dimension of an organization's footprint has become more than just a line item to be checked off during environmental scanning exercises. It is a full-fledged and multifaceted stakeholder with as much power to challenge, shut down, and damage an organization's reputation as a lack of cash or other assets. The days of operating under the assumption that social concerns are a low priority are over. Organizations must begin operating according to the Brundtland Commission's 1989 definition of sustainability—"meeting the needs of the present without compromising the needs of future generations."[8]

Thanks to globalization, it is no longer just a matter of what the United States, Japanese, and European societies think. Prior to the emergence of the technological and globalization trends, China, Vietnam, Indonesia, India, South Africa, Brazil, Russia, and Turkey were of little concern. They were just foreign countries with unique cultures, negligible economies, and small markets that were full of natural resources at cheap prices.

What a difference a decade makes! Now, apparel retailers such as Gap and Nike must design, manufacture, distribute, and sell their goods in ways that support freedom of association, labor's right to organize, and a country's quality of life in every part of their supply chains. Manufacturers, such as Flextronics and

Intel, must assemble products in ways that provide employment but do so in ways that do not destroy cultural values in multiple countries.

The social dimension also refers to an organization's relationship with its employees. When CCOs dump job security as part of their employment deal, they are left with an unattractive employee value proposition. With their emphasis on specialized jobs and top-down leadership and control, CCOs struggle to find competent employees who are motivated by the kind of human resource management practices that are offered. Today's employees resist the rigidity and conformity of this management approach, particularly now that most CCOs have made it clear that loyalty to the company is not reciprocated.

Academics and researchers have led the argument that organizations should be held accountable for the quality of work life they create.[9] It is not just that organizations have a moral duty to care about people (although they do); it is that organizations that treat people badly dump the costs of poor health, stress, mortality, and family conflict on society. HIOs became popular partly because CCOs failed to create a high quality of work life, but like their CCO cousins, HIOs also focus more on their own welfare than on that of their employees.

It is not just that organizations have a moral duty to care about people (although they do); it is that organizations that treat people badly dump the costs of poor health, stress, mortality, and family conflict on society.

If there is one issue that is more potent than social concerns it is ecological concerns. While organizations have for a long time had the ability to ruin land, forests, lakes, and rivers through bad practices, it is only recently that they have had the ability to do environmental damage on a global scale. The 2007 report from the Intergovernmental Panel on Climate Change (IPCC) placed global warming, greenhouse gas emissions, and carbon footprint issues squarely in front of us.[10]

Although there are those who continue to challenge the IPCC findings and the urgency with which we must respond, most right-minded people and organizations recognize the implications. We can no longer extract energy from the earth's crust with impunity. We can no longer place toxic chemicals or pollutants into the biosphere. The very resources that sustain life—not just organizations!—are in shorter supply and damaged condition.

Over 70 percent of Chinese rivers, lakes, and seashores are polluted, and 90 percent of underground water in Chinese cities is polluted; secondhand smoke is linked to respiratory disease; the levels of lead in fish and water continue to rise; and we continue to put carbon into the air we breathe. The fishing industry has become a kind of mining activity and has done long-term damage to what should be a renewable resource. Dependence on ever-more-expensive oil can produce problems far greater than the bursting of the finance bubble. Society will no longer accept that organizations should be exempt from caring about the health of the planet. Nongovernmental organizations have achieved enough power to demand organization action.

The social and ecological components of the environment have taken on the status of stakeholders as powerful and demanding as shareholders. The BP oil leak in the Gulf of Mexico had a game-changing impact on global oil companies and their employees, the communities in which they operate, their shareholders, and the environment and economy of an entire region. It is a chilling example of the interdependency among social, economic, and environmental issues.

Some argue that CCOs and HIOs have always served multiple stakeholders. Despite any rhetoric you may have heard, the CCO approach does not respect people; and while the HIO approach respects employees, it does not treat society or the natural environment as stakeholders. In both CCOs and HIOs, meeting the needs of all stakeholders is mainly done in the context of compliance, and even that is often up for debate if the cost of fines is less than the cost of respecting the rights of society or the planet's environment. This is to be expected, given that a board of directors primarily represents one stakeholder, the shareholders.

A Reset Requires an Integrated Approach

In high technology, a "kludge" is an inelegant and ultimately unworkable innovation that is the result of pieces not working together. It is the fashion equivalent of putting lipstick on a pig. To be sustainably effective, organizations must be both agile and responsible. They can only achieve this by adopting designs in which policies and practices work together to produce sustainable performance.

Technology and globalization pressures are not changes in the stakeholder mix demanding attention. They are forces to which organizations must adapt. Social and environmental stakeholders are different than owners. They demand a different set of objectives. Therefore, independent changes aimed at agility or responsibility will produce a kludge, not an SMO.

CCOs and HIOs are built on the assumption of stability and in particular on the assumption of stable growth in demand. Only under the assumption that the population will continue to increase, that new markets will always be created, that lesser developed economies will continue to emerge, and that consumers will continue to buy more and more can the logic of CCOs and HIOs be successful without having to account for change.

No industry is more locked into a continuous cycle of growth and greed than the finance industry, and its spectacular failure taught people from Florida to Latvia that housing prices and stocks do not go up forever. Only "the house" wins in gambling. Similarly, the world's population, global fishing, oil production, and so on cannot go up endlessly. Take away the belief in unending growth and there is little economic justification for organizations designed to pursue stability.

CCOs' and HIOs' values, strategies, and economic logic acknowledge social and environmental demands with only a wink and a nod. They point to philanthropic orchestra sponsorship and recycling programs but do not change their goals, work flows, supply chains, or reward systems. More important, they do not view these stakeholder domains as sources of innovation and profit. Their only comeback to the challenge of being more responsible is "We'll have to charge more"—which demonstrates how foreign the idea is to their economic model.

Facing the Challenge

The case is clear. A management reset is needed. It is needed in order to develop organizations that will be sustainably effective in today's and tomorrow's world—a rapidly changing, very demanding world that is not particularly forgiving of organizations that don't measure up to its standards. We have made the case that it is not demanding an upgraded version of the command and control management style or a more advanced version of the high involvement management style. It is demanding a new approach that integrates agility and responsibility into what we call sustainable management.

Sustainable management is an evolving management style that we believe is the right one for many companies because of how well it responds to today's stakeholder demands as well as the demands of the future. We have chosen to call it sustainable management because it is focused on creating organizations that consistently perform well financially, socially, and environmentally.

The specifics of the sustainable management style are not as fully developed as are those of its two "competitors"; that will come with time and experience. However, as we will show in the chapters that follow, there is enough known about it so that it can be practiced today.

| Sustainable Management

It is not enough for organizations to be good at just execution or innovation or change management or sustainability. They need to be good at multiple types of performance: Speed, yes! Change, yes! Innovation, yes! Sustainability, yes! Execution, yes! Social responsibility, yes! If they are not, their very existence is threatened.

Management commentator Richard D'Aveni coined the term *hypercompetitive* to describe today's highly complex and challenging business environment.[1] The reality is that organizations face a global, socially connected, 24/7, environmentally conscious, and financial-performance-obsessed world, and they must be designed to perform effectively in it.

There is no single management practice or organization structure that can make an organization perform effectively. It takes a "family" of practices that converge to create an organization that has the "right" performance capabilities. While we have criticized command and control organizations (CCOs) and high involvement organizations (HIOs), one thing they do right is fit together a family of practices that reinforce each other.

The CCOs' top-down management, tight budget controls, and clear job descriptions all fit together so that they are able to perform reasonably well—in some settings. Similarly, the teams, egalitarian culture, and employee-oriented development policies that are found in HIOs are part of a family of practices that work together in a complementary way. To be sustainably effective, sustainable management organizations (SMOs) also need to have a whole suite of practices that fit together and meet the demands of today's multi-stakeholder business environment.

In Chapter One, we considered the major reasons the command and control style and the high involvement management style are outdated. We focused this discussion on the many changes that are driving a new definition of organization effectiveness and requiring a major management reset.

In this chapter, we lay out the primary elements of sustainable management. We contrast how sustainable management differs from high involvement management and command and control management in four management areas: the way value is created, the way work is organized, the way people are treated, and the way behavior is "guided." In the chapters that follow, we will explore these key management areas in much greater depth by looking at the specific practices, policies, and structures that support them and bring them to life.

The Way Value Is Created

Fundamental to the operation, effectiveness, and survival of every organization is value creation. Organizations must create value to exist. The value they create and how it is created must fit the world in which they operate. Society is increasingly calling for the creation of value that goes beyond financial value to include social and ecological value. SMOs recognize this and define their effectiveness by the extent to which they create these three kinds of value—what we call sustainable effectiveness.

While its strategies may change and where it looks for competitive advantage may shift, an SMO is always driven and guided by a clear sense of what it is. It creates value in the domains of people, planet, and profit. SMOs have an internal compass that always points them toward their true north. They may change their route, but they always head toward sustainable effectiveness.

Identity and Purpose

All organizations have an identity and purpose no matter how they are managed. Understanding how an organization creates value begins with its identity. Identity is a summary statement of how an organization operates—what it stands for and what it aspires to accomplish.[2] It is part brand promise, part culture, part reputation, and part values. Together they describe how an organization creates value and what kind of value it creates.

SMOs need to be very aware of their identity. It should include that they are a good neighbor and community member, a good place to work, a good financial performer, and a friend of the environment. Their identity must also be supportive of change, adaptation, and innovation.

Philips's corporate identity is expressed in its marketing slogan "sense and simplicity." It describes its brand promise, how Philips intends to design its products and services, and how it wants to relate to a variety of stakeholders. It also describes how it thinks about managing people and its approach to organization design. "Sense and simplicity" continues a long Philips tradition of this kind of thinking and relating to the environment. Prior to sense and simplicity, Philips was concerned with "let's make things better."

Whereas *identity* describes the "how" or the long-term strategy of an organization, *purpose* describes the direction or goal. CCOs typically focus on satisfying one group of stakeholders, owners, through profits. HIOs typically focus on owners and employees. The purpose that best describes SMOs is sustainable effectiveness, the achievement of objectives that contribute to people, planet, and profit. Sustainable effectiveness involves an organization not just living within the demands of the natural environment but doing so in a way that meets the needs of the workforce, the communities in which it operates, and its shareholders.

Clearly defining and developing an identity and a purpose is particularly critical to the performance and success of SMOs. Their effectiveness rests on their having a compelling purpose that attracts the right employees and motivates them. The combination of attracting the right employees and having them involved in the organization allows SMOs to rely less on rules, regulations, and extrinsic rewards than do CCOs or for that matter HIOs.

The advantage of a purpose that focuses on sustainable effectiveness is its applicability to a wide range of businesses and situations. It is also likely to increase in appeal as environmental sustainability issues become more and more front and center in everyone's mind. The specific focus of an organization's sustainability purpose must be driven by the business it is in. For example, a forest products company such as Weyerhaeuser may choose to focus more heavily on the environment while an intellectual property company such as Microsoft may choose to emphasize people and social goals.

Strategizing

Find a sustainable competitive advantage—this is the advice that companies have been given for years. There is little doubt that if an organization can find one, there is great wisdom in seizing it. But what differentiates SMOs from CCOs and HIOs is that SMOs will not exploit an advantage, even a sustainable one, if it contributes to social or environmental harm. Further, they recognize that the world is changing so fast that few competitive advantages last for very long. What fits better with today's business environment is a series of competitive advantages that are based on economic, social, and natural environment capabilities.

It is increasingly difficult if not impossible to find anything resembling a sustainable competitive advantage.

Because of their different way of thinking about strategy, an SMO's strategizing process differs from that of CCOs and HIOs in important ways. First, the strategizing process in SMOs is based on a process of "futuring." New technologies, innovative product features, creative marketing, and effective implementation can duplicate or trump an existing competitive advantage in relatively short order. Thus it is increasingly difficult if not impossible to find anything resembling a sustainable competitive advantage. Witness what has happened to Kodak, Xerox, Blockbuster, and even MySpace. Because of this, most of an SMO's strategizing process time should be spent on thinking about what might happen and what should be done if it did.

Second, calendar-driven strategizing processes should be eliminated. They are a huge impediment to the ongoing adaptability that organizations need in order to adjust to rapidly changing business environments. Organizations need to constantly and continuously look at their strategy with an eye toward evolving, developing, and of course implementing it.

Third, the strategizing process in SMOs needs to include more than just the board of directors and senior executives. For multiple reasons, individuals throughout the organization as well as other stakeholders should be active participants in the strategy process. Individuals throughout SMOs have valuable data about what is happening not only inside the firm but also outside its surroundings. Their knowledge and observations can provide important inputs that generate momentary advantages along multiple dimensions. In addition, members of the community, customers, regulators, and representatives of the natural environment can help to shape effective strategies.

Broad participation in the ongoing strategizing process is important. It ensures that all stakeholders are not only involved in the business but understand the why and the how of where the business is heading. This of course is critical to their being engaged in the business and as a result behaving in ways that will support their organization's ongoing development and implementation of its strategy.

Value Creation Differences

The different approaches to value creation among the three management approaches are highlighted in Table 2.1. They start from very different positions with respect to the role each type of organization plays in the world. CCOs have identities that focus primarily on being predictable and reliable. Society can count on CCOs to be stable providers of goods and services.

HIOs are tied to their workforce commitment. Society can count on HIOs to be good places to work where employee skills and knowledge are leveraged and developed.

SMOs are adaptable and focus on sustainable effectiveness. Society can count on them to adjust to change in ways that maintain

Table 2.1. The Way Value Is Created

	Management Approach		
	Command and Control	High Involvement	Sustainable
Identity and Purpose	Profit: Predictability wins	Profit and employee involvement: Commitment wins	People, planet, and profit: Adaptability wins
Strategizing	Sustainable efficiency advantage	Sustainable human capital advantage	Series of momentary advantages

their economic viability, contribute positively to society, and act as good stewards of the natural environment.

As a result of their very different identities, CCOs, HIOs, and SMOs differ in how they think about strategy. Particularly critical is the difference in where they look for competitive advantage and how long they expect a competitive advantage to last. Unlike CCOs and HIOs, SMOs look for momentary advantages.

The Way Work Is Organized

Organizing is about dividing, structuring, and coordinating work to create value and accomplish the purpose of an organization. Most organizations have formal structures that specify who does what; others use informal and formal collaborative processes to accomplish it. All organizations have control systems and information systems that help divide, coordinate, and measure their work.

CCOs, HIOs, and SMOs differ greatly in how they divide work, what they measure, and how they distribute the information they gather. However, they do have one feature in common. At the top of all are boards, and how their boards operate is a key factor in determining how they are managed.

Corporate Governance

The role of corporate boards in SMOs is different from and in many respects more challenging than that of boards in other organizations. SMO boards need to understand and shape the identity, purpose, strategy, and structure of their organizations more deeply than do the boards of most organizations.

Good SMO boards do more than review financial numbers, monitor CEO performance, and deal with reporting requirements. They also look carefully at the future and monitor the culture and management practices of the organization to be sure that these are consistent with sustainable effectiveness. They understand the organization well enough to be sure that the way it is operating is a positive contributor to its identity and sustainable effectiveness. They ask for and get metrics that look at whether the organization is living up to its commitment to sustainability and the importance of its human capital.

Boards in SMOs need to be effective representatives of the organization's stakeholders. These include the owners but go beyond that to include communities, employees, and representatives of the natural environment. To fulfill this role, SMO boards must have a mix of members different from the one that is typically found in CCOs and HIOs. Its members need to be more diverse and more expert in the areas of organization design, human capital management, and sustainability.

Structuring

It is critical that the structure of SMOs have a strong external focus, powerful collaboration capabilities, and clear decision-making processes. Let's look at external focus first.

To be motivated, knowledgeable, and contributing members of an SMO, employees need to understand how their organization deals with its external environment. Without question, the best way to be sure they do is to create an organization structure that minimizes the degrees of separation between individuals in the organization and the external environment. Nothing beats dealing directly with a customer complaint or other external stakeholder issue when it comes to individuals understanding the challenges their organization faces and what is happening in the external environment. It provides direct feedback and helps create a felt need for performance improvement and, in many cases, change.

In structuring an SMO, it is important to avoid creating the rigid features of CCOs. Traditional command and control design features, such as lengthy job descriptions, narrow spans of control, and formal rules and policies, have no place in SMOs. What does have a place are multiple reporting relationships for some individuals and businesses, relatively broad spans of control, and constantly changing team memberships and group affiliations. Because the structures of SMOs are focused on customers, capabilities, and communities, this doesn't lead to chaos; it leads to self-management and behavior that is directed toward sustainable effectiveness. Structuring an SMO should be an ongoing process that focuses on continuously evolving and changing the structure to reflect changes in its strategy and business environment.

Nothing beats dealing directly with a customer complaint or other external stakeholder issue when it comes to individuals understanding the challenges their organization faces and what is happening in the external environment.

Decision making in an SMO needs to reflect its identity as a highly adaptable organization and the sustainable effectiveness focus of its purpose. In comparison to CCOs and HIOs, SMOs should look less structured and more networked. They may look a little inefficient because some slack is visible. Limited slack is not only quite appropriate, it is desirable because it supports collaboration and innovation in the service of sustainable effectiveness goals.

In many cases, the structure needs to be supported by social networking systems and "spontaneous" coalitions that support collaboration, new directions, and new ideas for the business. It is important that slack resources not lead to wasted time, but time that is devoted to exploring product and service innovations, improving environmental footprints, and supporting communities.

Work

Work in SMOs is organized according to its purpose. SMOs not only must deliver on current strategies, they also must create new products, services, and processes. Work that drives current effectiveness must be done in reliable and efficient ways. The HIO management approach provides important lessons on the best way to design work that is productive, empowering, and relevant.[3] For their "production" work SMOs should follow what HIOs do—it works! But a lot of the work in an SMO must be concerned with innovation. This type of work requires a multi-stakeholder, project-based, temporary approach to work designs.

Individuals in an SMO should have input to major strategy and organization design decisions as well as considerable control over how they do their day-to-day work. This kind of input and control is vital to ensuring that they will be motivated to perform well and support the purpose and identity of the organization. It is an effective substitute for the expensive and ineffective command and control approach to managing behavior.

Information Transparency

A key component of SMOs is the management and sharing of performance information. Transparency should be a major feature of every SMO. Today, organizations can achieve a level of transparency that is far greater than was possible prior to the development and adoption of modern information technology. Without transparency, most of an SMO's other processes will not work. Talent cannot be developed effectively. Ongoing strategizing becomes an impossible process to operate. Structuring on an ongoing basis is not possible, and as a result an important substitute for hierarchy and bureaucracy is lacking.

Internally, a great amount of transparency is appropriate with respect to the organization's strategy, financial results, and human capital management activities. All members of an SMO ought to be made aware of key financial results so that there are no surprises. They should also receive information to help guide them in their career development and about how their performance affects the organization's performance. But above all they should receive information about how well they and their co-workers are performing against goals that are tied to the business strategy.

To make the commitment to sustainable effectiveness meaningful, good measures should be developed to assess the organization's performance on its sustainable effectiveness goals. The results of these measures should be shared with all employees. Transparency in this area is critical to making sustainable effectiveness meaningful, motivating, and a top agenda issue for people throughout the organization.

As far as information transparency with respect to the external world is concerned, it doesn't need to be nearly as high as it does for the internal world. Google has a saying that external transparency should be opaque with respect to the key operations of the organization. It is hard to disagree with the point that being opaque with respect to business plans, anticipated financial results, human capital, and a host of other issues has many advantages.

However, it is important for organizations to provide the outside world with enough information to understand what the key features of the organization's management approach are and how well the organization is fulfilling its stated purpose. This is necessary so that it can attract the right employees by building its identity as an attractive place to work. Of course, the right identity not only can attract the right employees, it can help attract the right customers—witness Nordstrom, Southwest Air, The Container Store, and other companies that are known to employ customer-oriented individuals.

Organizing Differences

The major differences in the way the three management approaches organize and manage work are highlighted in Table 2.2. SMOs are more externally focused and collaborative than CCOs. They also have more diverse structural and work arrangements. Both SMOs and HIOs use team-based structures and work designs, but SMOs also use more network and project-based principles. While committed to transparency, SMOs apply the principle in a contingent way.

Table 2.2. The Way Work Is Organized

	Management Approach		
	Command and Control	High Involvement	Sustainable
Governance	CEO dominant	CEO-led board	Multiple stakeholder Boards
Structure	Hierarchical	Team based— flat	Collaborative, networked
Work	Controlled by supervisor; simple and repetitive	Controlled by employees; input to many decisions	Controlled by employees and customers; input to some decisions
Business Information	Secretive	Widely shared	Transparent internal, opaque external

The Way People Are Treated

Talent is the most important asset of SMOs. They share this feature with high involvement organizations. Both rely heavily on talent as a source of competitive advantage. Both need to make excellent decisions about rewards and talent management. In many cases, it makes sense for individuals to be paid very well for their skills and capabilities. SMO managers need to know who their critical talent is and whether it is in the right positions within the organization. Of course, SMOs also need to know how well its talent is performing and developing, and what its commitment is to the organization. Finally, it is important for SMOs to treat their talent as individuals by giving them the opportunity to customize their work arrangements.

Managing Performance

All organizations need effective control systems. Behavior needs to be directed and guided so that it supports the strategy and effectiveness of the organization. But it doesn't have to be directed and guided by the methods that are used by CCOs and HIOs. In organizations that adopt the command and control approach, control is usually achieved by carefully specifying what individuals should do, measuring whether they do it, and rewarding or punishing them on the basis of the results of that measurement. Sounds good, but it is an inefficient and often ineffective approach.

In SMOs it is important to measure whether critical results are achieved and to use the results as a method of control and improvement. But the results of the measures should not be used in the same way they are used in CCOs. Instead of supervisors and managers using measures to direct behavior, the major emphasis needs to be placed on self-management and peer control. This kind of accountability is not present in CCOs but often is present in HIOs. It requires a combination of good metrics; commitment to the organization's purpose; and public information about goals, objectives, and performance.

Self-control is clearly the cheapest form of control and can be the most effective. It makes unnecessary the layers of management that are required when control is based on rules, regulations, rewards and punishment, and supervisory monitoring. It requires an effective goal-setting process, good metrics, and ongoing feedback in order for individuals to direct their behavior. It also requires making the results of performance measures public so that peers and others in the organization know how everyone is performing. This allows them to coordinate their behaviors and intervene when there is a problem.

Rewarding Performance

Rewarding performance is a key feature of effective organizations regardless of whether they are CCOs, HIOs, or SMOs. Rewarding performance correctly can result in a number of positives, including the most important one, motivating employees to perform well. SMOs need reward systems that reflect, complement, and recognize the degree to which the organization is honoring its identity, successfully implementing its strategy, and achieving sustainable effectiveness.

The reward system's *focus* is an important difference among CCOs, HIOs, and SMOs. Whereas CCOs prefer individual rewards and HIOs prefer team-based rewards, a mixture of these often is the best answer for SMOs. The key is fitting the reward system to the structure of the SMO and the types of behavior its strategy calls for. The kind of rewards an SMO gives, whether stock, cash, or some other tangible reward, also needs to be customized to the business strategy, the preferences of employees, and the setting in which the organization operates.

One of the major advantages that SMOs have when it comes to motivation is in the area of nonfinancial rewards. All too often nonfinancial rewards in CCOs come across as trite or contrived because they do not fit the purpose or identity of the organization. SMOs potentially can do much better. They can recognize contributions that fit their purpose and give rewards that reflect it. If individuals are strongly committed to the purpose of their organization, being recognized for their contribution to it can be very meaningful and valued.

Managing Talent

Talent management in SMOs needs to go well beyond and away from what is usually considered "good" HR practice. The same kind of rigor and analysis that goes into making important physical and financial capital decisions needs to go into human capital decisions. Talent management needs to involve analytic models and the use of decision science knowledge about how individuals should be trained, developed, and utilized.[4] In short, people need to be looked at as an important organizational asset, not as an expense or fixed cost that needs to be managed and controlled. Without this kind of thorough analysis, it is hard to see how any organization, much less an SMO, can respond effectively to the challenges it faces in the areas of change, cost effectiveness, product innovation, and environmental impact.

Perhaps the best way of stating what SMOs need to do with respect to attracting, retaining, developing, and utilizing talent is to say that they need an employment contract or deal that reflects the realities of their business strategy, purpose, identity, and what is happening in the external world. Unlike HIOs, this does not necessarily mean a promise of job security or career development, something that often is not possible given the rate of change most organizations face today. SMOs do need to compete vigorously for the talent they need, utilize it well, and as was discussed earlier, keep it informed.

The same kind of rigor and analysis that goes into making important physical and financial capital decisions needs to go into human capital decisions.

As a result of selecting the right people and developing them, SMOs build a workforce that is aligned with the values of sustainable effectiveness. The members of this workforce also have the skills to make integrated sustainable effectiveness decisions when multiple objectives are possible and to make trade-offs that don't always favor one type of result (such as financial).

Managing Diversity

Globalization, longer life spans, and immigration are just a few of the factors that are creating more diverse populations and workforces in most countries. Having a diverse workforce should be a major consideration in the design of all SMOs. A diverse workforce is needed to reflect today's complex business and social environments. It is helpful in bringing different viewpoints to discussions concerning strategizing and structuring. It also can lead to the kind of talent flexibility that makes it easier for an organization to change.

In the best of all circumstances, a diverse workforce can bring multiple ideas to bear in ways that produce innovative products and services. Having a diverse range of employees who are in contact with a wide variety of social, political, and environmental concerns can also be critical in ensuring that an SMO does not miss critical trends.

Any organization that operates globally must recognize the importance of having diverse practices. Using the same management practices and policies globally rarely makes sense, and although it is less often recognized, the same is true for practices within a single country.

Today's highly diverse workforce creates the necessity for differences in how people are treated, even in organizations that operate only in the United States and other developed countries. Organizations need to be able to differentiate with respect to how they treat their employees. People with different backgrounds and lifestyles want to be and need to be treated differently.[5] In SMOs, differentiated policies and practices are necessary in areas ranging from how people are led to how long they stay with the organization.

There is no question that creating a differentiated organization means creating a much more complicated and difficult to manage organization. However, in most cases, differentiation earns a high return in terms of organizational flexibility, attractiveness as a place to work, understanding of the environment, and innovation. Of course, it is possible to have too much differentiation in how people are treated, but this is definitely not the problem in most CCOs and HIOs. SMOs can distinguish themselves relatively easily by offering differentiation to their members that includes the type of careers they have, where they work, how they work, when they work, and what their reward and benefit packages consist of.

Talent Treatment Differences

The three management approaches differ greatly in how they treat the people who work for them. Table 2.3 provides an overview of the key differences. One of the most interesting differences involves talent and how it is treated by HIOs and SMOs. HIOs invest in talent development and offer long-term employment relationships. SMOs do not. They take a much more analytical look at talent and make talent development decisions that are based on performance and the talent marketplace.

The three management approaches also differ significantly in how they treat individuals when it comes to rewards and work arrangements. The sustainable management approach is the most strongly oriented to allowing employees the ability to individualize their work lives.

Table 2.3. The Way People Are Treated

	Management Approach		
	Command and Control	High Involvement	Sustainable
Performance Management	Rules, measures	Commitment	Goals, understanding of business
Rewards	Job-based Individual performance	Team-based individual skills	Individual- and team-performance-based; critical talent rewarded
Talent	Job-based vertical careers	Development and career focused	Strong commitment to talent that is strategic
Treatment of Individuals	Differences based on hierarchy	Egalitarian with limited choices	Flexible, many choices

The Way Behavior Is Guided

How organizations are led is an important, perhaps the most important, determinant of their performance. How an organization defines and executes leadership is a core feature of its management approach. SMOs conceive of leadership as an organization capacity rather than the trait of an individual. Building this capacity needs to be a major focus of an SMO. It needs to be a key part of the talent development activities and a part of an SMO's identity.

Leading

To operate effectively, SMOs need more leaders than other types of organizations, and they need leaders to behave differently. This does not mean that they need more individuals in management jobs; it means they need more individuals who engage in leadership behaviors such as suggesting to others what behaviors fit the purpose and direction of the business. It also means they need more individuals who can and will assume a leadership role when there are moments of ambiguity and questions about what to do. Individuals who correct and at times criticize people who are doing things that are not consistent with the ethics, strategy, and identity of the organization are another need. In short, leadership should be a shared responsibility that does not respect titles or positions in SMOs.[6]

Particularly critical leadership behaviors in SMOs are those that involve goal setting, directing, and explaining the relationship between the organization's identity and the behaviors that are expected. Because sustainable effectiveness depends on change, leadership in SMOs requires many people to define and describe the new behaviors that change requires and to encourage others to adopt them. Leaders should spend a lot of time thinking about what new behaviors will be needed and how those new behaviors should be motivated. Absent leaders providing a link, often individuals cannot see the connection between their behavior and the sustainable effectiveness of an SMO. Good leadership behaviors in SMOs therefore include establishing clear-cut goals for individuals that support the purpose of the organization and, of course, rewarding and recognizing goal accomplishment.

Transforming

The way an SMO guides behavior begins with the way it is created. If it involves transforming a CCO or HIO, the transformation must challenge and change all assumptions regarding the importance and centrality of stability. It also must prepare the organization to achieve sustainable effectiveness and to make it clear that change will occur over and over again.

Establishing a new identity is critical to guiding the behaviors necessary for sustainable effectiveness. Identity change may be the most difficult type of change an organization can attempt. It is a long-term process. In the case of an SMO it can only be considered successful when organization members believe sustainable management is the way the organization will operate from that point on. To achieve this, leaders must consistently model and describe the behaviors required by the new identity and encourage their development and occurrence.

Identity change and the transformation to an SMO are facilitated by the specification of new goals, a new strategy, and a flexible organization. To guide behavior successfully, organization members need to know what is to be achieved. Accomplishing this requires leaders to clearly state how people, planet, and profit goals will be balanced and prioritized. It also requires that leaders clearly articulate and describe a strategy that will achieve these goals.

Establishing a new identity is critical
to guiding the behaviors necessary
for sustainable effectiveness.

PepsiCo has recently begun its transformation to a sustainably effective organization. For decades it has produced products that were high in calories, and it packaged them in ways that were not environmentally friendly. Today, it is trying to change its identity by stating a purpose that serves people with healthy foods and drinks and that is committed to environmentally sustainable production methods and packaging. Senior management sees this dual focus as a win-win. Using new packaging and production methods can reduce costs, improve environmental impact, and contribute to a change in consumer perceptions. Changing the company's identity will take concerted effort, time, and money, but perhaps most of all, good leadership.

Guiding Behavior Differences

The three management styles take very different approaches to leadership and transformation, as shown in Table 2.4. HIOs and SMOs are somewhat similar, but there are important differences. Both call for the frequent use of participative decision making, but HIOs are likely to use it more often.

The approaches to leadership that CCOs, HIOs, and SMOs have reflect their very different ways of influencing behavior. The top-down leadership style of CCOs reflects their single-stakeholder-oriented purpose. Their commitment to stability means that change

Table 2.4. The Way Behavior Is Guided

	Management Approach		
	Command and Control	High Involvement	Sustainable
Leading	Top down	Participative	Shared
Transforming	Evolution and revolution	Incremental change and improvement	Learning

occurs in fits and starts. Long periods of little or no change are punctuated by short periods of transformational change.

HIOs are more participative in the way they lead, and that supports their purpose of serving both shareholders and employees. Although HIOs also believe in stability, they approach change participatively and hope that small, consistent improvements will accumulate to create important adaptations.

SMOs are unique in their emphasis on sharing leadership responsibility throughout the organization. In combination with their externally focused and networked structures, this leadership approach supports the multi-stakeholder purpose of pursuing economic, social, and environmental goals. Transformation to an SMO includes the building of shared leadership and other capabilities that allow them to be agile. As a result, SMOs can implement both the small and large changes that are required to achieve sustainable effectiveness.

Integration Is Needed

SMOs require an integrated set of practices, policies, structures, and systems. No single practice, process, structure, or system can be viewed as a stand-alone "best practice," no matter how good it is. Ultimately, only the complete picture counts. An organization is only as effective as the degree to which its practices, processes, and structures fit and work with each other. The key to designing SMOs then is creating a totality of systems, practices, processes, and structures that work together to create a coherent management approach that delivers sustainable effectiveness.

It is the totality of an SMO that most differentiates it from CCOs and from HIOs. All three types of organizations share some features, but when the whole is considered, they are very different from each other in the way they create value, organize, treat people, and guide behavior. It is because of the way they are designed that SMOs can meet the changing demands of customers and be sustainably effective. All too often, individuals who make organization design decisions do not think about design in a big-picture way. Faced with the demands of the day and their jobs, they focus on one or another feature of an organization and end up creating management approaches that lack integration and coherence. The result is a poorly performing organization.

In the chapters that follow, we will discuss the major design features of SMOs separately, but this should not be taken as an indication that they are stand-alone best practices. Quite the opposite is true; they are best practices only when they are combined to create a sustainable approach to managing complex organizations.

PART ONE

The Way Value Is Created

CHAPTER THREE

Strategies for Sustainable Effectiveness

For much of its existence, but especially over the fourteen-year span between 1982 and 1996, the WR Grace Corporation was widely admired. It engineered a number of acquisitions and assembled an impressive portfolio of specialty chemical businesses. Grace returned over 500 percent to investors during that period, but was it an effective organization?

According to traditional financial measures it was. WR Grace effectively pursued the goal of maximizing shareholder return. But those who have watched the film *A Civil Action* or read about the asbestos-related lawsuits that drove the firm into bankruptcy know there is more to the WR Grace story than just a period of successful financial performance. Evaluating an organization's sustainable effectiveness requires looking beyond the single lens of economic returns. It is only a narrow and, in the case of WR Grace, misleading indicator of performance.

Robust Strategies

When we wrote *Built to Change* in 2006, we described robust strategies as consisting of clear identities and intents.[1] An organization's identity is the long-term feature of its strategy that describes "who it is" and "what it stands for." It guides and explains an organization's effectiveness over long periods of time. An organization's strategic intent, however, is the short-term aspect of strategy that describes how an organization will win in the marketplace. The choice of its intent and how well an organization executes it determines an organization's current effectiveness.

Since we wrote *Built to Change*, we have continued to work with organizations to understand value creation. Our conclusion is that identity and intent hold up very well as the keys to understanding what robust strategies consist of. Nevertheless, to paraphrase Microsoft's CEO Steve Ballmer, "We reserve the right to be smarter today than we were yesterday." So, while we believe robustness is still about identity and intent, looking back, we realize that we were too narrow in our definition of value. Since then, we have refined the concepts of identity and intent and, more important, added depth and richness to them so that they embrace the sustainable management perspective of value.

Sustainable management begins with a different view of strategy. SMOs don't have sustainability strategies; they have identities and strategic intents that describe the means to achieve sustainable effectiveness. To have a "sustainability strategy" is to imply that achieving green or socially responsible outcomes is somehow distinct from economic outcomes. SMOs reject this and instead view people, planet, and profit outcomes in an integrated way that recognizes the interdependencies among them while acknowledging that sometimes they conflict with each other.

This is the first of two chapters that focus on the way value is created in SMOs. In this chapter, we focus on the definition of value and effectiveness in an SMO, what robust strategies in an SMO look like, and how they are different from goals and strategies in command and control and in high involvement organizations. In the next chapter, we will focus on how SMOs go about developing strategies and in particular how they go about crafting the strategic intents and capabilities that support them.

A New Perspective on Creating Value

In contrast to CCO's and HIO's focus on financial performance, SMOs assert that creating social and ecological value should have equal standing with creating economic value. While there is increasing agreement with this position, it is not the foundation upon which most corporations build their strategies. SMOs do build on this foundation, however, and as a result have a very different perspective on profitability, growth, and risk.

Perspective on Creating Economic Value

Let there be no doubt, SMOs know they must create *economic* value to survive. They know they must operate in a way that leads to revenues meeting or exceeding expenses. Organizations that cannot meet this test of value cannot survive, let alone create other types of value. Our argument is not that organizations should be unprofitable; it has to do with how they make a profit, how much profit they make, and toward what end that profit is used. Maximizing shareholder returns is a simple and elegant goal, but it does not take into account the potential environmental and social costs of its pursuit. The environmental damage, concentration of wealth, and social injustices that all too often are incurred in the name of maximizing shareholder return warrant taking a new approach to profitability.

SMOs explicitly reject the goal of maximizing shareholder returns and set sustainable goals for profit and profitability. They recognize that achieving social and environmental goals will require investment dollars that may not be available under a profit-maximizing philosophy. J&J CEO William Weldon has stated the SMO goal well. According to him, shareholders are due a fair return, not the absolutely best return. Weldon asserts that J&J has responsibilities to patients, customers, staff, and the community that may prevent it from providing the best possible return, at least in the short term.[2]

SMOs explicitly reject the goal of maximizing shareholder returns and set sustainable goals for profit and profitability.

Reflecting a similar perspective, Kenneth Chenault, the CEO of American Express, in his 2010 commencement speech at Northeastern University said, "In exchange for permission to pursue profits, business must behave and act in ways that protect and enhance the world we live in. You cannot just look at the bottom line."[3] Laws providing corporations with the right to exist with limited owner liability (the shareholders of WR Grace could only lose the value of their investment no matter how much harm Grace did to others) are a gift to investors; they owe society something in return.

As long as financial returns are reasonable, shareholders and board members of SMOs have no basis for expecting them to squeeze out additional unsustainable financial returns. This position is driven by two factors. First, if you consider the long term, you know that unsustainably high rates of return are not that desirable. They can damage long-term results by undermining investment in the organizational capabilities that are needed to sustain the organization over time. They can also cause organizations to take unreasonable risks and stick with strategies for too long. Pushing too hard for high rates of financial return is also likely to undermine social and environmental returns.

SMOs are not willing to give up environmental and social results to serve a shortsighted focus on financial goals. In the case of WR Grace, if it had been an SMO, it would have been alert to the social impact of asbestos, not just for liability reasons but because SMOs value social outcomes as part of their purpose and identity. As it turned out, the blindness to social concerns was fatal.

The reality that blindness to social and ecological value has an economic cost is becoming more and more obvious. For example, Nestlé recently suffered a "kit-astrophe" of bad PR when Greenpeace publicized the link between the popular Kit Kat candy bar and the destruction of rain forests. Nestlé was buying large quantities of palm oil from companies that have routinely destroyed the rain forest to build larger plantations. It no doubt sourced an inexpensive supply of palm oil, but its blindness to environmental factors damaged Nestlé's reputation and provoked a boycott of its products. Today, many organizations still claim that pursuing sustainability costs too much and greatly reduces profitability. But such a claim distracts from the point. Overly aggressive, short-term profit maximization is the wrong goal, because in the long term it costs too much.

In *The Living Company*, Arie de Geus notes that long-lived companies are financially conservative.[4] To achieve economic sustainability, an organization needs to be able to weather hard times and that means keeping debt low and profit goals reasonable. This is quite a different approach from seeking to maximize shareholder value by leveraging debt, giving incentives to salesforces and executives to achieve "big hairy audacious goals," or pursuing acquisitions to "gain important synergies" that rarely materialize.

Perspective on Risk

SMOs set achievable financial goals that are in line with their financially conservative risk preferences. It is not that SMOs are more risk averse than CCOs and HIOs. The real difference is in the understanding of the risks being taken. Risk can come in many forms, including financial, organizational, strategic, and interpersonal, yet each one can be understood and managed. CCOs and HIOs constrain their view of risk to economic and technological risks. They tend to ignore the other types. SMOs are cognizant of more types of risk, have a better understanding of the risks they take, and bring that understanding of risk into strategic decision making.

SMOs know that setting high, difficult-to-achieve economic goals requires organizations to allocate most of their resources to achieving those goals and may limit the creation of other kinds of value. It may also cause employees to take unreasonable risks to achieve stretch financial goals. Equally important, the primacy of financial goals steals employees' mindshare from other goals and may lead to them behaving unethically and illegally in pursuit of them.

SMOs are constantly aware that any competitive advantage they have is temporary; they are aware that without warning that advantage may disappear. The strategy process of futuring that will be described in Chapter Four requires that organizations develop a portfolio of options. If one course of action does not generate sufficient returns, there are other opportunities already identified. Intel's Andy Grove is famous for saying "only the paranoid survive"; that is a pretty good motto for risk management in an SMO.

Perspective on Growth

By itself, recommending that organizations back away from the maximization of shareholder return as the sole objective of corporations is radical and provocative, perhaps even socialistic in some people's view. Even more radical is the stance that SMOs take to growth. While profit and risk are short-term issues, growth is a long-term issue for SMOs.

Growth is one of the least examined strategic objectives in organizations. At some level, it is hard to imagine a strategy that is not trying to grow the organization along some dimension: size, profits, revenues, market share, or influence. There is a big difference, however, between aggressiveness that is directed toward taking advantage of a short-term market opportunity and aggressiveness that pursues organizational growth rates that greatly exceed the rate of market growth, the market's capacity to sustain growth, or the organization's capacity to support growth.

We see too many organizations promising shareholders that they can and should sustain double-digit growth regardless of what is happening to the market for their products and services. The performance records across multiple industries clearly support the conclusion that rapid growth and supra-normal profitability are not sustainable. Organizations that embrace sustainable management must be leery of an intent that supports high growth as a consistent goal. We are not saying rapid growth cannot be a temporary strategic intent, but SMOs must be much more cautious about calling for fast growth than other organizations.

Tartan Yachts occupies a relatively small niche in the sailboat industry. Unlike sales volume leaders such as Beneteau, Hunter, and Catalina, Tartan builds a relatively low volume of high-quality performance cruising sailboats. Its success over the years has tempted it to expand rapidly. In the early 2000s, the growth of the overall economy and its own success at building a strong brand and image around quality resulted in more orders than its plant in Ohio could produce in a timely fashion. Management's conversation quickly turned to "Should we support this increase in demand and success by building another production facility?" In the end, they decided not to.

Tartan managers realized that one of the keys to their success was the relationships they built with their customers. The sales manager told us, "I know every person who has purchased a Tartan since 2003." They also realized that quality was very much a function of keeping things sized appropriately. The wisdom of their conservative growth approach paid off handsomely during the economic downturn that began in 2008. They did not have to go through the painful and disruptive downsizing that many of their competitors did.

In sum, we will paint, in the pages that follow, a rather rosy picture of the sure-footed SMO nimbly jumping from one momentary competitive advantage to the next. It is important to remember, however, that while SMOs are doing this they are guided by conservative financial goals and approaches to growth that are designed to achieve an integrated set of goals. SMOs embrace change and do take risks. However, the risks SMOs take are mitigated by futuring processes and a portfolio of options, rapid testing of ideas, and the ability to quickly scale up or withdraw from a market depending on the results.

Perspective on Creating Ecological Value

SMOs should create positive ecological value, although we suspect that most organizations that pursue sustainable effectiveness may need to start by setting an initial goal of not destroying it. SMOs are keenly aware of their carbon footprint and their overall contribution to the environment. They recognize that economic models based on rapid growth cannot reconcile the increasing demand for finite and fundamental natural resources with the decreasing supply of those resources.[5] This incompatibility is a central source of SMO strategies; how the organization creates economic and social value without compromising the natural environment differentiates SMOs' strategies from those of other organizations. Creating ecological value suggests that business strategies built around the productive use of natural resources can solve environmental problems at a profit.[6]

Perspective on Creating Social Value

SMOs should create positive social value. This goal mandates that organizations contribute to human and cultural well-being and recognize the role social issues play in innovation and long-term adaptability. Social value includes the way an organization treats its workforce. HIOs strongly support treating the workforce as a key stakeholder, but that view must be expanded to include the communities, cultures, governments, and countries in which an organization operates. SMOs need to act in ways that have a positive impact on their health and ability to perform.

The traditional view of economic growth and globalization embedded in CCOs and HIOs values predictability and control over operational flexibility. One way predictability can and has been achieved is through standardization of behavior. When an organization has no perspective on social value and culture, standardization can lead to resentment and the destruction of cultures.

When Disney opened Disneyland Paris, it basically duplicated its parks in the United States and expected European visitors to act and react in the same way North Americans do. Because Disney applied the same rules and regulations without acknowledging local customs, the park was shunned for years.

When Microsoft wanted to introduce Windows 3.0 into China, it chose a Taiwan firm to localize the program. As a result, the program came out in traditional Chinese characters favored by the Taiwanese and not the simplified characters required by the mainland government. Microsoft sales in China flopped, piracy was higher than normal, and the government was not inclined to help. Not until Microsoft translated the program into simplified characters and reshaped its China strategy in collaboration with the government did the operating system get accepted.

Although promoting social value is important in its own right, it clearly supports other elements of an SMO's strategy. For example, cultural diversity can be a real source of creativity and innovation. MTV has been very successful in non-U.S. markets by "glocalizing" its shows and using local talent to host them. GE, Philips, and Siemens also have been successful globally because they spend a lot of time understanding local cultures and how their products can be adapted to suit different country markets.

Perspective on Sustainable Effectiveness

What is sustainable—and what SMOs should try to achieve—is consistently above-average economic performance and above-average levels of social and environmental performance. Traditional strategies focus too much on economic outcomes, hoping that the theoretically elegant principles of perfect competition and growth will eliminate any negative social and ecological externalities. SMOs are committed to being sustainable and effective by pursuing an integrated set of economic, social, and environmental goals.

Identity as a Guidepost for Strategy

Microsoft is one of the most successful software firms in the world, and the stories of great strategic moves that have put them at the top of their industry are legendary. There is the one about how Bill Gates "connected the dots" by purchasing the DOS program, rebranding it as MS-DOS, and licensing it to IBM as the PC's core operating system, or how Microsoft bundled previously independent software applications, such as Word and PowerPoint, into Microsoft Office. You could get Excel for $200 or four different applications for $250. Duh!

But we think Microsoft's success goes deeper than the intriguing and entertaining stories of shrewd strategic decision making. There is a pattern in the way Microsoft operates that explains why it has maintained a high level of performance for so long.

There is a pattern in the way Microsoft operates that explains why it has maintained a high level of performance for so long.

Released in January 1983, Lotus 1-2-3 was the dominant spreadsheet application (replacing VisiCalc), with over 90 percent market share in 1991. Corporations, small businesses, and individuals were busy learning how to manipulate rows and columns, and there was even a specialized language among heavy users: "backslash," "plus," "sum," "data range," "enter." By 1997, however, Microsoft's Excel share of the market was over 70 percent.

In the mid-1990s, Netscape was the dominant Internet browser, with over 90 percent "usage share"—of all the websites visited, over 90 percent of them were accessed with Netscape's Navigator software. When the company went public in August 1995, it created several millionaires and made Marc Andreessen a household name. In that same year, Bill Gates wrote his famous "the internet is a tidal wave" memo after being blasted by an employee for not recognizing the Internet's importance, and Microsoft quickly developed Internet Explorer. Internet Explorer rocketed to a usage share of 95 percent in 2005. Since then it has faced legal challenges and stiff competition from Mozilla Firefox and Google Chrome but remains the leading browser, with about 60 percent usage share in 2009.

There are similar stories about Microsoft Word, which rapidly displaced the dominant WordPerfect and enjoys over 90 percent market share. Microsoft's Xbox now competes as an equal against the formerly dominant Sony PlayStation series and Nintendo machines (although Nintendo's Wii temporarily set a new standard in the industry).

Microsoft has been a strong follower in almost every product it has offered. Microsoft did not pioneer operating systems, GUI interfaces, spreadsheets, browsers, or gaming consoles. Rather, it is very good at identifying promising areas and refining its products over time. When you talk to Microsoft people, and you tell them, "You sure are a persistent bunch," they will all nod their heads in acknowledgment. It's an instinctive and involuntary reaction. "Yep, we are stubborn," they will say.

Persistence is the central concept in Microsoft's *identity.* If you want to understand how an organization tries to create value over a long period of time, you need to understand its sense of who it is and what inspires it. All organizations have an identity; what distinguishes the identities of SMOs is that they are (1) customized to the organization's history and industry and (2) support sustainable effectiveness. That is, an SMO's identity supports its long-term economic success as well as how it intends to achieve its environmental and social objectives. In addition, its identity is customized and has meaning for the organization. It may not look fancy or unique from the outside, but organization members understand it at a deep level.

If you knew that a core aspect of Microsoft's strategy was its persistence, would you bet against Microsoft when they entered the spreadsheet market? Would you bet against them when they entered the word processing market? Would you bet against them when they entered the Internet browser market or when they entered the gaming console market? Of course you wouldn't—but that's hindsight. Let's look at identity and why it has so much power as a core element of a robust strategy.

Identity and Culture

As shown in Figure 3.1, identity both flows from and helps create the internal culture and mission of the organization. Identity flows from the values that define an organization's culture and mission. Microsoft's culture, for example, prizes getting products shipped and out the door, employing really smart people, and criticizing everything. Identity also helps to create culture. It is the source of stories organization members tell each other about what the organization is.

At Microsoft, there are tons of stories about people staying up late to finish projects, heroic instances of customer service, and the dedication of people to complete software schedules. Together, these values and stories support the identity of Microsoft in which great work means dogged determination. Successful SMOs have identities that lead to performance that is right for their business, social, and natural environments.

Figure 3.1. The Elements of Identity

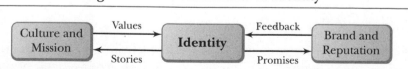

Source: Adapted from M. Hatch and M. Shultz, "The Dynamics of Organizational Identity," *Human Relations,* 2002, *55*(8), 989–1018.

Companies without a strong identity can be whipsawed by leaders with misguided agendas, suffer from a lack of consistent direction, and experience dysfunctional internal conflicts as different factions try to define what the organization is about. Until recently, Volvo's business was grounded in its traditional identity around safety and reliability; nobody ever accused Volvo of being sexy, and very few complained about its profitability. However, under Ford's ownership, Volvo's strong and socially relevant identity disappeared. Styling and performance won out over safety and quality and with it Volvo's unique claim to a revenue stream from a distinct customer segment.

Focusing on styling and performance moved Volvo out of a relatively protected niche and into direct competition with BMW, Mercedes, Lexus, and Infinity, where success depends on capabilities neither Ford nor Volvo possessed. Volvo's revenue initially increased but declined steadily for ten years; it became a weakened brand that China's Geely was able to acquire for a fraction of what Ford paid for it.

When organizations have a strong identity, they are less likely to propose adjustments to strategic intent (the second element of a robust strategy) that will not be supported by the organization's culture and are not in line with its brand image. On the other hand, when new strategic initiatives bubble up that honor identity, they are easily supported and implemented.

Harvey Golub recognized the importance of identity and capitalized on it when he became the new CEO of American Express. He spent a lot of time developing future leaders in the organization (including current CEO Kenneth Chenault) by asking them, "Does that strategy sound like 'American Express'?" He was teaching his managers to leverage the power of identity and propose strategies that would be understood, at a gut level, by the people who had to implement them.

Identity and Brand or Reputation

Figure 3.1 also suggests that identity flows from and helps to create an organization's reputation and brand promises. Its brand consists of messages about its products, services, and character. Like all organizations, SMOs must compete, and that means proactively communicating their mission—what they offer, what markets they serve, and what they stand for—to the marketplace. At Microsoft, there are enduring slogans, such as "Where do you want to go today?" and "Your potential is our passion." These messages suggest a brand promise that Microsoft products will help you achieve your goals.

The experience of consumers with an organization and its products provides an opportunity for it to test its brand promise and get feedback. Microsoft's "Where do you want to go today?" message sounds great until you get the dialog box that says, "We're sorry, an error has occurred in the program and we need to shut it down." As a last bit of insult, the screen asks, "Do you want to tell Microsoft about this problem?"

We don't know about you, but more than once, we have exercised our counterdependence and passive-aggressive tendencies and said, "no," but more often than not, we will say, "yes." So what does this have to do with Microsoft's identity? When you send that error message, it goes into a database where all the technical information is stored. Using data-mining programs, the analysts look for patterns—what build of the operating system was running, what other applications were being used, and so on—that might suggest a conflict among the programs. From time to time, they notice a pattern, the developers patch the software, and they make the correction available to consumers through updates.

Those really smart people keen to get the product out the door on schedule, who couldn't write a perfect program the first time, just keep plugging away at it until it works. Microsoft's "persistence" identity represents a strategically valuable integration of its internal culture (smart people, shipping of products, and so on) and external brand, image, and reputation (your potential is our passion, aggressive marketing and sales, occasional glitches). Anyone who works on large, complex software knows they are very unlikely to create a perfect product the first time around. What separates Microsoft—and has for a long time now—is that it keeps plugging away and eventually gets it right.

Identity is an important guidepost, helping organizations be successful over long periods of time. It can help an organization reorient itself in response to new situations. Without an identity guidepost, strategy can wander about instead of supporting decisive reactions. While identity is an important element in all organizations, it needs to take on special characteristics in SMOs so that it supports positive economic, social, and environmental outcomes simultaneously.

Identity in a Multi-Stakeholder World

To craft a sustainable, robust strategy SMOs need to take a special approach to identity. To have a strong sense of "who we are," the conversations in SMOs about "what we value" and "the stories we tell ourselves about ourselves" must align with the external communications about "who we want you to think we are" (brand promises) and "what your experience of us is." Getting this alignment right even in the best of circumstances is a tricky proposition. Whether an organization's identity will support sustainable effectiveness depends on (1) the existence and influence of sustainable effectiveness values in the culture, (2) a brand promise of sustainable effectiveness, and (3) the consistency of the organization's responses to external stakeholder feedback about its behavior.

There is an effective three-step method for discovering an organization's identity and exploring its consistency. First, organizations need to look backward over a long period and ask, "Have we been successful (or simply survived) because our orientation was on efficiency or because we were special?" By applying the traditional strategy concepts of low cost (efficiency) or differentiation (special), an organization can gain a quick insight into the part of its identity that supports economic outcomes. Although this is a good first step in discovering an identity, we believe that it is too crude a place to stop. Part of an SMO's identity should be unique to its long-term approach to success. Thus the second step should be customizing the economic identity of an organization to its history and industry. For example, it is one thing to say that Microsoft's identity is low cost and quite another to say that the basis of its success is "persistence." In most organizations, there are stories told, metaphors used, and a reputation in the marketplace that can be used to develop a customized identity.

The final step in understanding an organization's identity is to determine whether its identity extends to all aspects of its sustainable effectiveness. SMOs need to ask, "Is our orientation toward social responsibility and the natural environment the same as our economic orientation?" Microsoft's identity of persistence indicates something about its culture and reputation, and how it explains economic success. However, it may not necessarily reflect a stance toward social or environmental issues.

The real key to an identity that supports sustainable effectiveness, however, is whether these messages line up with the actual behavior of the organization and whether the values influence the way employees behave.

At DaVita, a Fortune 500 corporation that provides kidney care services, its "we're a 'village' first and a company second" identity reflects an integrated conversation between its values-in-use and its image, brand, and reputation. Internally, there is a clear understanding that taking care of patients and each other—maintaining the village—will lead to revenue and profit. Externally, analysts know that the first five minutes of the quarterly earnings call will begin not with financial results but with clinical outcomes.

DaVita extends the village metaphor to its relationship with the community and the natural environment. It has a mind-boggling array of internal employee support programs, a strong health care reform agenda, several external philanthropy efforts that focus on social accountability, and a clear understanding of its environmental responsibilities. Its managers are very aware of the environmental impact of the company's clinical treatments and actively implement steps to reduce or eliminate the toxic wastes from its dialysis treatment processes. To do otherwise would poison the village water well (figuratively) and fail to create the conditions for long-term survival.

It is relatively easy for most organizations to project an image of sustainability through their advertising messages about green products and the social issues they support through sponsorships and other philanthropy. The real key to an identity that supports sustainable effectiveness, however, is whether these messages line up with the actual behavior of the organization and whether the values influence the way employees behave.

Microsoft has extended its identity to the natural environment. Greenpeace gives it poor marks on a range of regulatory, consumer, and green-house gas programs; however, Microsoft has for years been a steadfast (read persistent) supporter of good environmental practices. From grassroots recycling efforts to systematic separation of glass, aluminum, paper, and other materials as well as broader social and environmental schemes, such as shared ride programs and public transportation systems, the organization has been a positive corporate model. Nor is Bill Gates letting his money lie idle. The Gates Foundation has an innovative philanthropic model that leverages grant money to address health care and educational problems around the globe.

Agile organizations have change and innovation friendly identities; SMOs do also, but they don't stop there. In addition, they have identities that support "doing well and doing good over the long run." SMOs have missions that are about more than just financial success. This is how we know they are an SMO: their identity addresses purpose, innovation and change, and sustainable effectiveness. Cisco's long-standing purpose of "changing the way we work, live, play, and learn" is a great example. It not only drives the company's economic value creation activities, it also informs its stance with respect to social responsibility and ecological health; it describes why Cisco does what it does along multiple dimensions. It also represents an additional performance standard that SMOs have to meet.

Strategic Intent Links Strategy to Execution

We were sitting in Beijing's original Starbucks—one of many there now—in the China World center with the CFO of a consumer products company. He was giving us his view of how China's economy was developing. It was a very compelling story of how China's development paralleled that of the United States following World War II, only at a much faster pace. As the excitement of the conversation waned, it dawned on us how similar this experience was to the other experiences we have had at a Starbucks.

A lot of people are surprised to find out that Starbucks's identity has relatively little to do with coffee. Its identity is best captured by the phrase, "creating great experiences." Internally, the organization pays higher-than-average salaries and provides health care benefits for even part-time employees. Baristas are trained extensively and encouraged to be customer focused. Externally, the Starbucks brand is associated with high quality, diverse flavors and smells, and good service.

But an experience at Starbucks, like the one we had in the Beijing store, has a variety of facets. While in Starbucks, a customer can have a coffee experience, a social experience, a technical experience, a musical experience, and even an eating experience.

The Dimensions of Intent

When SMOs say they are changing their strategy, they are not referring to their identity. Rather, they are referring to their strategic intent—a flexible, momentary strategic advantage that describes a way to win in the marketplace. Strategic intents and momentary advantages have a "hit and run" or "entry and exit" logic that is responsive to changes in the business environment. They are key to SMOs being agile.

When SMOs say they are changing their strategy . . . they are referring to their strategic intent—a flexible, momentary strategic advantage that describes a way to win in the marketplace.

When an opportunity to profitably offer new or existing products and services appears, SMOs commit resources to it. For example, Garmin, a leading global positioning satellite (GPS) firm, recently entered the mobile telephone market, adapting its handheld GPS units. Lured by the (assumed) profit potential in this market and the relatively low mobility barriers it faces, Garmin is carving out a niche position leveraging its GPS applications. Should it fail in its attempt, it can easily exit the market and retreat to the traditionally profitable GPS business, but it may very well succeed and generate an incremental profit stream.

This same logic can apply to the command and control and the high involvement management styles, but as described in Chapters One and Two, their commitment to stability and execution as a means of generating profit limits their ability to change and innovate. Research suggests that CCOs and HIOs do not pursue compelling opportunities when their financial performance is already high. Their belief in stability drives them to think, "It does not make sense to move into a new market with risky returns when our existing recipe is working so well." CCOs in particular often need to be in a state of crisis before they make major shifts in strategy, and by that time, it is often too late. Their shifts are poorly executed and highly risky.

SMOs, on the other hand, can say "yes" to change more often and more quickly, and they are able to withdraw more effectively if they make a bad choice. As a new entrant to a product or market, SMOs move quickly and monetize the identified advantage. As an existing player in a market, SMOs stay as long as it makes sense by imitating or innovating to extend an advantage, or exiting if a new entrant makes significant inroads. An SMO has less attachment to an existing market than other firms, which often face difficult decisions about levels of commitment and whether a new strategic intent means going after different customers or alienating an existing customer base. (The futuring process we will describe in Chapter Four ensures that SMOs have some place to go!)

Contrast the SMO approach to what is taught in business schools. Traditional strategy-related economics tells executives to identify sustainable competitive advantages. It says to focus attention and resources on establishing entry or mobility barriers, building up switching costs, and increasing bargaining power. We think counting on these mechanisms to protect profitability for any significant length of time is a misguided commitment to stability and in most cases a waste of time.

Because any source of advantage is fleeting, SMOs adopt a set of assumptions that are based on innovation and change rather than stability. In SMOs, strategic intent and momentary advantages are achieved by tinkering with the breadth, aggressiveness, and differentiation features of their product or market orientation. *Breadth* refers to the range of products and services offered, the number of markets served, the scope of the distribution network, and the different types of technologies that represent the organization's core competencies. A change to any of these increases or decreases the breadth of the advantage. *Aggressiveness* describes the amount of urgency, enthusiasm, and resources an organization throws behind the communication, marketing, and execution of its strategy. Finally, *differentiation* describes the product and service features that distinguish the organization's offerings from competitors, including price, quality, warranty, after-sale support, and other characteristics.

For any set of product or service features, an organization can have a broad or narrow product line and can be relatively aggressive or passive in its approach. For example, WD40, the lubricant manufacturer, relies on its difficult-to-imitate product features for differentiation, but is narrow in product-line breadth and relatively passive in its market approach. Disney has strong brand differentiation that it leverages across a broad range of products, services, and markets in a relatively aggressive manner.

Over time, Starbucks's "creating great experiences" identity has been translated into a series of momentary advantages. Each of these advantages has built upon the other. Starbucks's initial strategic intent was a great "coffee" experience. The momentary advantage was built from a relatively narrow breadth—the company focused on domestic markets and a small range of coffee drinks. It aggressively pursued that advantage by growing the number of stores quickly and supported the advantage with great coffee smells, good-tasting coffee, and a customer-focused experience.

Significantly, Starbucks's coffee experience had more than just economic overtones. The company consistently pointed out its pro-labor stance with respect to coffee growers and its use of recycled materials, both of which made the coffee experience more meaningful. The coffee was expensive, but worth it in multiple ways.

The success of the great coffee experience identity led customers to ask their friends and colleagues to socialize at a

Starbucks. To support the social experience, Starbucks furnished its retail locations with comfortable chairs and tables to encourage conversation. The social experience was upgraded with a technical experience in which work could get done. Starbucks partnered with T-Mobile to create hotspots so that people could surf the Web, work on their emails, and generally stay connected to their business and social networks.

Eventually, while drinking coffee or having a conversation, you notice the music. You say to the barista, "Who is that playing that music? Can I get a copy of that CD?" Moreover, if you stay there long enough, you get hungry. So Starbucks continued to expand the great experiences you can have by adding food, which generated a new stream of revenue for its stores but, as we will discuss later, also has created some problems.

Momentary Advantages in a Multi-Stakeholder World

To craft a sustainable, robust strategy, SMOs need to adopt an integrated set of value creation goals. In turn, the dimensions of strategic intent—breadth, aggressiveness, and differentiation— must be explored by SMOs for their relationship to the sustainable effectiveness outcomes they are committed to achieving. Product, service, technology, and market breadth can have a positive or negative impact on social, environmental, and economic performance.

The breadth of the markets an organization chooses to participate in—especially with respect to global markets—is an important input to the organization's "footprint." It also represents an opportunity to contribute to or detract from social and ecological outcomes. Starbucks's global footprint means that its supply chain must source and distribute coffee and other ingredients around the world. There is some opportunity to source local ingredients, but there is little doubt that its carbon footprint is larger because of the geographic breadth it has chosen.

An organization's identity can help to guide its choices about strategic breadth. For example, Intel has high product and technology breadth that involves a variety of manufacturing plants in Asia and other parts of the world. Where Intel's economic objectives align with Intel's clear and strong cultural values and with the local population's cultural orientation, its plants have been very successful. When these elements do not align, Intel has had to engage in intense conversations about which parts of the organization's culture are critical for economic success and which parts can be adapted to support local customs, suppliers, labor pools, and energy and environmental concerns.

Rather than aggressive growth or "big, hairy, audacious goals" that encourage the firm to reach beyond its grasp, SMOs take a [goal setting] approach that can be defended from ecological and social as well as economic perspectives.

The aggressiveness dimension of strategy has a clear relationship to sustainable effectiveness. Remember, aggressively pursuing a momentary advantage is not the same as an aggressive identity. There are times when aggressiveness in strategic intent is necessary to capture the benefits of an advantage. But aggressiveness may be negatively related to social and environmental objectives. A more aggressive intent often means more travel (carbon footprint), more advertising (potential social issues), more investment in plant and equipment (positive employment benefit, negative energy), and so on.

Rather than aggressive growth or "big, hairy, audacious goals" that encourage the firm to reach beyond its grasp, SMOs take an approach that can be defended from ecological and social as well as economic perspectives. Toyota's missteps in 2008 and 2009, its massive recalls, and its damaged reputation would appear to have been a perfect opportunity for Honda to step on Toyota while it was down. Honda's response, however, was quite measured: little increase in advertising, minimal expansion in production, and few sales incentives. Honda stuck to its message and its way of operating. It experienced some short-term gains, but it did not overstep the opportunity and commit to a nonsustainable approach.

A second aspect of aggressiveness, one that dovetails nicely with differentiation, is how organizations approach new product development. An overly aggressive innovation objective that does not include triple-bottom-line criteria can support economic over social and environmental outcomes. For example, technological advances, low materials costs, and planned obsolescence in most electronic equipment result in about fifty million tons of "e-waste" each year: the United States alone discards thirty million computers and Europe disposes of a hundred million phones.

If computer companies asked their designers to make computers last one year longer or enticed buyers to stay with their brand by offering a lower price for reusing their power cord, for example, the reduction of waste would be substantial. Given that much of the heavy metal in landfills comes from electronics, there would be an environmental benefit as well. If GM had been as concerned with ecological issues as it was with economic returns, would it have bought its now failed Hummer brand and discontinued its electric car, the EV1?

Finally, the differentiation dimension of strategic intent is important because an organization can choose a variety of product or service features that are environmentally or socially sensitive. Supporting its identity of customer intimacy and emotional connection, the Victoria's Secret (VS) division of Limited Brands has developed a sophisticated set of potential and actual differentiation advantages. By constantly asking, "What's new, what's next?" VS has created a stream of innovations in its core intimate apparel line that maintains a strong emotional connection to its customers.

VS has a complex global supply chain of factories that meet or exceed local labor laws and social conditions. By using sound and fair employment practices, VS is making important connections with customers who are looking for responsible operational decisions. At the retail end, the store experience, facilities design and maintenance, and product placements contribute to all three triple-bottom-line outcomes.

Victoria's Secret's marketing differentiation is partially based on printed catalogs and other paper materials. When VS was challenged by the NGO ForestEthics for using paper from nonsustainable growth forests, it had a choice to make. It could fight the NGO or adjust its strategy to create a new momentary advantage. Choosing the latter and working with ForestEthics, VS shifted its paper supply policies and began promoting responsible environmental practices. Similarly, VS works with textile suppliers and manufacturers to be sure it uses materials that are environmentally friendly.

The concept of strategic intent is inseparable from the concept of identity. A robust strategy consists of a stable identity that defines "who we are" and aligns actions through changeable short-term strategic intents. The clear distinction between identity and intent keeps organizations agile. Extending these concepts to incorporate sustainable effectiveness goals requires some conscious adjustments, integration, and even some trade-offs but is a must do for SMOs.

The Rest of the Story

We left our Starbucks story a few pages ago drawing a very positive picture of satisfying experiences building on each other. The astute reader was no doubt thinking, "But Starbucks's performance started to decline in 2007." And you'd be right. We want to close this chapter with the rest of the story as an important reflection on and integration of the concepts in this chapter.

An analysis of Starbucks's recent struggles points out the power of identity and intent. Their difficulties are extremely germane to the sustainable management perspective we are describing. Starbucks was sustainably effective when all of the dimensions of its momentary advantages were in balance. Once aggressive growth moved from an element of strategic intent to a proxy for its identity, as it did in the middle of the last decade, the company's performance started to decline.

Starbucks let the internal and external pressures for growth distract it from its identity. Aggressive growth became a goal and part of who it was instead of an element of intent. Its drive for more stores both domestically and internationally became more important than creating great experiences.

Following the addition of technical and musical experiences, it tried to create a food experience with muffins, rolls, and other breakfast items. This led to other drinks, yogurt, sandwiches, and salads. The baristas were happy to heat the muffins and do other minor preparation work; they were trained and expected to be customer focused, but they were also very proud of their ability to create a cup of coffee just for you—the core experience.

With the addition of the other food and drink items in the store, baristas were expected to not only make coffee but prepare food, stock shelves, manage inventory, and arrange point-of-purchase displays for coffee makers, coffee cups, and other products. The baristas complained that it was too hard to make a great cup of coffee *and* help with food. Instead of focusing on the experience, growth became the overriding objective.

In the pursuit of more revenue growth per store, Starbucks said, "OK, we hear you, we'll make it easier for you to make a great cup of coffee" and they replaced the one-cup-of-coffee-at-a-time system with an automated coffee machine. The barista could make Mr. Robinson's vente, latte, extra hot with a double shot of vanilla, with the push of a button.

Starbucks redesigned the stores to lower the counter so the baristas could see more of the customer and increase the high-touch customer experience. Which all sounds good until you realize that the substitution of technology for labor ruins the experience. The baristas were not making a cup of coffee just for you, they were making just another cup of coffee. The whole experience became routinized and, in the ultimate disgrace to a differentiated experience, was easily imitated by McDonald's at a lower price point!

The comedian Lewis Black tells a great joke about thinking that he might be coming down with early Alzheimer's disease when upon leaving one Starbucks he looked up and saw another one on the opposite corner.

When Starbucks became enamored with growth, it became distracted from defending and leveraging its identity. Aggressive growth did not sit well or align with a brand promise or mission of responsibility—"To inspire and nurture the human spirit—one person, one cup, and one neighborhood at a time." The company lost its focus on drawing incremental revenues through a disciplined approach to understanding momentary advantages.

Perhaps not by accident, Starbucks's focus on economic growth was associated with an increase in criticism from the environmental and social sectors. Starbucks has done a good job, in general, vis-à-vis sustainability—using recycled material in its coffee cups and working with NGOs to ensure sustainable growing, harvesting, and labor practices in the field. But it also has been criticized for taking a lazy approach to recycling and water use.

The Starbucks case illustrates how rapid growth can distract an organization from its core identity and the true basis of its success. Similarly, Toyota's quality problems that became very visible in 2009 and 2010 were no doubt linked to its siren call to be the world's largest auto manufacturer when its managers realized in the middle of the decade they were close to surpassing GM in size. Toyota succeeded, but has lost billions in market value and brand reputation because of how it got its growth.

Conclusion

Sustainable strategies rely on a business model fundamentally different from the ones used by CCOs and HIOs. In the command and control style, effectiveness is a function of stability, predictability, alignment, and growth, the cornerstones of bureaucratic efficiency. In an HIO firm, effectiveness derives from the productivity of engaged and committed people. In contrast, SMOs expect effectiveness to be achieved through change. They are guided by an identity that remains stable over time but is also change, socially, and environmentally friendly. They create value from a flexible strategic intent and the speed and effectiveness with which they orchestrate transitions from one momentary advantage to another. In other words, the ability to change drives performance because no advantage is expected to last.

Assessment Questions

1. If you asked your colleagues, "Even in turbulent times, what won't change about our company?" what kind of answer would you get?

   a. "Anything could change!"

   b. "Gee, I'll have to really think about that."

c. Wildly different answers from different people.

d. Reasonably consistent answers that agree with the top management view.

Here is what the answers imply:

a. Implies there is no sense that an identity exists.

b. Implies that if there is an identity it is not well understood.

c. Implies there is no consensus on identity.

d. Implies a strong, clear identity.

2. What do senior leaders talk about with respect to competitive strategy?

a. They use traditional language about being a low-cost provider or a customer friendly firm.

b. They talk in generalities such as about striving to provide the highest-quality products at the lowest possible price.

c. They talk about short-term tactics and responding to opportunities and threats.

d. They are clear about having both a long-term strategy and a short-term way of winning.

Here is what the answers imply:

a. The organization remains mired in the view that the world is reasonably stable. A significant rethinking of what strategy means in the twenty-first century is required.

b. The organization does not have a clear strategy. This may reflect dissatisfaction with approaches to strategy that assume a stable world.

c. The long-term view is missing; the organization needs to develop an identity.

d. The organization has a good framework for creating a robust strategy.

3. How does your organization think about growth?

a. It's the lifeblood of the organization. Each year we are given "stretch goals" for growth.

b. As long as we are not losing market share no one complains too much.

c. Our growth goals vary significantly from year to year depending on perceived opportunity.

d. Our leaders are keenly aware of the dangers of rapid growth.

Here is what the answers imply:

a. Becoming an SMO will be like a cold splash of water.

b. While not an optimal approach, this mind-set can keep you out of trouble.

c. This is the best way to operate, taking a very conscious approach to growth.

d. Hopefully you ticked this choice as well as "c." If leaders don't recognize the dangers of rapid growth, then the future of your organization is at risk.

| Developing a Strategy

If you are employed by the U.S. Secret Service detail that protects the president of the United States, your job is pretty clear. You do whatever it takes, including taking a bullet, to see that the president remains safe. But what do you do when you are not actually guarding the president? We were fascinated to learn that agents spend a lot of their time worrying about how the president *might* be attacked, what they would do, and how to prevent it. (We envision a room where agents sit around reading Robert Ludlum and Vince Flynn novels.) Thinking about the when, where, and how questions is an important part of the job.

Every once in a while, the agents come up with a radical, clever attack scenario and create a simulation (real or imaginary) in which they act out their roles and responses. "If terrorists come at us this way, what do our rules say we should do?" "Does that make sense?" "Are we or the president vulnerable?" After they walk through the simulation, they debrief. "What was your response?" "Why was it successful or not?" and "What would we do differently?" They also wonder about how they could intervene earlier or prepare better.

We think this is a great example of the key feature of strategizing in an SMO: using a sophisticated "futuring" process to prepare for an uncertain world. While many organizations have processes for environmental scanning, too few actually use them, think beyond current trends, or incorporate social and environmental issues. We think SMOs need to make futuring a central part of how they operate. They need to look at multiple future time frames and integrate a broader spectrum of issues. But first, let's finish the Secret Service story, since there is a surprising twist.

Because of their preparation and early interventions, the Secret Service has deterred or preempted many attacks. But when an attack has occurred, it has never resembled any of the practice scenarios dreamed up by the Secret Service. The way it happened, where it happened, and when it happened were complete surprises to the people who were doing the protecting. Despite this, the Secret Service responded effectively. How do they do it?

The agents say it is the preparation that pays off. The scenarios they create and the discussions they have about how to respond give them a chance to develop options, consider different behaviors and tactics, and learn about their fellow agents' reactions. When a truly new situation arises, they are prepared because they have considered multiple options and have a sense of what their fellow agents might do.

Current performance is as much a function of preparation as it is execution.

The preparation and practice of responding to unknown situations builds up a repertoire of potential actions that allows the agents to quickly adapt. It generates effective behaviors when unknown situations actually occur.

The Secret Service story teaches us three important lessons that are the backbone of strategy development in SMOs. First, current performance is as much a function of preparation as it is execution. Futuring is about building the capacity to deal with what you cannot plan for. For the Secret Service, preparing means discussion, practice, and debriefs—but we don't expect most organizations to practice responding to terrorist attacks! What organizations can do is develop a cadre of options, decisions, and actions they might take if something unexpected happens. Without preparing for alternative futures, even the most capable organizations will not be ready and will be too slow to capitalize on an opportunity or respond to a threat.

Second, looking at the future has to be a regular process, not an add-on, every-once-in-a-while event. The Secret Service is thinking about alternative futures all the time; getting ready for the future is part of the job, not an extra.

Third, it is important to spend time learning and reflecting on practice. When a situation does occur, the Secret Service wants to know what happened, why it happened, whether their responses worked, or why their responses didn't work. They want to know what they could do to respond better.

In Chapter Three we saw that the way SMOs create value in terms of identity and strategic intent is quite different from how CCOs and HIOs do it. We also saw that many of the perspectives on what makes a good strategy for SMOs are different (for example, more willingness to change, a high awareness of risk, more concern about all the stakeholders, being cautious about recklessly chasing growth and profits). In this chapter, we will consider how SMOs can explore the future context for strategic intents and begin building the capabilities that will allow them to be successful.

Build a Strong Future Focus

It is no surprise that the subject of futuring is a popular topic these days. Many organizations were "surprised" by the financial and economic crisis that occurred in 2008. This is hardly the first time that organizations have been surprised by economic and business changes. GM and Ford were surprised by the Japanese auto industry's growth and success, Microsoft was surprised by the Internet tidal wave, and Kodak was surprised by digital photography. Given all the research and practice in scenario planning, why are so many firms "surprised" by events, and why are so many organizations so slow to respond?

The purpose of spending time on the future is to prevent becoming overly focused on the present. If you are a parent, you are familiar with this problem. Your kids are sitting on the couch watching their favorite TV show, and you tell them they need to take out the trash. You may get a response, usually in the form of a grunt, or not. Twenty minutes later you return, the kids are still there, and you ask them if they took out the trash. They look at you with that "what?" look.

That's what psychologists call "inattentional blindness."[1] People can become so consumed by their current task (such as watching TV) that they are blind to what's going on around them. This is a likely explanation for Starbucks's problems. It became so focused on growth that it forgot its identity.

To avoid inattentional blindness and to create future value, SMOs need to use a futuring process that is differentiated along two lines: time and goals. First, as shown in Table 4.1, SMOs need to look at short-, medium-, and long-term business horizons, and there is a specific purpose for each. The long-term view considers possible future strategic intents and the operating assumptions that will drive them whereas short-term futuring guides adjustments to the current strategic intent. The actual time frame attached to each of these horizons is somewhat arbitrary but should be a function of the industry. In retail and high technology organizations, the short term can be measured in weeks whereas in industries with large, fixed assets, the short term can be one to two years.

To capitalize on a series of momentary advantages, SMOs have to attend to all three horizons, and they must do so in a very deliberate way. This is no small task, as any member of an organization who has tried to get time to practice disaster preparedness responses will tell you. However, it is the only way to reduce the problems that come from being blindsided by "unforeseeable" events.

Second, SMOs focus their futuring process on three effectiveness areas: financial performance, social value, and the natural environment. SMOs expand existing sensing capabilities by developing specific scenarios about social and environmental issues and integrating these perspectives into short, medium, and long-term economic scenarios. Organizations designed for sustainable effectiveness add NGO activities, government policies related to social and environmental issues, and social trends to their future-focused data collection and sensing activities. This increases the amount of social and environmental information available to decision-making processes and increases their saliency.

Broadening the information available can be accomplished by expanding the existing environmental scanning processes to include search routines in areas beyond market demand, customer

Table 4.1. Elements of a Futuring Process for Sustainable Effectiveness

	Short Term	Medium Term	Long Term
Purpose	Identify adjustments to current strategic intent to optimize sustainable effectiveness	Develop boundaries for next version of robust strategic intent	Identify future business assumptions and develop range of possible future strategic intents
Key Outputs	Operating decisions that change breadth, aggressiveness, and differentiation	Identify capability investments	Identify potential capabilities Build a cadre of responses
Tools	Traditional environmental scanning tools Prediction markets Extreme strategizing	Ecosystem mapping Base, best-, and worse-case forecasts	Future scenarios
Who Is Involved	Top management (20 percent of their futuring time) Any boundary-spanner Current customers and relevant stakeholders	Top management (50 percent of their futuring time) Network and ecosystem community	Top management (30 percent of their futuring time) Board (75 percent of their futuring time) High-level government, NGO, and community representatives; futurists
Number of Scenarios	Zero; use goals instead	Three in current trajectory Surprise scenarios	Three to five scenarios of diverse conditions

requirements, and regulatory trends to include social and community impacts and ecological implications. It also can be accomplished by creating specialized units, such as corporate social responsibility departments, and charging them with gathering these data and integrating them with traditional data during strategizing meetings.

SMOs spend a lot more time thinking about the future than CCOs and HIOs because they accept and embrace the frequently repeated admonition that the world is changing faster and faster. They believe that the "new normal" is more and more change. CCOs and HIOs may give lip service to this "new normal," but they act "as if" everything is stable and wait until they are forced to change.

SMOs spend a lot more time thinking about the future than CCOs and HIOs because they accept and embrace the frequently repeated admonition that the world is changing faster and faster.

SMOs involve a lot of people in their futuring processes. People from their organization and from external groups are involved, so they understand all the sustainable effectiveness issues they may face. This is particularly true of the long-term futuring process, which we will look at next before we consider the medium- and short-term processes.

Long-Term Futuring

SMOs recognize that their circumstances will change in many unforeseen ways. To create value in an uncertain future, they "play" with a variety of possible scenarios in order to develop a cadre of responses. In other words, the long-term futuring process is about decreasing the number of surprises and about increasing the number of options available to a firm when an unknowable future happens.

Scenario planning is the best method for considering possible future situations, exposing changing business assumptions, and developing a cadre of options to draw on in the future. Futurists say that there is nothing wrong with traditional forecasting tools because forecasting is generally pretty accurate. The problem with forecasting is that it rarely challenges the assumptions underneath the forecast. Betting your mobile phone company on the growth of third-generation (3G) demand is a pretty safe bet, but it is the wrong bet if 4G services are about to be announced. Becoming aware of the changing business assumptions is the purpose of long-term futuring.

The key output of a long-term futuring process should be a list of capabilities that the organization will explore and a set of alternative action plans "just in case." As shown in Table 4.1, and as we will discuss further in Chapter Five, the long-term scenario process should be owned by the board. This is a radical idea, and we don't want to gloss over it. In an SMO the board, not the top management team, is responsible for ensuring the long-term viability of the organization.

Because an SMO changes more often than a CCO or HIO, it is important that the top management team's focus be on the execution of strategic intents and transitions from one momentary advantage to another, not on how business assumptions might change in the long term. The medium-term forecasting and short-term scanning processes that will be discussed later are more relevant to the futuring process for the task of executing a strategic intent and therefore should be the responsibility of senior management.

The top management team should be involved in long-range thinking; it is just not their primary responsibility. Why do senior managers need to spend most of their strategic thinking time on the medium term? Because spending most of their time thinking about the medium-term future means that SMO executives will have little time to worry about the present—and as most operating managers will tell you, that's a good thing.

Playing with the Future

The best-known example of long-term scenario planning is Royal Dutch Shell's use of it in the late 1960s and early 1970s. A group of Shell strategic planners were concerned that executives held two very questionable assumptions about the marketplace: that there was plenty of oil and that the price of oil would stay low. On the basis of these assumptions, Shell executives were making long-term infrastructure investments and resource allocation decisions. The group used those assumptions to identify events that would affect the price and supply of oil to create three scenarios for strategic decision making.

One scenario assumed that U.S. oil reserves were rapidly declining at the same time demand was increasing. This gave OPEC important bargaining leverage over supply and price. Another scenario described how a Saudi Arabian oil pipeline was accidentally damaged, resulting in lower supply and decreased production. The situation created a market in which oil prices increased and allowed OPEC nations to pump less oil but make more money. A third scenario suggested that many OPEC country governments would become increasingly aggressive. The question posed by the scenario was not whether OPEC would demand much higher oil prices but when.

Each of the scenarios described the implications of supply and price events and included stories about the possibility of OPEC governments taking over Shell's oil fields. The scenarios sparked a vigorous conversation among executives about what the company might do if any of these scenarios actually came to pass.

In October 1973, in response to the U.S. decision to resupply the Israeli armed forces during the Yom Kippur War, OPEC decided to suspend oil shipments to the United States. Within weeks, the price of oil jumped from $3 per barrel to $12 per barrel. As these events unfolded, managers at Shell began to see a pattern that, although different from the specifics of any of their scenarios, resembled the scenario well enough to help them make some decisions. Among the more important ones was a decision to lower their refining investments and to shift those investments to other locations. As a result, Shell did not suffer from the industry's subsequent overcapacity in refining and significantly outperformed the industry.

Shell's timely and quick response to the 1973 oil crisis was an important contributor to its movement from being one of the weakest oil companies to being the second largest and most profitable. Their scenario planning work helped Shell executives interpret a series of events and decisions as part of a pattern, appreciate the implications, and make quick decisions. In fact, like our Secret Service example, none of Shell's scenarios matched the actual events that happened, but were quite similar to the conditions that Shell encountered. The conversations about "What would we do if the unthinkable happened?" prepared them well when the unimaginable occurred.

The Process of Scenario Planning

SMO corporate boards should spend up to 75 percent of their strategy time thinking about the long term. They should ask in-house and external resources (such as futurists and industry analysts) to generate a set of possible futures. In the Shell example, price and supply were key assumptions in the energy business and formed the core of the different economic scenarios, although they could have just as easily been assumptions about environmental attitudes and regulation (Was Exxon prepared for the Valdez oil spill?) or relationships with local communities (Did Chernobyl's, Union Carbide's, BP's, or Toyota's managements have good responses?).

Good scenarios are not based on things you know, like whether people will demand faster and more user-friendly mobile web experiences or whether the Chinese economy will continue a high rate of growth in the future. Long-term scenarios are best constructed around key uncertainties that will have a big impact.

Good scenarios for the financial services industry are based on whether the world will adopt a global monetary standard; good scenarios for an automobile manufacturer are based on whether a breakthrough fuel cell technology will occur before 2015; and good scenarios for any organization are based on whether global warming will be arrested in our lifetimes. Making assumptions about uncertainties; describing the competitive, social, and ecological conditions implied by those assumptions; and understanding those implications for strategic intent and decision-making contexts can shed light on and generate insights into what might be done and what is likely to be successful.

Scenarios should be broad and diverse in nature (not small, medium, and large), linked to or triggered by possible key events, and specific and concrete in their description. Scenario diversity is important. Some scenarios should be terribly optimistic, while others should be disastrous. They should account for economic, social, and environmental trends, and they should "play" with events outside the normal range of factors considered in the industry. What condom manufacturer thought it would be in the disease prevention business and not just the pregnancy prevention business? Good scenarios are specific. The Shell scenarios were linked to real groups (OPEC) and real, plausible events (OPEC decisions, pipeline accidents). Long-term futuring is not about being right, it is about generating insight and conversation, increasing awareness, and creating options.

Finally, scenarios should not just be developed and then trashed. Part of the responsibility of the board and the strategic planning function in an SMO is the collection, revision, and refinement of scenarios. For the Secret Service, scenario planning is a routine; it represents an important organizational learning process.

When the board and top management team revisit scenarios, some may get discarded but only after thought is given to questions such as "What did we learn?" "What did we see (or not see)?" and "How can we do better?" As an organization moves from long-term to medium-term thinking, scenarios can be used to help senior executives understand their blind spots ("What didn't we see?") and to remind them of their strategic assumptions.

Output of Long-Term Futuring

The board and senior management should have a variety of conversations about the implications of the scenarios. "What decisions should we make if this were to happen?" "If this did happen, would we be able to respond?" "How might our government, community, and NGO partners respond?" "What can we do today to encourage or prevent some scenarios from happening?" "What capabilities would we need (that we do not have today) to develop?" The decisions, actions, and processes should be captured, shared, and catalogued.

The capabilities discussion in particular is crucial. The discussion isn't expected to generate specific strategic intents. Rather, the key output is the elaboration of what the organization needs to learn to be successful under these conditions.

Following an assessment of event probability and available resources, the next step is to create a variety of small capability initiatives. The team assigned to each initiative should be led by a member of top management and populated by relevant managers from throughout the organization, as well as external stakeholders such as government representatives, NGOs, customers, and community members. The team's task should be to understand the capability, including the knowledge and skills that underlie it; the structures, systems, and processes necessary to support it; and the kinds of learning and experiences necessary to be good at it. Where appropriate, this may involve some small acquisitions (as an offensive move to shape the structure of the future industry or as a defensive move to lock up resources), key talent hires, or business plan development.

Medium-Term Futuring

The medium-term future is critical because it is the likely time for creation of the next strategic intent (constellation of breadth, aggressiveness, and differentiation) or series of momentary advantages. A strong medium-term futuring process generates forecasts of likely business environments under best, base, and pessimistic scenarios. In addition, medium-term futuring processes should look for a range of surprises. The processes should be run by the top management team—which should spend half of its futuring time on this activity—and the key output should be a list of capabilities the organization needs to develop and a clear path to building or acquiring them.

Forecasting the Future

Let's look at an example of a medium-term futuring process that was designed to produce the innovations needed for a company to be sustainably effective. Nokia is the worldwide leader in mobile phones, with a global market share of 37 percent at the end of 2009. In Europe, Africa, and Asia, Nokia phones are ubiquitous, but not in the United States, where the company has struggled.

Nokia's current profitability—along with that of its competitors—is clearly down, but its long-term performance profile meets the objective for sustainable effectiveness we outlined in Chapter Three. Nokia has been consistently, but not significantly, above average in profitability for fourteen of the fifteen years from 1993 through 2008. It has avoided the boom-bust cycle that has plagued other mobile device manufacturers such as Motorola and Apple.

A broader look at Nokia is even more revealing. In addition to being recognized at January's (2010) World Economic Forum as the fifth most sustainable company and topping Greenpeace's electronics index several years running, look at what the Dow Jones Sustainability Index report had to say:

> In 2009, Nokia emerged as the sustainability leader in the technology sector [*Author's note: they have been a leader in this index for years*], scoring high in all three sustainability dimensions. . . . Nokia's solid management system is highlighted by above average corporate governance, risk and crisis management as well as unparalleled supplier management strategies. A clear and well-managed innovation process also contributed to its outstanding score in the economic dimension. Innovation at Nokia is not just aimed at improving technological leadership: environmental and social aspects play an important role in the research and development process. The company's research spending showed a relevant increase over the last three years, with focus on developing technically feasible products based on the concept of "Design for Environment." Nokia's commitment to environmental sustainability becomes apparent in activities such as establishing "environmental teams" in each business unit and regularly auditing all environmental data. The company has launched programs, such as "re-made" to utilize recycled material, and has funded research on radio-frequency and health through the Finnish National Research Program. The company also stands out in the social dimension with special focus on digital inclusion and stakeholder engagement. In an effort to reduce the digital divide in society, the company has many initiatives in place to improve the affordability of telecommunications focusing on remote regions and on socially challenged people.[2]

One of the reasons Nokia has been able to maintain such a consistent level of sustainable effectiveness is that it spends a lot of time collecting data about the medium term and developing forecasts about the likely future conditions that it will face. Of importance, these same processes make valued social contributions along the way.

One of the reasons Nokia has been able to maintain such a consistent level of sustainable effectiveness is that it spends a lot of time collecting data about the medium term and developing forecasts about the likely future conditions that it will face.

The Nokia Research Center (NRC) has the mandate of leading Nokia into the future as "the global leader of open innovation for the human mobility systems of the fused physical and digital world, giving birth to the growth of businesses for Nokia." The NRC does research with a variety of partners that goes well beyond any current business model to intentionally disrupt the status quo. It is important to note that the mission is driven by the "open innovation" model used by Procter & Gamble, IBM, HP, and others.[3] It suggests that important work will happen outside the boundaries of the NRC. The mission also broadly defines the space that NRC works in (human mobility systems and fused physical and digital world).

One of NRC's more interesting initiatives in this vein is the work of Nokia behavioral researcher Jan Chipchase.[4] He wanders around the world looking for how communication technologies are being used and exploring the implications.

The Nokia Open Studio experiments are intended to understand the implications of a "digital divide," in which some countries enjoy a variety of technologies while others have little access to them. Specifically, the goal of the project is to explore "opportunities for new products, applications, [and] services that would be viable within 3–15 years timeframe . . . *not* to generate concepts to be fed into the design process."

In 2007, the Open Studio established "design studios"—small storefronts in local communities in India, Brazil, and Ghana—and

sponsored a design contest. People from these mostly impov-
erished neighborhoods were given access to designers and
encouraged to think about their "ideal phone." "What does it
look like?" "What does it do?" "How will you use it?" "When and
where will you use it?"

The design submissions were driven by a variety of motives,
including cost savings, convenience, status, problem solving, and
vision of a better future. While involvement was driven initially by
the opportunity to win prizes or by general curiosity, according
to Nokia, community members participated "to have their opin-
ion heard—a nontrivial issue in communities that are often stig-
matized by outsiders; a chance to elevate their standing within
the community through contact with a respected corporation; a
chance to show off creative skills; a mental and physical space to
reflect on their own life, their relationship with their peer group,
and community; and a fun family activity."

The Nokia Open Studio project demonstrates several benefits. First, it represented a way for Nokia to gain insight into
how developing markets think about the use of technology and how
its technology should adapt. Second, the actual process of collecting information about the future generated positive social benefits.
Locals were hired to run the studios, and the studios became a
place for people to convene. While that was an immediate benefit
for the community, the project also benefited Nokia. It generated
data about the use of technology and how technology might get
diffused as well as building long-term goodwill.

The Process of Forecasting

The medium-term futuring process forecasts the economic,
social, and ecological contexts that are likely to dominate the
next planning horizon. For many firms, this is a two-to-three-year
period. Whereas the long-term planning process is about playing with the future, attempting to identify changing assumptions,
developing a cadre of options, and making low-risk investments
in future capabilities, the medium-term process is about forecasting the likely conditions under which the organization will have
to compete. This is accomplished by participating in four different
conversations (Figure 4.1).

Figure 4.1. Value Creation–Value Capture Matrix

		Value Creation	
		In-House	**Community Driven**
Value Capture	**Company**	A large enough percentage of products and services to generate economic success	Participate in networks to identify trends and innovations that can be important ideas for new products, services, markets, and businesses
	Ecosystem	Use innovations that do not contribute to the firm's future value proposition to contribute to the economic, social, and ecological sustainability of the business ecosystem	Support formal and informal participation in a variety of networks for personal, professional, and social development

In 2003, Henry Chesbrough suggested that the range of innovations organizations have to deal with is too complex for a single organization to control, especially with respect to all the necessary knowledge needed to successfully innovate. He proposed that organizations collaborate and share resources so that a whole network could innovate and prosper together.

Figure 4.1 describes how strategists can use Chesbrough's "open innovation" concept to gain important insights into medium-term conditions.[5] Organizations interested in their medium-term future need to understand (1) where and how value will be created and (2) where and how value will be captured. Our addition here is to link these ideas to an organization's current and future offerings and describe how such a view can generate sustainable effectiveness.

In the upper left quadrant, the organization engages in activity during which value is created "in-house" and that value is expected to be captured by the "company." As a medium-term forecasting issue, the organization asks, "What resources and capabilities are we developing that are likely to yield new businesses or new technologies?" or "What are the emerging social and environmental issues that our resources and capabilities can address?" As we will describe in Chapter Six, senior executives need to give special attention to these forecasting projects so that overly bureaucratic processes do not smother them at this early stage of development. A large part of the NRC's work is devoted to this kind of development, as implied by its mission statement.

In the lower left quadrant, value is created "in-house" but that value is captured by the "ecosystem," where *ecosystem* refers to the web of businesses, customers, governments, NGOs, and other stakeholders that operate together—consciously or unconsciously. That is, the organization thinks about the work it is performing that will benefit others. As employees (managers, individual contributors, or researchers) engage in innovative activity for their firm, they often generate valuable ideas that do not contribute substantively to expected future strategic intents of their firms, but they can be used by others without harm to the organization's performance.

The Aravind Eye Clinic in India has developed a remarkable process for doing cataract surgery and addressing preventable blindness.[6] Whereas many surgeons only perform one or two surgeries per day, the Aravind doctors perform eleven to fifteen per day with fantastic quality results. The process innovations that were created internally have been shared with others.

The clinic takes its process on the road, delivering cataract surgeries throughout India; the profits from paying customers are used to subsidize the surgeries in less fortunate parts of the country. As a result, the Aravind Eye Clinic has dramatically reduced the amount of preventable blindness. Other clinics, such as the He Eye Hospital in Shenyang, China, have picked up on the innovation and begun to address the preventable blindness in China. In this case, innovative, future-focused activity that began as in-house/company value was extended to in-house/ecosystem value.

In the upper right quadrant, the "community" creates the value and the "company" captures it. As the obverse of the "in-house/ecosystem" quadrant, organization members participate (on company time) in different networks in which new ideas are being developed. As a result, the organization becomes aware of opportunities and trends that can help it develop future value-added strategic intents.

Many firms, including Cisco, Intel, Microsoft, and GE, take a small ownership stake in a variety of other firms to extend their reach and knowledge of future opportunities. This idea can be easily extended to sustainable effectiveness. For example, having managers and employees sit on nonprofit boards for social and environmental issues exposes them to likely future markets, business ideas, and regulations. The Open Studio experiments clearly show this process at work. By sponsoring ideal phone design contests, the value was generated in and by the community (Nokia had a clear and transparent intellectual property process in place) even though the ideas might eventually generate value and be captured by Nokia.

Finally, in the lower right quadrant, value is created by the "community" and captured by the "ecosystem." The open source movement, famous for its Linux operating system, is the result of people (many working on their own time and not as part of an employment relationship with an organization) developing and improving the software. The software is distributed free, and contributions to it are rewarded with the inclusion of the contributor's name as one of the authors. Similarly, marketing functions and corporate communications departments are quickly learning how to leverage social networking sites, such as YouTube, Facebook, and a variety of sites where people post reactions to products and services, in order to gain insights into emerging trends. We heard one marketing manager worry that her million dollar marketing campaigns can be made worthless by social networking sites where product defects are quickly identified.

Viral marketing, Google Analytics, Tweets, and blogs are not only useful for immediate information, they can be used to identify "weak signals" regarding future opportunities. Again, the Open Studio experiments reflect the process well. Not only did Nokia gain insight about its technology for its experiments, but the way it conducted them also generated social value for the community that was captured by the community.

The value creation–value capture matrix provides important guidelines for medium-term futuring processes. The top management team of an SMO must be responsible for governing this process. The executives must allocate enough of their time and involve a broad enough range of external stakeholders to ensure that all quadrants are covered. SMO strategizing processes should include enough emphasis on the in-house/company quadrant to generate future revenues and profits. In addition, the organization should participate appropriately in the other three cells to generate information, innovations, and knowledge to increase their awareness of other potential products and services.

The matrix defines areas where organizations should look for trends and emerging opportunities. CCOs operate largely in the in-house/company quadrant, trying to "go it alone" and generating innovations for primarily economic gain. HIOs also work primarily in this quadrant, but in the pursuit of generating an engaged and knowledgeable workforce, may encourage some people to participate in professional and technical communities.

The logic of SMOs calls for an external focus. In a world changing rapidly, it is highly unlikely that an organization can do it all on its own. No organization can employ all the smart people (scarce and expensive resources), and so, to understand emerging opportunities, it makes sense to gather observations about the future in collaboration with others. The strategizing process must create the opportunity to capture ideas from other places and give organizations a chance to contribute to other organizations' products and services. Innovation, it turns out, isn't an efficient process, but this approach can help organizations figure out how to benefit from that inefficiency. As a result of using it, social good is produced alongside economic progress.

Output of Medium-Term Futuring

The output of the medium-term futuring process is a range of expected conditions, a set of robust strategic intents, and specific investments in the resources and capabilities that will support sustainable effectiveness. First, the top management team must collect the data generated by participating in the different value creation–value capture quadrants, and they must systematically analyze it. "Where is the market heading?" "What new markets appear to be emerging faster than we expected?" "What would the best and worst cases look like from our point of view and what would appear to be the key events most likely to trigger these scenarios?"

Second, looking across the pessimistic, expected, and optimistic forecasts, executives should identify choices of breadth, aggressiveness, and differentiation that are likely to be success-ful under most or all of the scenarios. For example, despite the passing of a health care reform bill, there are still a large number of uncertainties facing hospitals and other health care firms. At Alliance Imaging, a provider of mobile and outsourced imaging services, disciplined aggressiveness is considered to be the smart play in terms of entering a new market (oncology) and defend-ing its traditional CT and MRI markets. No matter how the health care reform process unfolds, an aggressive intent—not an aggressive identity—is the most robust intent.

Finally, the top management team needs to decide on the investments they need to make to build the knowledge, skill, infrastructures, processes, and systems to support capability devel-opment. In the Alliance Imaging case, managers' understanding of the importance of disciplined aggressiveness led to decisions about building the company's sales, marketing, and servicing capabilities. Must-do activities included thinking through and developing the necessary organization structures, hiring and reten-tion strategies, and operation processes that would keep current customers loyal and allow the sales force to pursue new accounts.

Short-Term Futuring

The short-term performance time frame is controlled by the cur-rent strategic intent. It generates current revenue and profit, and drives ecological and social benefits (or harm). It is the result of actions taken or not taken in the past. Too many CCOs and HIOs spend most of their time trying to understand current trends in the business environment and do not spend enough time con-sidering longer-term issues. While making adjustments to their current strategic intent, they miss important signals about the need to adapt, and, as a result, their ability to adapt is severely constrained. They don't have any insight into why the changes are happening. To avoid this problem, SMOs complement tradi-tional environmental scanning techniques, such as SWOT analyses (strengths, weaknesses, opportunities, threats) and identifying current social, technical, economic, ecological, and political trends, with tools such as prediction markets and the extreme strategizing process.

In SMOs, senior executives spend only about 20 percent of their futuring time thinking about short-term trends. Instead, they rely on operating managers who are in much closer contact with the marketplace. In too many CCOs and HIOs, executives get involved in short-term processes because of their impact on current financial outcomes. In the vernacular, they let the "urgent drive out the important." Operating managers, not senior executives, should handle adjustments to a strategic intent, such as increasing or decreasing the aggressiveness with which the firm attempts to drive an advantage, changing a product or service feature to build a short-run differentiation advantage, or entering adjacent market segments to increase breadth. The organization's identity plays a crucial role here in guiding decisions according to the cultural values and brand promise.

Operating managers, not senior executives, should handle adjustments to a strategic intent, such as increasing or decreasing the aggressiveness with which the firm attempts to drive an advantage, changing a product or service feature to build a short-run differentiation advantage, or entering adjacent market segments to increase breadth.

The Future Is Now

Southwest Airlines has done a great job letting operating managers handle short-term futuring processes and modifications to its strategic intent. Southwest has a clear identity and strategic intent around the concept of "freedom." It leverages its identity (gives customers more freedom) with changes in breadth (for example, entering and exiting city markets). In addition, it differentiates itself and contributes to customer freedom with low fares, on-time departures, and friendly customer service.

Southwest—especially its operating managers—monitors certain trends for changes that can affect its strategic intent. Those trends include fuel prices, economic forecasts, seasonal changes (more vacations!), and competitor moves. When the economy went into recession in 2008 and the other airlines announced fees to check bags in an attempt to boost revenue, Southwest quickly ran advertisements highlighting its policy of not charging for checked bags. It was an aggressive move that was made with Southwest employees in mind (if they had charged for baggage, it would be the employees taking the brunt of questions and complaints). The top management team didn't suggest the advertising theme, middle managers did—they are and should be more concerned about where the industry is headed.

The Process of Scanning

Despite all the long- and medium-term crystal ball work, every organization must still execute in the short term. As shown in the Southwest story, short-term futuring processes must stay close enough to the current trends and issues in the competitive environment that adjustments to the current strategic intent can be made quickly. In many ways this facet of the futuring process relies on the nature and characteristics of the organization's structure, which will be discussed in Chapter Six. In that chapter, we will describe how a structure's "surface area" needs to be maximized to capture as much information as possible from the external environment. Using that information, transparent decision-making and flexible resource-allocation processes can be used to adjust the current strategic intent to optimize profits, social value, and environmental health.

What does a short-term, future-focused, transparent-decision-making, and resource-allocation process look like? One great example is a "prediction market." These virtual markets gather together a diverse range of stakeholders to bid on the likely outcomes of specific questions. If you google "prediction markets," you find a wide range of ongoing discussions. Recently we found prediction markets for "Will the global average temperature in 2019 be 0.1 degree Celsius (or more) than 2009?" "Will the highest marginal single-filer Federal income tax rate be equal or greater than 40% in 2013?", and a number of markets concerned about who will win this year's Emmy awards. While these prediction markets are for public input and entertainment, similar ones can easily be set up for organizations.

If an organization wants to understand whether customers will pay more for products that either incorporate recycled components or are produced with lower-carbon-footprint processes or have a socially responsible supply chain, they could establish a prediction market around these questions. The market would invite employees, customers, salespeople, regulators, and other stakeholders to "buy" or "sell" probabilities.

For example, let's say the question is "Will customers pay 10 percent more for our product if they know our supply chain is socially responsible and environmentally healthy?" Let's say the current "price" is 30 percent agreement or "yes" to the question. A customer who logs onto the market and believes that his or her firm is willing to pay more would see that price as too low and would work to buy that probability to increase it to a higher percentage.

The interesting thing about prediction markets is their accuracy. Studies suggest that well-run prediction markets are consistently more accurate than expert predictions. Accurate short-term forecasts can be used to change differentiation features of a product or service or increase or decrease the aggressiveness of different initiatives. Such adjustments to the firm's strategic intent allow firms to achieve reasonable profits, support change, and develop more sustainable outcomes.

A second approach, known as "extreme strategizing," calls for an organization to reengineer its environmental scanning system to rapidly collect and disseminate customer, regulatory, social, and natural environment trends to strategic decision makers through its employees.[7] The key to extreme strategizing processes is the rapid cycle of data exchange and dialogue between the organization and its stakeholders. The essence of this approach is the realization that it's not just the feedback of data from stakeholders to the organization, and not just the communication from the organization to stakeholders, but the feedback and communication together that drive better and faster actions and decisions.

Employees in HR, sales and marketing, operations, and corporate responsibility develop routines to engage stakeholders in data-driven dialogue. There is a conversation about questions such as "What's going on in our different worlds?" "How do you see our organization's behavior in the marketplace?" (great data for understanding the organization's identity!), "What do we need to pay attention to?" and "What do we need to do better?" The conversation is driven by data and a concern over what they mean.

The data and dialogue results are then integrated, summarized, and presented to decision makers in a regular cycle of assessment and adjustment. A great example of how this pattern works is the experience of PayPal. The organization initially was focused on creating a system that would allow people to make payments with Palm Pilots. Realizing this market was small, it put its payment transfer software on the Web. The service was picked up by online auctions—a service and function it was never intended to provide—to facilitate payments between buyers and sellers. PayPal's exchanges with eBay and other auction sites, their customers, and the marketplace allowed the organization to recognize the opportunity and focus its attention and resources on it.

Over time, operating managers and senior executives work with the extreme strategizing data to generate two important outputs. The first is a set of conclusions and observations that are fed back to employees for use in the next round of sensing. The second output is decisions regarding any changes to the organization's breadth, aggressiveness, and differentiation features of its strategic intent.

Output of Short-Term Futuring

The output of the short-term futuring process is aimed at changing the dimensions of strategic intent to improve current value. These decisions are fed directly into the operating processes of the organization to drive financial, social, and ecological value. For example, UPS's "on demand" process mobilizes its resources and logistics expertise to ensure that food, water, medicines, and other relief supplies can get to areas affected by an earthquake, tsunami, hurricane, or other natural disaster. It is just one part of an overall sustainability orientation that drives social value.

Conclusion

The futuring process is an important complement to the definition of a robust strategy. SMOs create value through a long-term identity and short-term series of temporary advantages. When the elements of a robust strategy are paired with the outputs of short-, medium-, and long-term futuring processes, an SMO has the means to generate sustainable effectiveness.

Assessment Questions

1. How do you approach futuring?
    a. Our managers are reasonably well-informed and we do have strategic planning meetings, but looking out beyond twelve months is not an important part of our approach to management.
    b. We do have a futuring process in which we do things like scenario planning, but I'm not sure how the information is used.
    c. We are very future-oriented and have the culture and the processes that support futuring.

    Here is what the answers imply:
    a. A futuring process should exist in any complex organization just like there are processes for hiring, crisis management, product development, and so on. The lack of good futuring process leads to constantly being late in seizing temporary competitive advantages.
    b. If the futuring process exists but is ineffective it is probably due to lack of senior management and board involvement; without their involvement no futuring process can be effective in identifying new strategic intents.
    c. This is the right place to be. We hope the futuring process has created a sustainable effective organization.
2. Does futuring embrace inputs from outside the organization or is there a secretive "behind closed doors" mind-set?

a. We are very secretive about futuring and do not involve outside partners.

b. While there are some secrets, we are generally open and keen to collaborate with others on inventing the future.

c. We actively pursue a strategy of openness and collaboration in futuring.

Here is what the answers imply:

a. A few firms do well with a highly secretive, internally driven futuring process, but typically it's a poor model for futuring.

b. A thoughtful attitude toward what needs to be secret and what does not opens up more doors and should lead to successful futuring.

c. An active strategy of openness and collaboration is the way to turn the organization's futuring capability into a strategic advantage.

PART TWO

The Way Work Is Organized

| Board Governance

All too often, today's corporate boards perform poorly. A close look at them suggests that most are ill-prepared to govern complex organizations.[1] They failed to prevent Lehman Brothers and other financial institutions from making risky decisions that led to their bankruptcies and government bailouts. At Lehman the risk committee of the board met just twice a year during the two years before the company went bankrupt as a result of its high-risk failed investments.

In the cases of Enron and Tyco, illegal activities were overlooked or not detected by the board before they went bankrupt. The board of BP has consistently failed to deal with its poor safety record and now faces decades-long litigation and reputation damage as a result of the Gulf of Mexico oil well explosion.

Board decision making with respect to the hiring and firing of CEOs all too often has been at best irresponsible. One particularly outrageous example occurred at Tyco. In 2001, CEO Dennis Kozlowski got a new contract which specified that even conviction on a felony charge was not grounds for termination. Four years later he was convicted of numerous felony charges and sentenced to twenty-five years in prison. It is hard to understand how any board could have agreed to a contract with this provision in it.

The record of U.S. boards is particularly poor when it comes to executive compensation. It is not just that on the average it has increased dramatically over the past twenty years; all too often the amount paid is not related to performance. At Lehman, the CEO received over $480 million of compensation in the eight years prior to the company declaring bankruptcy. Then there is the case of Ray Irani, the CEO of Occidental Petroleum. He was the second-highest-paid U.S. CEO for the decade starting in 2000, despite the fact that he was not managing one of the largest oil companies and that the company was not an outstanding performer. At least the highest-paid CEO for this period, Larry Ellison at $1.8 billion, built a large, very successful software company, Oracle.

The one thing that boards rarely have been accused of is unlawful behavior (Tyco is an exception here), but that simply is not good enough. Boards do not just need to behave legally, they have to behave responsibly and ensure that their corporations perform effectively.

The corporate governance model in most developed countries makes boards a key actor. In theory, it is their "job" to see that the interests of the major corporate stakeholders are considered, taken into account, and furthered.[2] They are expected to provide direction, guidance, leadership, and oversight. Specifying what boards should do is relatively easy. Specifying how they need to be staffed, structured, and designed in order to do it is quite another matter.

Let's start our consideration of governance with what boards should do to make an organization effective. What they need to do with respect to corporate governance depends on the management approach a corporation takes. CCOs and HIOs do not differ greatly from each other with respect to the way their boards are expected to govern, but SMOs do differ from both in terms of the issues to be considered and the decisions to be made. How boards operate is particularly critical in the case of SMOs. They need to role model the types of mission focus, problem-solving capability, and team effectiveness that is required throughout the organization.

The Role of Boards

Before we get into the details of how boards need to be designed and to operate in an SMO, it is important to establish what they need to accomplish. The primary function of boards has always been to represent the shareholders or owners of the organization. This is true of CCOs and HIOs. The boards of SMOs, however, should represent the organization's major stakeholders, not just its owners because they are responsible for their organization's sustainable effectiveness, not just its financial performance.

A second and very critical role concerns the organization's strategy. Using input from the CEO and the management team, board members are responsible for establishing the organization's identity and approving strategic intents that are aligned with that identity. They are responsible for ensuring that their organization's strategic intent is aligned with its purpose. As we stressed in our discussion of strategizing, the boards of SMOs should take a strong leadership role in exploring long-term economic, social, and environmental assumptions through a scenario-planning process.

Boards need to approve their organization's strategic intent and how it is managed. With respect to the strategic intent, the board needs to decide what business the organization is in, what its competitive approach will be, and, of course, the way the business processes will be executed.

In developing and evaluating the strategic intent of its organization, the board needs to take into account its major stakeholders. These usually include its customers, its employees, the communities where it operates, and of course, its investors. How much and what kind of influence each of these groups has on the strategy should be determined by the board and should reflect the nature of the business the organization is in and how it is managed. The board should also strongly influence what management approach the organization operates with. When the sustainable management approach is chosen, the board needs to be an articulate and persuasive voice of the major stakeholders in the organization. It should define a strategic direction that will serve all stakeholders' interests, not just those of senior management and the owners.

As we have already pointed out, to be effective in today's business environment, an organization needs both an identity to guide its long-term strategic decisions and a strategic intent to guide short-term decisions. Given the rate of change in the world, it is necessary for a company's strategic intent to evolve and change over time. A company's purpose and identity are less likely to change, but it is possible, and when change is needed, the board should take a leadership role.

Given the lack of long-term sources of competitive advantage and the continuous changes in knowledge and markets that exist today, boards need to constantly evaluate and potentially change some of the elements of their company's strategic intent. In the best of all worlds, companies can stick to a strategic intent and perform well simply by adjusting and tweaking the elements of the intent (breadth, aggressiveness, and differentiation), but in many cases, more significant changes are needed. As we have already established in our discussion of strategizing it is unrealistic to expect that any SMO's strategic intent will stay the same for very long in today's rapidly changing global business environment.

To be sure the company's identity remains viable, the board needs to carefully monitor the external environment and the company's strategic assumptions using the process of scenario planning that was described in the previous chapter. The board needs to regularly review data about how key features of the external environment are changing and consider how they relate to the company's identity and to its strategic intent. To get the right kind of information to do this, boards need to demand and receive frequent ongoing company and environmental data. They need updates on the financial condition of their company's markets, the condition of its human capital, the environmental impact of their company's operations and products, and, of course, how effectively the company is operating.

Particularly in the case of SMOs, boards need to be fully aware of not just whether their company is accomplishing its strategic objectives but of how it is accomplishing them. This should include looking at the way the company is managed. To do this, the board needs data from company sources as well as such key independent external sources as customers, regulators, the NGO community, and other stakeholders.

There simply is no substitute for the boards of SMOs receiving valid comprehensive company performance data and data that show the company's impact on its key stakeholders. They need to know how well the company's strategic plan and performance capabilities fit the business environment. Three of the biggest U.S. bankruptcies ever—Enron, WorldCom, and Conseco—occurred in part because the companies used accounting practices that their boards did not know about or did not understand. As a result, their boards were unable to monitor their performance and prevent management from making a number of bad decisions.

Three of the biggest U.S. bankruptcies ever—Enron, WorldCom, and Conseco—occurred in part because the companies used accounting practices that their boards did not know about or did not understand.

The board of the now defunct Washington Mutual did not get valid data about the level of risk that existed in its loan portfolio. Board members were "caught by surprise" when the country's largest savings and loan was taken over by the government and sold to J.P. Morgan Chase.

Because SMOs are designed to gain a competitive advantage by the way they are managed, it is particularly important that their boards get data about how and how effectively they are managed.[3] For example, they need to get data on the skills and competencies of the workforce as well as on its motivation and commitment. The boards of SMOs should get information on the condition of the company's competencies and capabilities.

A board cannot be content to simply "monitor" its company's performance. It needs to act decisively and effectively when a change in strategic intent is needed as well as when execution is poor or inappropriate. Sometimes the poor execution is a strategy problem, and of course, as already mentioned, that may mean changing one or more parts of the strategy. In some cases the strategy may be the right one but improved execution is needed. Boards should be adept at spotting poor execution and at improving it so that it is supportive of the company's strategic intent.

Boards often fail to operate effectively as strategy setters.[4] Instead of worrying about the larger picture and the long term, they try to micromanage the corporation and end up being resented by senior managers. As a result, they do not get the data, information, and insights that they need in order to be effective setters of the organization's strategic direction. Finally, all too often, they fail to recognize the major changes that need to be made in their company's products and services.

The recession of 2008 served to highlight just how many boards are poorly prepared to deal with economic change and adversity. Most were not prepared for a major economic downturn and struggled with the task of adjusting their company's strategic direction to deal with the recession. In extreme cases, the poor performance of boards resulted in bankruptcy and government takeovers.

During this period, it was surprising how little attention was focused on the failure of boards. Instead, most business writers focused on the members of senior management and their high levels of pay. Clearly, senior executives deserved a considerable amount of the blame, but many corporate boards also deserved a great deal of blame. They were responsible for who was in the senior positions and for many of the major decisions that determined how their companies performed during the recession.

Admittedly, the recession was an extraordinary event, and the failure of many boards to deal with it effectively does not necessarily mean they typically perform poorly. What is more damning is how often over the past several decades they have failed to deal effectively with CEO succession issues, excessive executive compensation levels, sustainability issues, and corporate fraud. One can only imagine what the board members of Home Depot were thinking when CEO Robert Nardelli told them not to come to their company's annual meeting and they agreed. Perhaps the poster child of poor performance is the General Motors board. It failed to prevent decades of decline that finally resulted in the once dominant auto company filing for bankruptcy.

Finally, in some organizations, the most important role of the board is to serve as a crisis manager. It should not be a "standard operating procedure" for the board of any company, much less an SMO, to run it—far from it. Boards should avoid micromanagement and meddling in the company's activities on a day-to-day basis, but sometimes this cannot be avoided because a crisis occurs.

Not surprisingly, many boards fail when they have to deal with a crisis. They simply don't have the time or the talent needed to intervene when a crisis strikes. In the case of an unexpected crisis such as the death of a CEO or the collapse of a company's financial performance, the board should be able to take immediate corrective action and, in some cases, even take over running the company. To do this they may need to designate one of their members as an interim CEO or to replace some of the key managers in the company. This can be an incredibly demanding role for a board member or members to fill and one that can lead to serious disruption in their lives. But every board should be prepared to deal with a crisis that demands that one of its members take an operational role in the company. They may never need to, but they need to be prepared to.

To accomplish their objectives, the board of an SMO needs a number of identifiable features. In the rest of this chapter, we will discuss how the boards of SMOs need to be staffed, designed, and operated in order to be effective in today's business environment. Many of the points we will make are applicable to organizations that are not managed with a sustainable management approach because they are simply good practices for most boards to engage in. But we will also discuss some practices that are a good fit for just SMOs.

Board Membership

It is easy to make the case that many U.S. corporate failures were the result of boards failing to do their "jobs" in part because they lacked the needed expertise. Let us return to the case of Lehman Brothers. Lehman, like most large corporations, was a very complex global corporation with exotic financial products. To understand its business, the board needed deep expertise in the following: corporate finance, organization design, accounting, risk management, economics, international relations, and talent management.

Instead of staffing its board with individuals that had expertise in these areas, Lehman Brothers chose to staff its board with a theatrical producer, an actress, and a retired admiral. The result was a board that had almost no expertise in the exotic financial instruments and transactions that led to its downfall. For eighteen years the actress and heiress (E.F. Hutton and Post

Cereals) Dina Merrill sat on the board and the compensation committee that approved the CEO's extraordinary compensation package.

Lehman Brothers chose to staff its board with a theatrical producer, an actress, and a retired admiral. The result was a board that had almost no expertise in the exotic financial instruments and transactions that led to its downfall.

Who is on a board makes a great difference in its credibility, its access to knowledge, and its ability to bring the correct perspective to strategic planning, and indeed, it is critical to all of the things that a board must do to be effective. Putting together the right combination of board members clearly is not an easy task. It is not simply a matter of picking people with the right areas of expertise. Rather, it is a matter of picking people who can work together and, as a total group, perform the functions that an effective board needs to do well.[5] In this respect, it is a little like putting together a basketball team or other sports team in which the members are highly interdependent and the performance of the team reflects very much the degree to which the team members fill different roles and complement each other. Boards should have between nine and fifteen members, so there are a number of tough membership choices that have to be made.

Boards are critical to many features of SMOs, particularly to developing and fulfilling the purpose and intent of the organization, as well as how it operates and gets things done. As noted earlier, their most important role is to deal with issues concerning whether the strategy and the way the company does business is consistent with its purpose and identity. In SMOs boards must be in a particularly good position to understand and advise on how the business strategy and practices will affect key stakeholder groups.

Member Independence

Probably the most important feature of a board's membership, although it is hard to single out just one, is the degree to which it is made up of independent members. To be independent, an individual cannot be employed by the company. In addition, this individual should not have any business or family relationships with the company or the members of its senior management that might compromise his or her credibility and independence when it comes to key decisions.

Some have argued that boards should be made up entirely of independent directors. It is easy to see how they have reached this conclusion, but it may be too extreme a position.[6] There are some clear advantages to having a few members of the board—the CEO and two or three others—who are not independent. Executives and others who work for the company can bring to the board a perspective and types of information that are not easily available to independent directors. This often is particularly true with respect to issues concerning how the company is managed and what the attitudes and the behaviors of the workforce are.

Having insiders on a board can also help with management succession. Board members can see potential CEOs in action, and CEO candidates can learn about how boards operate. The disadvantage of having individuals on the board who are executives or who are otherwise "compromised" by their relationship with the company is that they may not be objective in their assessment of issues. Nevertheless, our belief is that in general it is useful to have at least one or two employees on the board, in addition to the CEO. Particularly in SMOs they are an important stakeholder group and can bring valuable information to bear on the issues boards address.

Key Stakeholders

A membership issue that greatly distinguishes what should be the membership of SMO boards from that of CCO and HIO boards is the presence of representatives from the organization's key stakeholder groups. This includes, in most cases, the investment community, the local communities or countries where the organization does business, employees of the company, and members of organizations that represent the environmental impact footprint of the organization. All of these groups are affected by board decisions and warrant a board position in an SMO, something they rarely if ever have in CCOs and only occasionally have in HIOs, which sometimes have a nonmanagement employee on them.

In the case of large complex SMOs it is not practical to have members that represent all of the key stakeholder groups—there simply are too many. When this is true, it is important that boards find other ways to hear from those groups that are not represented on the board. They can, for example, invite representatives to come to board meetings, have committees that gather data from them, and meet with them.

Diversity

Closely related but somewhat different from the issue of key stakeholders being present on the board is the issue of diversity. What constitutes the correct kind and amount of diversity is to a degree a function of where an organization does business and what kind of business it is in. In almost every case, there is a strong argument for diversity in gender, race, and ethnicity. In many companies, a strong case also can be made for international diversity. Particularly in today's global economy, it is difficult to think of many companies that are not affected by what is happening in multiple countries and multiple regions of the world.

Getting the right kind and mix of diversity is not easy. Clearly it needs to vary by company, and consideration needs to be given to how diversity will influence the decision-making effectiveness of the board. Diversity can be very positive in terms of bringing more viewpoints to the table and allowing issues to be raised that would not "normally" be raised. Thus it is often worth seeking diversity in order to improve the decision-making process of boards as well as to ensure that there is representation of the key stakeholder groups.

Diversity has to be balanced against the ability of the board to operate as a smoothly functioning group. In many important respects, boards are teams and need a spirit of cooperation, mutual sharing, and common goals. This may not exist automatically with a diverse group, but can potentially be created through team building and group development work.

Some countries have passed laws that require gender diversity on boards. For example, in Norway and Spain a percentage of all board members must be women. It is easy to understand why these laws have been passed; in most countries boards have not awakened to the reality that diversity is a key to board effectiveness in all organizations and particularly in SMOs. Nevertheless, we do not think SMOs should have quotas. They are simply too blunt an instrument, particularly in a country such as the United States with its many racial and ethnic minorities. Simply stated, diversity needs to be strategically targeted to each organization, not determined by a mandate. Overall, in the case of SMOs, almost whatever needs to be done to create a diverse and yet smoothly functioning board is worth the investment.

Expertise

The independent members of boards in U.S. companies typically have been drawn from among executives in other companies. The assumption is that they will have a good understanding of the business problems and therefore have the necessary expertise to be on the company's board. We have no argument with the idea that CEOs bring value to a board and that some CEO representation on an SMO board is desirable, providing the CEO understands sustainable effectiveness.

However, all too often the boards of CCOs and HIOS have three or more CEOs on them, and as a result there are not enough board seats left for individuals with other areas of expertise. Particularly in SMOs it is important to fill some board positions with individuals who are experts in organizational effectiveness and the human capital side of an organization. This area of expertise may overlap with other kinds of expertise so that a "specialist" is not needed, but it does need to be planned for when boards are staffed.

Because human capital performance is a critical difference maker in HIOs and SMOs, it is very important to have board members who understand what effective human capital management is and what an effective organization design is. In our research, when we ask board members whom they rely on for advice on human capital management, they often cite the CEOs of other companies who are on their board. In most cases, this is a serious mistake.

In our research, when we ask board members whom they rely on for advice on human capital management, they often cite the CEOs of other companies who are on their board. In most cases, this is a serious mistake.

Most CEOs have some knowledge of human capital management, but they are rarely experts in it, even though they manage large firms. What is needed are board members who have the kind of in-depth knowledge of human capital management and organizational effectiveness that one gains as a result of being an HR executive in an SMO or HIO. An alternative is someone who has consulting or research in human capital management experience.

Deep content knowledge is critical; without it, SMO boards cannot be expected to make good decisions about how the strategy and talent management practices of their organization should fit together in order to create a sustainably effective organization or to deal with key senior executive talent management issues. Further, in-depth knowledge of the interface between talent management and organization design is critical to a board being able to determine how well a company is being managed.

Currently, about 80 percent of the boards of Fortune 1000 companies do not have a member who is an expert in human capital management, much less human capital management in SMOs. Most boards do recognize the importance of having a member with deep financial knowledge and have at least one. No doubt financial assets are one of the most critical assets that most companies have and, of course, they need to be monitored and effectively managed. Our point is that the same thing is true of an SMO's human capital and that this should be recognized at the board level.

Finally, it is important to include on a board individuals who are expert in the core competencies of the organization. A software company, for example, needs software engineers, a chemical company needs chemists, and an educational firm needs one or more individuals with a background in learning and knowledge, and so on. In the case of an SMO that has a major environmental impact, the board should have a member who has expertise in that feature of the natural environment.

Number of Board Memberships

All too often individuals are on multiple boards, not just two or three but six, seven, or more. Historically in the United States there have been some individuals who are in what is called the "corporate board club." They serve on multiple large corporate boards; an extreme example is Vernon Jordan, who at one point was on ten major corporate boards. Football star Willie Davis at one point ran his own company and served on eleven boards at the same time. In addition to being the president of a major university, Shirley Ann Jackson sat on five corporate boards in 2009. Her income for these board memberships totaled over $1.3 million.

Having multiple board memberships may be acceptable in the case of CCOs and HIOs (although we don't think it is), but it certainly is not okay in the case of SMOs. Being a board member in an SMO is a very demanding job, not one that can be done in the two hundred or so hours a year board members in CCOs and HIOs spend doing it.

To be an effective board member in an SMO, no one should be on more than two other boards if they do not have a "day job" and on one or perhaps no other if they do. There simply are not enough hours in the year for someone to do what is required of a board member in an SMO and to be on multiple other boards as well as have a "day job."

The Way Board Members Are Chosen

What we have done so far is to specify some of the types of individuals who should be on boards in a sustainable organization. Each organization needs its own unique blend of directors who are independent, possess the right areas of knowledge and expertise, have the right amount and kind of diversity, and can work together. Creating a board like this begins and to some extent ends with having the right selection process.

Choosing the right board members needs to be done in a credible, transparent way. In the case of most U.S. corporations, a committee of the board picks one nominee for each board seat. The list of board candidates is then given to the total board for its approval. The company then submits an unopposed list of directors to the shareholders for a vote. In some respects this process makes sense, particularly if the nomination committee is aware of the needs of the board for member skills and knowledge, has engaged in a good search-and-interview process so that it knows a great deal about the individuals it is proposing to be on the board, and has carefully assessed their qualifications.

The danger with this board nomination process is that members of the company executive team, especially the CEO or a special interest group, may dominate it and steer it toward picking individuals who are overly favorable to the CEO and other members of senior management. The last thing a board needs is members who are unwilling to raise tough questions and bring independent views to the boardroom. Thus it is very important that any board member selection committee be made up solely of independent directors. They need to have a good understanding of the expertise required of board members in order for them to deal with the many issues that need to be considered in establishing an effective, team-oriented board.

It is important that key stakeholders have a "say" in the board member selection process. To get shareholder input, for example, Pfizer and United Health have established advisory nominating committees that are made up of their largest shareholders. This appears to be a good way to give one group of stakeholders—shareholders—a voice; others could be given one if employees and environment NGOs were asked for their input, as they should be in an SMO.

The second step in most board selection processes is a vote by the shareholders on board membership. In many U.S. corporations, this vote is far from a true "democratic" election. Yes, shareholders are given a vote on whether to approve or not approve board members. But it is extremely difficult for groups who would like to run alternative candidates to get their candidate on the ballot. As a result, in almost every case, board members run for election with no opposition. In addition, in many board elections, shareholders cannot vote yes or no on individuals. Instead, they are asked to ratify the entire slate, and if they do not vote, it is considered to be favorable. Not surprisingly, directors who are nominated by boards almost always are elected.

In an SMO, the whole board election process should mirror a classic democratic election processes. It ought to be relatively easy for individuals who want to run against the existing directors to get their name on the ballot. In addition, each individual board member should run independently and should only be elected if they get a majority of the votes cast. Admittedly, in many cases the votes will still be in favor of the board members nominated by the company. This is hardly a negative, however, since it most likely means that shareholders are relatively happy with how the board and the company have been performing.

Having democratic elections is not about SMOs that are performing well. It is about those instances when the company, and in particular the senior management team, has been performing poorly. For them, it is critical that shareholders have a chance to vote out members of the board. This is consistent with the overall management approach in an SMO because it holds individuals accountable for their results and introduces accountability at the board level. The principles of accountability and results are integral to SMOs, and thus having them practiced from the top to the bottom of the organization is vital to creating a culture of accountability and performance.

We would be remiss if we did not mention a major problem with, as is required by law, having only shareholders elect the board members of an SMO. It means that the other key stakeholders of the organization do not have a direct say in who is on the board. This may not be a major problem if the nomination process produces the "right" candidates. Thus it is particularly important that all the major stakeholder groups have a say in who is nominated to run for board seats. Until there is a change in the law that opens board elections to all stakeholders, this is the best that SMOs can do to be sure their boards have the right members.

Board Leadership

SMO boards require a special type of leadership.[7] Board chairs need to be able to bring an independent and objective viewpoint to board discussions involving a wide range of issues. They also need to be able to facilitate group discussions and adroitly schedule and facilitate decision making. Finally, they need to have a good understanding of business and what it takes to effectively manage a corporation. The key question is, where should boards look for the type of leader who can handle the complexities, stresses, and time commitment needed to be an effective board chair?

One place to look is to the company's CEO. In the majority of U.S. companies, this has been where most boards have looked, and still do, for a chair. The CEO role and the board chair role are combined in most U.S. companies. The alternative approach, which is being taken by an increasing number of U.S. companies and has already been taken by many European companies, is to split the roles of the board chair and CEO.[8]

There are a number of reasons why splitting these two roles fits SMOs better than having them be combined. Having a chair in place who can act as an objective outsider when it comes to making decisions about sustainable effectiveness, business strategy, succession, CEO performance, executive compensation, board appointments, board membership, performance appraisals of board members, and a host of other issues simply makes more sense and is likely to lead to better and more objective decisions.

Expecting the CEO to have an active role in managing an SMO and to fill the board chair's role is asking too much. All too often, it puts the CEO in a situation that is rife with conflicts of interest and excessive time demands. Particularly in question when the CEO holds both roles is the evaluation of the CEO and the determination of his or her compensation. Simply stated, it is unreasonable to expect someone to evaluate their own performance and decide how it should be rewarded. The CEO should work for the board, not, as is so often the case in CCOs and HIOs, the reverse. As one board activist recently noted, "The board is not the CEO's friend—it is the CEO's boss."

Not only should the CEO and board chair roles be separate, it is important that the board chairperson be independent of the organization's management.[9] All too often in the United States and in other countries (for example, the United Kingdom), the chair of the board is either the former CEO or someone who has a strong historical involvement with the company. Although this type of appointment may increase the relevant knowledge that the chair brings to the position, it seriously damages the ability of the chair to be objective and to provide the kind of external visibility that speaks to accountability and objectivity.

Simply stated, it is critical that the board chairs of SMOs be independent. SMOs need to have cultures of objectivity, assessment, and accountability. Having an independent chair reinforces this element of the corporate culture starting at the top. It creates a situation in which decisions about the CEO's career and the company's strategy are the responsibility of someone who has an uncompromised perspective on the company's performance and that of its CEO. It promises to bring objective decision making to bear on succession, compensation, and performance evaluation issues that involve members of the board and the CEO. Perhaps less important but still an advantage of having an outsider as the board chair are the issues of time demands and responding to a crisis.

Boards are facing more and more demands. Just preparing for board meetings and participating in them can involve a considerable amount of time. In major corporations, boards need to meet at least eight to ten times per year for a day or more, and there are a number of committee meetings as well. As mentioned earlier, the time demands are particularly great for the boards of SMOs. They are expected to deal with a broad range of sustainable effectiveness issues and, as we will discuss next, they have more committees. Given this, it is particularly appropriate to have someone as a board chair who can spend a third or more of his or her time on board business. This is difficult for somebody who is also performing the CEO job.

It is desirable to have a board chair who can take on the CEO job when a crisis occurs that makes it impossible or undesirable for the CEO to perform this job. A CEO's performance or health problems can make it necessary to replace the CEO with little or no notice; thus it is very desirable to have a "standby CEO."

Finally, there is the matter of where to find an independent board chair for an SMO. In many cases, the former CEOs of other companies are good choices. They are used to assessing strategy and dealing with large, complex issues, and they have a good network of individuals they can go to for advice and input. Often they also are able to step in and run the company when and if a crisis requires leadership from the board chair.

The major "watch out" when choosing a CEO to be the board chair of an SMO is the individual's management style. If this person is a command and control executive, he or she should not be the chair of an SMO! The situation is different for executives who have a high involvement management style; there is a good chance they can be successful chairs of SMOs, but of course the best choice is someone who has led an SMO.

Committee Structure

The committee structure of an SMO board needs to reflect the new realities of the external world and its commitment to sustainable effectiveness. Today most boards do not have a committee structure that does. Let's take a look at the committees an SMO should have that CCOs and HIOs typically do not have.

Sustainability

Few boards in the United States have a sustainability committee. The good news is that U.S. board members do appear to be assigning more importance to environmental sustainability. Our recent survey of U.S. board members shows that a majority now think that environmental sustainability is an important issue for their corporation. In this case, board members in the United States appear to be catching up with their European counterparts.

Given the importance of sustainability to sustainable effectiveness, it is appropriate to have a sustainability committee of the board. This committee needs to review the data on the environmental performance of the company, make recommendations to the total board on how environmental sustainability should influence the company's strategy, and generally oversee the environmental performance of the company with respect to its operations and products. They should meet regularly with the members of the company who are focused on sustainability so that they understand what they are doing and, of course, what kind of approach the company is taking. An ideal member of this committee is someone who has a good knowledge of sustainability issues and the company business strategy, and knows external experts in the area of sustainability.

Given the importance of sustainability . . . , it is appropriate to have a sustainability committee of the board.

Social Responsibility

Most boards do not have a social responsibility committee or subcommittee. For SMOs, this is not acceptable. They need a committee that collects data on the social impact of the organization, reviews the social performance of the organization, and makes recommendations to the board about how it can be improved. It should review major board decisions that have an impact on the communities where it operates and suggest actions that will have a positive impact on communities and customers.

Human Resources

Today, most U.S. boards have a committee that is focused on executive compensation and, to some degree, executive (CEO) succession management. Sometimes this committee is called the human resource committee, though in most cases, its focus is mainly or only on the compensation of very top executives, not on the company's overall approach to talent management.

SMOs need a human resource committee that has a broad and comprehensive charter. It needs to have responsibility for the key talent management issues that face the corporation. Yes, it needs to look at executive compensation, but it also needs to take responsibility for the talent management programs the company has. It needs to be sure that the right succession planning processes are in place for the key management and technical positions. This analysis should be driven by a talent management program that focuses on critical positions and difference-making individuals.

The committee should ask the human resource function for a human capital scorecard that regularly reviews and shows the talent currently on hand in the organization, the projected future needs for talent, and what talent is available in the external market. The committee needs to monitor the talent in the company and how it is being managed and developed. The existing talent needs to be mapped against the core competencies and capabilities of the organization and how they ultimately relate to the strategic plan of the organization. In essence, the human resources committee needs to be sure that the company will have the talent supply that it needs in order to be sustainably effective.

Our research suggests that at this time, most boards do not get the information they need in order to monitor their company's talent, and they know it! Table 5.1 presents data gathered by us from board members of large U.S. corporations.[10] A significant number report not receiving, but wanting to receive, data on employee attitudes, recruiting, turnover, and succession management for key technical positions. Somewhat surprising is the result that almost 20 percent say they don't get and shouldn't get data on key technical positions. Hopefully this response is coming from directors of companies that are in low-tech or simple service businesses.

A key issue with respect to the human resource committee of the board is what type of individuals should be on the committee and how the committee should be supported. First, particularly when dealing with executive compensation issues, the committee should include only independent board members. A larger human capital committee may include a few insiders, but whichever group, a subcommittee or the committee as a whole, deals

Table 5.1. Information Given to the Board

	Get and Should	Get but Shouldn't	Don't Get but Should	Don't Get and Shouldn't
Succession planning data for most management positions	73.1	0	24.4	2.6
Succession planning data for key technical positions	46.8	1.3	32.5	19.5
Metrics on turnover	59.0	3.8	33.3	3.8
Metrics on recruiting success	49.4	5.2	36.4	9.1
Attitude survey data	51.9	1.3	42.9	3.9

with executive compensation should be made up of only outsiders. This is critical to good decision making with respect to executive compensation and to the credibility of the decisions made with respect to executive compensation.

Earlier it was mentioned that it is critical that one or more board members have expertise in human capital management. One of the reasons for this, of course, is that someone or better yet more than one person on this committee needs to have depth expertise in talent management, and in most cases, that person or persons should be the chair of the committee.

In addition to having one or more members of the committee with good knowledge of talent management, the board should receive two kinds of support so that their expertise level in human capital management is high. Board members should be supported by the company chief human resource officer and by the company staff experts in human capital management and executive compensation. They should also have access to independent consulting help, particularly when it comes to making decisions about executive compensation. This and other areas of human capital management are extremely complex and involve decisions that need to reflect, among other things, what is going on in other companies that are competing for top human capital.

In essence, this committee needs a staff and a budget for external consultants to support its activities.

Finally, it is important that the committee be responsible for reporting the results of its analyses to the whole board. Boards need a regular update on the condition of their organization's human capital just as they need a report on its financial and physical capital.

Organizational Effectiveness

SMOs need a committee of the board that focuses on organizational effectiveness. Today few boards have a committee that does this; if the issue is dealt with at all (often it isn't), it is handled by the entire board. In an SMO, it deserves more attention than the whole board can give it. Thus we feel a separate committee is needed.

The organizational effectiveness committee should be responsible for the strategizing work the board needs to do. It is the logical place to do much of the work needed to prepare the full board to discuss long-term strategizing. In addition, it should be charged with looking at the sustainable effectiveness of the organization with respect to the management practices the company uses and how they interface with each other and the strategy.

Do these practices complement each other in ways that produce the organizational capabilities and competencies the organization needs? Do they lead to the type and levels of sustainable effectiveness that are called for by the business strategy? Do they lead to dangerous risk taking on the part of employees? Do they lead to an overly short-term orientation? The answers to these questions are central to the board fulfilling its oversight role with respect to how well an SMO is operating and whether the practices used are providing a competitive advantage.

The membership of the organizational effectiveness committee needs to consist of experts in strategizing, organization design, and the way companies are managed. It needs to receive company balanced scorecard data and needs to be able to collect its own performance data. Like the human resource committee, it needs to be able to hire consultants and commission studies of the company's management effectiveness.

Succession Management

It is said that the most important thing boards do is pick the next CEO of its organization. Often this is true, although it may not be as true in an SMO as it is in organizations that are managed with more of a focus on the CEO providing direction and making the major decisions. The shared leadership approach, which we will discuss in Chapter Eleven, argues that the CEO is a critical culture setter and definer, but perhaps not as important as the CEO is in other management approaches. Nevertheless, the human resource committee and the board in general should regularly discuss succession issues. They should be sure that multiple individuals are being developed for the CEO role and that those individuals have a commitment to the shared leadership approach and to sustainable management.

In general, the best candidates for the CEO job in an SMO are to be found internally. The emphasis of SMOs on talent development and the importance of talent should lead to an organization with a very effective competency-driven talent model. It also should lead to an organization that has a number of potential CEOs and senior executives who understand the management approach, are committed to it, and can take a shared leadership approach. Bringing someone to a senior leadership position from outside is often quite risky. It may take an outsider a great deal of time to understand the sustainable management approach, and they may prefer a more imperial approach to how the CEO role is performed.

Evaluation and Rewards

Central to SMO boards should be accountability and rewards that are based on sustainable effectiveness. This needs to start at the very top or it will never be an important part of the culture, and it should be practiced throughout the organization. Yes, boards need to evaluate the performance of the CEO, but they need to do more. They need to review the performance of the senior management group. This is an important part of their succession management process and their ensuring that there are individuals in the organization who are available to fill key management positions. It also is a sign of how important they believe the talent management process is. Their involvement speaks loudly and clearly to the organization about the importance of doing talent management and doing good performance reviews.

But what about the board and the individual board members? Should the boards of SMOs be evaluated? Should individual members of SMO boards be evaluated? The answers are yes and yes. It doesn't happen in many CCOs and HIOs, but there is no question that consistency with respect to how the sustainable management style is implemented requires that board members, and the board as a whole, be evaluated on their performance.

Should the boards of SMOs be evaluated?
Should individual members of SMO boards be
evaluated? The answers are yes and yes.

It is already a regulatory requirement in some countries that the board evaluate its performance. Much less common is an evaluation of the performance of individual board members.[11] We have talked to many board chairs and CEOs of CCOs who strongly resist this because they feel it demeans the board members and may be "insulting" to them. This may be true, but this reaction is more an indication of the fact that the board is poorly constituted or that the CEO does not practice sustainable management than that board members shouldn't be individually evaluated. Being a board member is a job, a well-paid one at that, and as result, individuals who do it should be accountable for how well they do it.

Evaluating individual board members is quite consistent with the sustainable management approach to accountability and to rewards. Individuals need feedback about their performance, and they need to change their behavior on the basis of it. We have done a number of board member assessments that resulted in behavioral change. The changes have included being more attentive at board meetings, not interrupting other board members, and taking courses in finance and talent management.

We also have seen board members refuse to change, and in some cases this has resulted in their not being allowed to continue as board members.

It makes sense to reward board members on the basis of sustainable effectiveness. However, given the high level of interdependence among board members, it may not make sense to use evaluations of the individual board members to determine the compensation of individuals. But it certainly makes sense to evaluate their performance and give them feedback.

Boards are a good place to use a 360-degree appraisal process in which board members comment on each other's performance. When appropriate, members of the management team and external stakeholders also should comment on the performance of individual board members and the overall board's performance. Ignoring performance issues that exist with individuals, or the board as a whole for that matter, means running a very great risk of poor board performance and represents a glaring inconsistency with how sustainable management should be operationalized. Again, the call is for accountability and rewards that are based on performance. This needs to be true at the board level in SMOs just as it needs to be true throughout.

If a good performance appraisal process is in place, age and term limits for board members are not needed. In many cases, they are in place mainly to make it easy for boards to remove poor performers, but they come with a high cost, the elimination of valuable board members who perform well but happen to be "too old." They also tend to undermine the evaluation process because they make good evaluations unnecessary in the case of individuals who are required to leave the board. Age and term limits are a "solution" to some performance problems, but they make having a good performance management system less important and cause other problems.

Let's turn for a moment to the type of reward system that should be in place for board members. This is a clear case of when it is important to have relatively long-term rewards in place and rewards that reflect the sustainable effectiveness of the organization relative to its peer companies. Many of the decisions that board members make are long-term decisions and are intended to improve their company's performance against industry competitors. This suggests very strongly that board members should be rewarded primarily on the basis of their organizations' sustainable effectiveness. In most cases, the best way to judge an SMO's performance is how it performs over the long term relative to its peers.

Perhaps the best way to combine long-term compensation with rewards for performance is to have three components to a board member's compensation package. The first is a relatively small base pay package that covers board membership and meeting attendance. Second, board members should receive stock grants and stock options that have a relatively long-term perspective; five to ten years is probably the right length of time for most board members. Third, board members should have a cash bonus plan that pays out annually on the basis of the organization's sustainable effectiveness against peer companies.

Long-term stock plans are a critical part of the reward package for board members of SMOs because they call attention to the longtime perspective board members are expected to have. Boards need to do long-term strategizing, so it makes sense to reward them on the basis of how well they do it. They also are key to risk management; rewarding them for long-term sustainable effectiveness is the best way to be sure they don't try to inflate short-term financial performance by making highly risky investment and operational decisions.

There are many ways to structure bonus plans. One approach that makes sense for board members involves calibrating company incentives against peer companies so that a bonus is paid out only when an organization's effectiveness betters that of peer companies on multiple indicators of sustainability. Here is where financial incentives and the triple-bottom line should come into play. For board members to get maximum bonus, their organization should have to outperform the average performance of its peers on all of the three major elements of sustainable effectiveness for multiple years.

Recognizing the importance of total performance, in 2010 a Dutch company, TNT, introduced a bonus plan that pays its top executives bonuses on the basis of triple-bottom-line performance. It uses measures of customer satisfaction and environmental impact (such as energy use and emissions).

Finally, there is the question of how much board members should be paid. Board member compensation has risen quite a bit over the past two decades. Still, the highest-paid board members in the United States usually make less than a million dollars. Many do make well over a quarter of a million and some over half a million, however—not bad for part-time work, but small compared to what most CEOs make!

Given the important role of boards in SMOs, the critical issue, in our minds, is not how much they are paid, it is how they are paid. If they are paid on the basis of the effectiveness of their corporation, amounts up to a half million dollars a year are reasonable. However, it is unacceptable if they are highly paid because they have de facto deals with the CEO that involve their paying the CEO highly and the CEO supporting their being paid highly.

Boards Must Be Effective

SMOs must have effective boards. The way boards operate has a strong influence on the way their organization operates. In addition, they make some of the most important decisions concerning the way their company adds value, treats people, is organized, and behaves. Not surprisingly, SMO boards must look and operate very differently from the way boards do in CCOs and HIOs. They need different information, leadership, structures, and reward systems in order for them to be successful in governing SMOs.

Although SMO boards operate differently from the way most boards operate, none of the features of SMO boards are untested or impossible to implement. They also align quite well with what many corporate governance experts and activists say boards should do. Thus there is every reason to believe they can be put into place and can lead to improved board and corporate performance.

Assessment Questions

1. How important is the board in your organization?

   a. If the board were to disappear, it's not clear it would be missed.

b. Board members do an okay job with CEO succession, executive compensation, and preventing major strategic missteps.

c. The board is a leadership group that keeps the organization sustainable and effective.

Here is what the answers imply:

a. If you answered "a," you are probably in the majority. All too often, the board often seems to be more a ceremonial body than one offering significant value added.

b. Your board has fulfilled its mission in the context of mainstream management thinking.

c. You have an organizational advantage over other firms due to excellent governance.

2. How diverse is the know-how and perspective of the board?

a. Our board is composed of people with financial, legal, and general business expertise.

b. Our board has diversity in backgrounds and expertise beyond the usual suspects.

c. Board members are selected with diversity in mind, including members representing different cultures, stakeholder perspectives, and expertise.

Here is what the answers imply:

a. When boards lack diversity in expertise they are not able to provide governance in a world in which serving multiple stakeholders and managing organizations is essential.

b. The organization has clearly recognized the value of some diverse thinking but failed to take it to its logical conclusion.

c. The organization is serious about creating a highly capable representative board that understands what it means to be sustainably effective.

CHAPTER SIX

Structures for Sustainable Effectiveness

There is a popular story about how John Chambers, CEO of Cisco Systems, settled on a way to make Cisco more flexible and customer focused. While participating in a small-group visioning exercise at the 2007 World Economic Forum in Davos, Switzerland, in which executives from a variety of industries and countries were tasked with thinking about the future, it dawned on him that this wasn't a bad way to make creative decisions.

Chambers had recently reorganized Cisco—the third major reorganization since the company's founding in 1990—from a decentralized business unit organization where each customer-facing unit had a full complement of staff functions into a centralized functional structure.[1] In the wake of the dot.com bust of the early 2000s, the duplication of resources in the customer-focused structure was seen as too expensive.

Chambers worried that like most functional organizations Cisco would be too inwardly focused and not sufficiently customer-centric. To avoid this, he had been experimenting with cross-functional overlay teams, or what Jay Galbraith calls "lateral integration mechanisms."[2] These cross-functional teams, or as Cisco calls them, "councils and boards," were not so much a new design as a radical bet on collaboration as a complement to hierarchy.

Cisco is a $40 billion Internet hardware and solutions provider. Its identity is nicely summarized by its vision—changing the way people live, play, work, and learn—and its strategy is often characterized as "managing market transitions." Since the firm began, it has watched for and facilitated a number of major technological transitions, such as the integration of voice and video, making the network a platform, and driving collaboration, in ways that add significant value for its customers. These transitions defined periods of strategic intent for Cisco, and they created a series of momentary advantages.

For each momentary advantage, Cisco adjusted its breadth (currently increasing), aggressiveness (always pretty high), and differentiation (varies by product line and market). Cisco has posted impressive economic returns, and a strong record of social and environmental results. For example, it recently was listed as the number one firm on Greenpeace's "Cool IT" leaderboard.

This chapter describes three organization structures that support the achievement of an integrated set of sustainable effectiveness goals (economic success, positive social value, and ecological health) and also reflect an organization's identity. First, we will describe how Cisco has adapted the traditional functional structure. Second, we will describe how Harris Corporation's Broadcast Communications Division has created an ambidextrous structure that balances innovation and efficiency. Finally, we will describe how W. L. Gore created a network organization that balances flexibility and execution. Each structure applies and leverages three adaptations—surface area, resource allocation, and decision making—that help SMOs perform in complex, uncertain, and unpredictable business environments.

Ambidextrous and network structures are not commonly used in organizations today. However, the emergence of new views of power and status, the sophistication of information technology, and their clear advantages with respect to supporting sustainable effectiveness have created a compelling case for their use. Thus we expect to see more and more organizations adopting these structures.

Sustainable Functional Structures

Most people think of structure as an organization chart with boxes and lines showing reporting relationships and work assignments, but a more enlightened view is that structure is the way organizations focus attention and manage resources.[3] Functional organizations focus attention and resources on technical specialties such as finance, research and development, manufacturing, and marketing; divisional structures focus resources on products, customers, or regions; matrix structures focus them on multiple dimensions.

For SMOs to be effective, two questions need to be answered: "Focus attention on what issues?" and "Focus what resources on what compelling issues?" The answers need to support the integrated objectives of economic performance, positive social value, and environmental performance. In the context of the issues discussed in the prior chapters, the short list of answers includes

- Customers
- Environmental trends (natural, social, and economic)
- NGOs, governments, and regulators
- Vendors, suppliers, partners, and employees
- The interactions among the units of the organization (functional or business)

The Cisco case is a clear example of how a traditional functional structure was adapted to focus attention and resources on these issues and support sustainable effectiveness outcomes. Cisco made three important adaptations to their functional structure, adaptations that led to the right focus for an SMO. They increased the structure's surface area with cross-functional teams, enabled collaboration with flexible resource allocation processes, and improved decision making with transparent information policies.

Maximum Surface Area

Organization structures traditionally have been designed to focus on meeting shareholders' needs. The recent shift toward customer-centric organizations is a step in the right direction, but we are arguing for an even more radical leap. SMOs need to listen to multiple stakeholders, not just the ones who buy their products and services. They need to listen to employees, the communities and countries they operate in, and the needs of the planet.

SMOs can facilitate the gathering of information by implementing maximum surface area structures that are flatter and full of roles that are expected to bring stakeholder input into strategic and operational decision making.[4] In SMOs, all or at least most employees should have few, if any, degrees of separation from the external environment. A good rule of thumb is that no employee should be more than two connections away from a customer or key stakeholder. The reason for this is straightforward.

A good rule of thumb is that no employee should be more than two connections away from a customer or key stakeholder.

Direct exposure to how well an organization is satisfying its stakeholders provides employees with credible and powerful feedback about performance and provides key inputs to the short-term futuring process described in Chapter Four. Putting organization members in "direct contact" with stakeholders shifts attention from a focus on what you do to whom you need to satisfy.

This may seem an obvious and simple idea, but in many ways it is radical and difficult to execute. How many organizations have systems that put human resources, research and development, production, accounting, audit, or procurement representatives in touch with customers, or even with someone who deals with customers? How many organizations have automated telephone answering systems that are designed to buffer organization members from contact with customers?

Now extend the idea of contact further. How many organizations put HR, R&D, operations, and finance people in touch with the communities in which they operate or with the NGOs who are considering the air, water, and carbon footprint impact of their business? How many organizations put their employees in touch with investment analysts? And finally, how many organizations that have these contacts actually pull together all the available information to make integrated decisions that optimize their strategic intent? This is the essence of the short-term futuring process we discussed in Chapter Four and will be a primary focus of the work systems we describe in Chapter Seven.

For a variety of reasons, organizations with a maximum surface area structure are much easier to change and better able to address social, ecological, and economic concerns than are internally focused structures. When Cisco moved to a centralized, functional organization, there was a lot of concern about it maintaining a customer focus. Cisco created a council and boards to preserve that orientation.

Creating councils and boards leveraged the customer-centric aspects of Cisco's identity. Cisco has a long history of being customer focused, and both its internal values and its external reputation as being customer-oriented have fueled the company's identity of "changing the way people live, work, play, and learn." Even as its managers abandoned a structure with an obvious customer orientation, they knew they could not abandon a very central part of who they were.

The councils and boards structure kept Cisco's focus on the external environment, including customers. It also allowed the company to focus on emerging markets, corporate responsibility, and the environmental impact of the business. Its councils and boards are a complement to Cisco's core functional structure. The "Operating Committee" (OC) has profit and loss responsibility for Cisco's global business and consists of Chambers and the executives who head up sales, marketing, manufacturing and supply chain, technology, finance, strategic planning, and engineering.

To ensure that the functional organization has a maximum surface area, Cisco created multiple cross-functional councils to address specific market demands and organization initiatives. These councils are groups of five to ten senior executives pulled from the different functions and tasked with creating and driving a strategy to achieve particular objectives. Councils are different from a task force because councils are relatively permanent. Councils are put into direct contact with specific markets and stakeholders. Cisco currently has nine councils, as is shown in Figure 6.1.

The original "segment" councils were formed around the very same customer segments that had defined Cisco's prior structure: large enterprises, small and medium businesses, and service providers. Eventually, the number of segment councils was expanded

Figure 6.1. Cisco's Council Structure

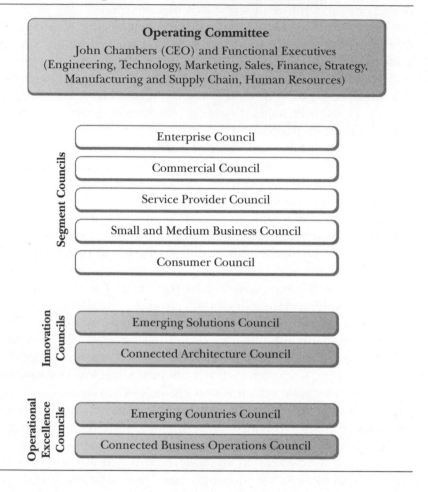

to five, demonstrating the flexibility of the structure. In pursuit of maximum surface area, Cisco also created councils to focus attention and resources on emerging solutions, new technologies, internal organizational processes and operations, and emerging markets.

The responsibility for establishing new councils rests with the OC. When the need for a new council is identified, the OC names the individuals who will be on the council, drawing on executives from the relevant functions. The council's first task is the creation of a vision, strategy, and execution (VSE) document. The VSE document is a statement of the council's belief about what's possible; how to achieve the vision; and the required resources, programs, and initiatives. It is a key document because it outlines the council's mandate or charter.

Once the VSE document is approved by the OC, the council can create one or more boards, and the boards can create one or more working groups, to focus on specific products, markets, or technologies. Boards, like councils, first create a VSE document to verify their charter and scope of responsibility.

One of the first boards created after the initial set of councils was formed was the "EcoBoard." The EcoBoard's vision—"if it can be connected to the Internet, it can be green"—dedicates Cisco to the goal of reducing greenhouse gas emissions 25 percent by 2012 (from a 2007 baseline). The EcoBoard intends to achieve its goal through environmentally conscious product designs, supply chain solutions, innovations to the network architecture to reduce power requirements, and sustainable company operations.

Like a council, a board normally has five to ten executives or managers from the functions considered necessary to drive specific elements of the council's strategy. Board members expect to spend about 30 percent of their time on board work.

Cisco's council and boards structure is a good example of a maximum surface area structure that puts members in touch with a broad variety of perspectives, reduces the number of surprises coming from the external environment, and makes members aware of a broad set of possibilities. It is a good way to increase the surface area of a functional organization.

Coordination and Resource Allocation Systems

All organization structures attempt to achieve multiple objectives. Being in touch with the different aspects of the external environment through a maximum surface area structure is one thing; coordinating what an organization does and allocating resources is another. In an ideal world, coordination and resource allocation are achieved by having all of the activities and processes necessary to create and deliver a product or service report to one manager and be visible to all employees. This is the holy grail of the high involvement organization, an achievable goal in a small, single product or service firm, and a key feature of W. L. Gore, as will be described later.

But in most large organizations, no matter how hard you try, you always run into some constraint or constraints—scale, scope, scarce resource, time—such that self-containment isn't possible. Can you imagine any structure that could put all the activities necessary to manufacture and test Boeing's 787 Dreamliner in one group?

Organizations have to address how they coordinate processes that run horizontally across their business units or functions. For example, how can a traditional functional organization made up of R&D, operations, marketing and sales, and administration coordinate the innovation process? Each function thinks they can, but R&D cannot do it without sales and marketing input, operations cannot do it without input from the other two, and so on.

In Cisco's case, the enterprise segment council has responsibility for crafting strategies and plans that grow and develop large corporate customers. To do that, council members must address two key horizontal coordination tasks. The first is coordination of the functions to deliver solutions to large enterprises. Growing and developing the enterprise market requires sales and marketing to provide information about customer demand. They need to coordinate that information with the technology and engineering functions in order to develop products and solutions that are attractive to this customer set. These coordination requirements do not just happen magically in a functional organization, they have to be actively managed.

The second coordination task involves interaction with the other segment councils, such as the small business or consumer councils, in order to allocate functional resources. Should the engineering and technology development functions prioritize large or small business products? How will they decide? SMOs address these questions with strong coordination and flexible resource allocation processes that overcome the lack of coordination that exists in most functionally structured organizations.

Coordination Processes

Coordination usually is accomplished by processes that help glue an organization together, including setting goals, defining schedules, and planning budgets. These basic coordination processes need to be designed to support a lot of sustainable practices. If goal setting does not include environmental objectives, they are not likely to be a concern. If budgets do not support social issues, where will the resources come from? To achieve the collaboration necessary to create an integrated set of outcomes, SMOs must be proficient at not only the basic coordination processes but also the more complex types of collaboration, such as project management, matrix relationships, cross-functional decision making, and prioritization.

More complex coordination processes are particularly important when the basic processes are not sufficient to handle the complexity of the business. For example, if goal setting, plans, and budgets are insufficient to handle the relationships among products, supply chains, and retail outlets, then a cross-functional team must be established to coordinate the flow of goods and services from sources to consumers.

Cross-functional decision making is a complex coordination process that requires special skills and knowledge, such as negotiation and the ability to see a whole system, and sophisticated management support processes, such as enterprise-wide information systems. In large organizations, the number and complexity of IT projects required to support different functions and product groups often exceeds the available resources. To coordinate the internal demand for IT support and optimize effectiveness, a "portfolio" decision-making process is required to prioritize the projects that should be funded, whether the criteria are economic, social, or environmental.

No organization has made a bigger bet on the process of collaboration than Cisco. The councils and boards represent large investments in cross-functional and portfolio decision making. The segment councils, for example, are tasked with coordinating the different functions toward goals that drive segment revenue and profit. The cross-segment innovation councils have the mission of developing new products, technologies, and solutions. By having functional representatives on each council, commitments can be taken back to the functional organization and prioritized. The councils also coordinate the boards in addressing specific segment and cross-segment issues and the work teams in addressing specific projects.

The VSE process, a basic coordination process, is key to supporting the more complex collaboration processes in the councils, boards, and functions. It identifies the necessary resources, creates a plan of record to monitor activity, serves as a communication device to the functions for their own prioritization and planning, and provides the OC with an important control mechanism.

No organization has made a bigger bet on the process of collaboration than Cisco. The councils and boards represent large investments in cross-functional and portfolio decision making.

Flexible Resource Allocation Systems

An organization such as Cisco with multiple councils creating new products and drawing up strategies for new markets will soon come apart at the seams unless there are coordination structures. The membership requirements and VSE process in Cisco are helpful here, but are not enough. To effectively coordinate activity, all of the processes described earlier assume a stable set of priorities and goals, but that is not a good assumption. SMOs must also have strong flexible resource allocation processes that move people, money, and assets to their most valued use when the business environment and priorities change. In most CCOs and HIOs, the enemy here is clear: the annual budget.

In most organizations, the annual budget is a fixed performance contract between one level of an organization and another. As a result, if an opportunity arises or a significant but unexpected event occurs, it is relatively difficult for a CCO or HIO to reprioritize attention and find the resources to adapt. Fixed annual budgets are primarily about control—in the negative sense of the term—and the operative word is *fixed,* which is why the "beyond budgeting" approach fits SMOs so well.[5]

At the heart of the beyond budgeting movement and any flexible resource allocation system is the insight that using budgets as a rigid control mechanism leads to an internal focus and counterproductive game playing. Two of the most common games are "padding the numbers" (such as, how can I know what will happen nine months from now; I need to add some contingency funds into my budget) and "creating shadow organizations" (for example, in a crunch, the IT group is too slow; I need some of my own IT resources working for me). These games may solve some problems but they do not recognize and address the real problem: fixed annual budgets are not suited for fast-changing organizations.

Budgeting restricts people's view of outcomes to financial metrics and their perspectives on resource allocation to vertical concerns. Budgets are financial metrics, and even when organizations move to a "balanced scorecard" that includes learning, customer satisfaction, or other categories, they retain a focus on financial returns. Similarly, since budgets (including revenues) always need to "roll up," the concern is almost always vertical, not horizontal and certainly not with customers and other stakeholders.

SMOs change the budget process in two ways. First, they focus on accountabilities. Goal-setting efforts address a broad set of economic objectives, social concerns, and ecological health outcomes. These goals must be reconciled by all the relevant structural dimensions of the organization. For a large multinational, this should include functions, products, and geographies. An SMO cannot pursue an integrated set of triple-bottom-line outcomes if part of the organization is working at cross-purposes with another part. The goal-setting process defines projects and operations that are resourced and budgeted. The process of defining projects and accountabilities should occur as often as necessary and not be just a once-a-year event.

Second, the process of setting outcomes against which people and teams will be held accountable is both vertical and horizontal. The beyond budgeting companies in Europe are experimenting with not having budgets at all. They are quite disciplined in their measurement of performance, the development of goals, and their accountability for results. However, they have eliminated the detailed line item budgeting process that sucks up management attention, produces organizational rigidity, and generates mountains of reports that are rarely looked at.

Cisco creates an annual long-range plan, and during that process, functional priorities are set with input from the councils. If significant opportunities emerge during the year—if a competitor launches an important new product or a new technology becomes commercially viable—or if councils change their aggressiveness, breadth, or differentiation—then the Operating Committee or the functions have to reprioritize.

Creating a formal mechanism to control the council and boards structure is something with which Cisco is struggling. For example, the functions and councils understand that the functions own the resources. However, that doesn't stop the councils from arguing that if they had a little budget to control, they could leverage activities more effectively and flexibly. In response, Cisco is developing a more effective portfolio management process.

As we described earlier, the complex coordination process involves the councils, representing different elements of the business environment, and the functions. As part of the long-range planning process, the budgeting process has evolved from one dominated by the functions to one in which the councils make inputs to functional budgets to one in which decisions are made on a portfolio basis. Each evolution of the process has been the result of an evaluation that recognized the organization's current resources and processes and its desired capabilities.

A totally functional budgeting process tended to allocate resources into shorter-term operations over longer-term investments. When the process involved inputs from the councils, the needs identified far exceeded the available capital. The emergence of a portfolio process recognizes the balance required to keep short- and long-term issues as well as efficiency and innovation in alignment. To do that, Cisco is considering whether portfolio optimization decisions should be made by the OC or by a Cisco Alignment Board that can also prioritize, plan, and track advancements on key strategic initiatives.

Transparent Decision-Making Processes

What differentiates SMOs, CCOs, and HIOs when it comes to decision making and information transparency is *who* offers input and *what* input is available. In a CCO, there is little doubt that the key strategic and operational decisions are made at the very highest levels of the organization. The reason for this is obvious—that is where the information exists and where the greatest decision-making and analytic expertise are. But when organizations adopt a maximum surface area structure and more sophisticated collaboration processes, good information exists in many parts of the organization and the information-processing and decision-making system of the organization must be adjusted.

Unlike CCOs and HIOs, SMOs try to optimize financial effectiveness as well as social and environmental effectiveness. A manufacturing plant in China that we worked with had to make a very real choice between operating the plant to provide jobs for the local economy and shutting down operations in order to stop polluting the local water supply. Asking why environmental equipment wasn't installed in the first place (a great question that provides important insight into the organization's identity and its business context) or recommending that they install equipment now (we did) doesn't help the plant manager decide what to do today.

Organizations that do not acknowledge social and environmental effectiveness have the luxury of ignoring and avoiding the complexity of multiple bottom lines. In this case the plant manager felt compelled to continue operations and wait for the environmental equipment to be installed even though watchdog NGO groups began publicizing the plant's polluting activities. The alternative—losing face among the members of his community— was an overriding concern.

Organizations that do not acknowledge social and environmental effectiveness have the luxury of ignoring and avoiding the complexity of multiple bottom lines.

To support a transparent decision-making process, Cisco's information systems measure key work process activities, organization performance, and stakeholder activities, including those of competitors, communities, regulators, customers, and others, and provide that information to everyone. This requires a system to organize and integrate the information, that everyone input what they know and hear, and that everyone uses the information for decision making to jointly optimize triple-bottom-line outcomes. Segment councils that do this are guided by Cisco's identity, the current strategic intent, and inputs from the other councils and boards. Looking ahead, in Chapters Eight and Nine we will describe how these systems interact with goal-setting and reward-system processes, but for now, what's important is the point that all SMOs should have information transparency.

With respect to transparency, some organizations are performing very well. Today, for example, there is good corporate social responsibility and sustainability reporting by many organizations, including DaVita (health care), UPS (logistics), Gap (retail), and Cisco (technology). Gap's reporting evolution is particularly noteworthy. It began with a simple brochure reporting on its activities and has evolved into a comprehensive website where its practices are described, metrics related to factory compliance are reported along with a variety of other data, comments from external stakeholders are published, and a larger community is created.

As important as transparency is when it comes to information, it is even more important when it comes to decision processes. Because of changes in the business environment, the best location for most decisions will change over time, although this is something that organizations rarely think about. At best, it comes up during reorganizations every few years. In SMOs, it is important that it be a regular topic of discussion and an important consideration when there is a strategy change.

For any organization to be effective, it needs to be clear who is making decisions and what the criteria are for deciding among conflicting alternatives and priorities. Cisco has done a good job of moving decisions to where the information and knowledge exist. There is a clear bias toward making decisions lower in the organization, and there is a clear bias toward integrating triple-bottom-line concerns. Implementing such a system is dependent on people in the organization being able to handle these types of decision-making processes as well as information transparency. Cisco can do it because it has both.

Summary

Cisco provides a good example of how traditional functional structures can be adapted to support sustainable effectiveness. By increasing the structural surface area through councils and boards, Cisco interfaces with the multiple stakeholders and the complexity in its environment. By improving its flexible resource allocation and collaboration processes, Cisco is able to move people, budgets, and work to their most valued use. By implementing transparent decision-making processes, it leverages its surface area and resource allocation processes for flexibility. There is little doubt that Cisco has created an effective but complex organization structure that does a good job supporting sustainable effectiveness. There are two other ways to accomplish this. Let's begin our look at them by considering the ambidextrous organization.

Ambidextrous Organization—Balancing Innovation and Efficiency

Established organizations must attend to the tension between activities that account for current performance and activities that will generate the innovations that are needed to meet future demands. Many CCOs are good at cranking out standardized products and services but lousy at innovation and adaptation. High involvement organizations are a little less programmed and a little more adaptable, but neither CCOs nor HIOs are particularly good at developing new businesses that require new competencies and capabilities.

For example, Sony missed the boat on MP3 players because its policies for protecting its music division got in the way of creating new products. Giving the right amount of attention to innovation and current products, as well as to the sometimes conflicting priorities of the triple-bottom line, requires a mental and operational agility that most organizations don't have. They simply are not structured in a way that develops this capability.

Two-Structure Design

In the face of an increasingly complex and uncertain business environment and the challenge of achieving sustainable effectiveness, one adaptation that some large organizations, such as IBM and HP, have made is the development of an "ambidextrous" organizational structure.[6] Ambidextrous organizations operate effectively in both slowly changing traditional businesses that require efficiency and businesses requiring transformational change and innovation. They use a maximum surface area structure and strong collaboration capabilities to achieve these objectives. But just as with people, few organizations are ambidextrous. Let's look at one that is.

Harris Corporation is a $5 billion, sixteen-thousand-employee communications and information technology company serving government and commercial markets worldwide. Its Broadcast Communications Division (BCD), with sales of $600 million, is one of six divisions and sells TV and radio transmission equipment, voice- and data-networking services, and fiber-optic solutions.[7] In the early 2000s, BCD was facing several important market transitions, including maturing digital markets in the United States and growing digital solutions opportunities internationally. To continue growing its core U.S. markets but also to pursue new "breakout" markets in governments, public safety, and live events (such as the Olympics, FIFA, and so on), BCD adopted an ambidextrous organization.

To achieve the goal of efficient growth in its core markets and rapid growth in new markets, BCD modified its structure to support two structures. The first—BCD's core structure—was designed to focus on efficiency. As shown in Figure 6.2, BCD's three business units provide products and solutions to its three regional sales organizations, who take them to market.

The core structure is good at producing and selling existing solutions but relatively poor at generating important innovations. It owns the budgets and the people; has a short-to-medium-term time frame; rewards technical and operational excellence; hires and develops people to be outstanding contributors; and is accountable for meeting efficiency goals. To support the business unit–sales collaboration necessary to pursue organizational efficiency, BCD business unit managers work hard to ensure that the sales organization is well trained in BCD products, including how the products from the different business units work together. It also provides the sales organization with technical support.

Figure 6.2. Harris Corporation's BCD Core Structure

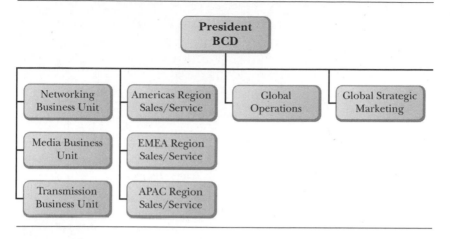

A second feature of the structure is new. It focuses on product development and innovation. As new product ideas emerge and pass divisional reviews for alignment with the strategy and future scenarios—no matter what business unit spawned the idea—a temporary organization is established (see Figure 6.3). Rather than having the new unit report to the business units or the sales regions, where they might not get the resources or attention they need, the innovation unit is assigned to the strategic marketing function, where it can operate outside the core structure's controls.

The temporary innovation unit has a clear mandate and design: drive development of the new product or market strategy; take a longer-term view; use staff with the appropriate talent from the different business units and functions; and get rewarded for creating new ideas and business development. The staffing model includes the possibility of drawing on expertise from other Harris divisions that might have a stake in the product's success. Thus the temporary innovation unit is not completely divorced from the core structure.

Independent Units

Organizations often find that the only viable approach to successfully starting new businesses within an existing organization is to

Figure 6.3. Harris Corporation's BCD Ambidextrous Structure

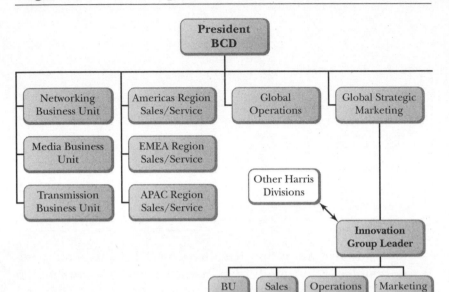

create special business units that are "independent" of the existing corporation, much like Apple and Lockheed Martin have successfully done with their Skunk Works organizations and IBM did with its PC business. The degree of independence can vary, but experience suggests that it needs to be high because new businesses in old organizations are often weighed down by the expenses and controls imposed on them by the existing corporate structure.

A high level of independence may mean that only the general manager of the new business venture reports to the CEO of the existing company. The rest of the new venture has no reporting relationship to the old organization, so that it is inoculated against parts of the old infecting it.

Highly independent organizations tend to create their own cultures. As a result, frequently anything they produce is rejected by the parent organization under the rule of NIH (not invented here). Further, the cultural differences can create internal jealousies that lend corporate executives to decide that the new unit should operate under the same rules as everyone else. For example, even though it was a successful "startup" as a separate division, Saturn eventually succumbed to the dominance of GM's command and control culture and ultimately was closed.

The risk associated with creating innovative business units can be reduced by building good links between the new organization and the very senior management levels of the existing organization. Harris's Broadcast Communications Division has done this. The temporary innovation unit is tasked with rapid product and market development and given significant freedom and resources, but it is still linked to the core structure. Although complex, this ambidextrous structure has paid off for BCD. It has launched a number of new products, grown market share, and transferred several new product ideas to the core structure. The division is currently addressing how to decide which business unit should house products that cut across business unit boundaries.

Ambidexterity allows large organizations to balance efficiency and innovation. It also enables organizations to support sustainable effectiveness if they are driven by triple-bottom-line objectives. Efficiency, for example, can have very solid ties to sustainability when it includes efforts to lower the carbon footprint of an organization, use recycled materials, eliminate waste, and pursue a more systemic approach to product design.

Innovation can be driven by technology and markets, as well as by social and environmental issues. For example, C. K. Prahalad's "fortune at the bottom of the pyramid" concept suggests that improving social conditions in emerging markets, different cultures, and less advantaged consumer segments can be an important source of product and business model innovation.[8] When GE's health care division considered expanding into countries that could not afford large investments in imaging equipment, it modified its designs to support higher patient throughput volumes and lower price points. Its modified equipment brought important social benefits to lesser-developed economies and new revenue to GE. Similarly, many consumer product companies, including Kraft and P&G, have modified packaging sizes to allow lower prices. They have not only stimulated demand, they have made toothpaste, eye care, and soap available to more people.

Lovins and his colleagues have described the "natural capitalism" model and demonstrated the economic potential of solving environmental problems.[9] Their primary suggestion is that organizations shift their business models from a "purchase our product" to a "rent our services" model. Multiple firms, including Interface Flooring Systems, United Technologies, and DOW Chemical, have shifted their business model to embrace this new services and solutions mind-set to gain more control over their environmental footprint. Innovation in an SMO can be guided by social, environmental, and economic outcomes. If the innovation parts of an ambidextrous organization are given incentives to drive sustainable innovation, sustainable effectiveness can result.

Summary

The ambidextrous organization structure approach has some advantages over a modified functional organization. First, it is not as complex. An existing organization can maintain its use of a more traditional structure, while it adds the ability to innovate quickly with the addition of innovation units. Innovation units do have to be protected, and this requires some political skill and commitment from senior managers, but this is much easier to get in place than the restructuring of an existing organization. Second, the flexibility of the innovation unit allows the organization to pursue products, solutions, process improvements, and services that address sustainable effectiveness. Finally, the innovative units can develop new behaviors and processes that the larger organization can adopt.

The Network Organization—Balancing Flexibility and Execution

A third structural option for an SMO is the network structure.[10] In the context of rapidly changing business environments and the demands for triple-bottom-line outcomes, a network structure can reliably produce effective outcomes and yet retain the flexibility to adapt and change. Unlike ambidexterity, in which two types of architectures are coordinated to pursue different purposes, a network organization's key capability is being able to reconfigure quickly and effectively.

Most existing organization structures can be described as networks. They are systems of relationships and exchanges among functions, geographies, products, programs, and individuals working together to accomplish a task. But they are very different from a "network organization."

The issue is the perspective. Hierarchical structures, such as functional or ambidextrous organizations, specify how managerial attention and scarce resources are focused and deployed. Network structures specify how managerial attention and resources are exchanged among the units to achieve certain outcomes. For example, instead of focusing on what role an individual plays— who is responsible for the European sales division or who heads up the corporate social responsibility function—network structures shift the focus to the relationships and exchanges that produce key outcomes. Networks are best described in terms of the work done or the outcomes sought—innovation, problem solving, career advancement, or labor relations.

The outcome desired can radically change the composition of a network but tells us little about the organization's hierarchy. For example, the people who are involved in making an acquisition decision may form a network in which certain individuals collect and summarize information that is provided to other people who analyze it and decide on a course of action. As a result, some people are central and others peripheral in the network. The network structure, however, says very little about the hierarchical structure of the organization, since someone central in the network may occupy a very low role in the organization's hierarchy.

There are informal networks in most organizations that do such things as give career advice and tell newcomers how to work around the formal system. The number of these networks has increased dramatically as the Web has become more and more accessible to most employees. Again, the formal organizational structure is irrelevant in this regard because advice can come from a senior executive or from a long-term employee with lots of expertise.

The ability to create network structures has been greatly facilitated by technological change. Prior to enterprise resource programs, web-based information systems, Web 2.0, and other social networking technologies, there was a great deal of reliance on vertical boss-subordinate communication. Today, managers and employees around the globe can find out what's happening in other parts of the organization with just a few keystrokes and mouse clicks—and pretty soon by just asking a mobile device.

A Network Organization

One of the most famous examples of a network organization is W. L. Gore.[11] It is a fifty-year-old, privately held, $2.5 billion organization with an uninterrupted string of annual profits, more than a thousand products, and thirteen consecutive years on *Fortune* magazine's list of the "Best Places to Work." Gore's strategic intent is grounded in innovation, and to support that, Gore has no organization chart, few titles, no job descriptions, no "bosses," and minimal budgets.

In Gore's way of thinking, if you cannot attract a team to work on an idea, the idea must not be that good.

Much of the work at Gore is done through project teams that form organically. Everyone at Gore is encouraged to play around with ideas in an unstructured way. When they believe they have an idea for a new product or process improvement, they gather interested people together. Pulling together a team of the right individuals or groups is facilitated by clustering plants and offices together geographically and keeping the number of employees in each group small. Gore is famous for breaking up groups into smaller units when they reach more than 150 to 200 people. This facilitates having a high level of communication and knowledge about what is happening in the organization and what types of talent and skills are available.

In Gore's way of thinking, if you cannot attract a team to work on an idea, the idea must not be that good. However, if people do commit to the project, there is a belief that the project has something to offer the corporation, such as access to a market, a lowered carbon footprint, a new product with profit potential, or a better way of doing things. In addition, it means the project has something to offer the individuals who sign up, including the opportunity to expand their skills or do interesting and meaningful work. In exchange, the individuals commit their energy and talent to determining whether the idea can be developed.

Creating Surface Area, Flexibility, and Transparency

Using what they call a "lattice" structure, Gore works through its four divisions (industrial, fabrics, medical, and electronics) to gain surface area by asking individuals, groups, and functions to think of themselves as bundles of valuable resources and competence. Gore achieves resource flexibility and accountability through commitments to teams and projects and a "real-win-worth" process, and it facilitates transparency through clusters of small plants and offices.

W. L. Gore's network organization is a maximum surface area structure because every individual and group is expected to seek out relationships with customers, suppliers, and collaborators inside the organization. That is the essence of a "lattice." Each individual and group recognizes the resources and talents they bring but acknowledges that they cannot achieve their growth, contribution, or development goals or add value to the company without exchanging resources with other people. Each person or unit has to be clear about his or her interdependencies—what they want from the others, both internally and externally, and what they can offer in return. They must understand the organization well enough to know where to find opportunities that suit their expertise.

A network structure achieves surface area in the same way a matrix structure does without the traditional problems of power being vested in a hierarchy and requiring balancing by senior managers. In a matrix structure, the needs of customers (represented by programs) and the requirements of the technology (represented by functions) are worked out through negotiations. An engineer who is deployed to a particular program performs work that is a negotiated outcome between the functional boss ("This is a good opportunity for him or her") and the program office management ("We need a more senior engineer with experience for this work").

The role of senior management is to "balance the matrix" so that each dimension, whether it is customer, function, or geography, has an equal voice and results in the "best of both worlds" (development and performance) optimization. In reality, senior management rarely performs the balancing function and the organization ends up with either a strong program or customer orientation or a strong technology focus. Under these circumstances, one dimension loses, politics rule, and the organization struggles to achieve its objectives. With the advent of multidimensional matrices as well as the insertion of a triple-bottom-line objective, this situation can get worse. In contrast to matrix structure, Gore uses the network concept to achieve surface area by asking each unit or individual to be in a relationship with as many other internal or external resources as necessary to make a contribution to the strategic intent.

Gore uses the network structure to achieve resource flexibility. People are pulled together into different projects. In networks, work is thought of as a project done by a group whose membership flexes with the task. For example, if the people involved in a particular innovation project cannot figure out a way to bring the idea to market, the functions, products, and geographies can be redeployed to a different innovation idea. The same people who try to sell a foreign government a slightly higher-priced solution that is more reliable, less polluting, and longer-lived do not have to be the same people who try to figure out how to bring a new product to market.

Network structures shift people's focus from the roles in the hierarchy to the exchanges among members and units. The currencies in these exchanges include capabilities, talent, goals, visions, opportunities, constraints, demand, information, and customer inputs—anything that has value in the context of the organization's identity and strategic intent. For example, anyone at Gore can propose a new product because the structure facilitates their awareness of information regarding the market, they understand the organization's identity and strategic intent, and they have the skills to convene the network. Members are added to the team on the basis of their interests and capabilities. The team grows and more exchanges occur if (1) each party gets what they need to pursue their purpose and add value in the network and

(2) the exchange aligns with identity and intent, including the pursuit of economic, social, and ecological outcomes.

To ensure alignment between actions and interest, W. L. Gore asks each innovation team to work within the real-win-worth process. When a project reaches the stage where it wants formal support from the organization, it has to prove the opportunity is real. There need to be markets with customers willing to pay money for the product. Once they establish that the opportunity is real, the team has to show that Gore is in a position to win in the marketplace. Does the organization have the technology, the organizational capabilities, and the resources to support it? Finally, the team must show that the effort will result in benefits to the organization. Will the margins be large enough to cover the costs of doing business? This is the governance mechanism in a network exchange.

Finally, execution and flexibility are both served by a high level of transparency in the organization's information flow. Because the exchange between nodes has to be mutually beneficial, there is a pressure on team members to keep their commitments and to make a contribution. Otherwise, and within limits, the parties can move to another exchange. Transparency contributes to execution because lots of information is available. Associates know what other associates can do, what they know, and how much they can be trusted.

Future of Networks

Networks represent a powerful alternative to hierarchy, but they also represent an important threat to existing authority in most organizations. Gary Hamel makes the point that Gore's network and innovation structure has been around for fifty years without being copied or replicated.[12] He believes this is because a network structure requires too big a shift in management thinking and is too threatening to the traditional definitions of power and status. Cisco achieves sophisticated collaboration capabilities while still under the control of the Operating Committee. Harris relies on the hierarchy to keep innovative units independent but still linked into the organization's resources. Why replace the most widely accepted and understood organizational logic for an unproven one?

But a second issue is more relevant and insidious to sustainable effectiveness. By replacing hierarchy with exchange, a network structure rewrites the traditional definitions of power and status. In hierarchy, authority and power derive from a manager's position and the right to give orders and control employees. The effective functioning of a network structure relies only on finding a relationship in which the goals of individuals are aligned with those of the organization and the exchange is mutually beneficial. When exchange is used instead of hierarchy for control, power flows to the people with critical knowledge and a reputation for getting things done.

Networks represent a powerful alternative to hierarchy, but they also represent an important threat to existing authority in most organizations.

Converting from hierarchy to networks is difficult because it requires confronting our views and definitions of power. Moving to a network structure without a commensurate adjustment in leadership style is an implementation error. Put another way, continuing to apply CCO leadership practices to a flexible, SMO structure is an accident waiting to happen, as the Challenger shuttle, Bhopal, Chernobyl, Exxon Valdez, the recent financial crisis, and BP's disasters demonstrate. In each case, a centralized command structure interested in efficiency and profit objectives ignored local knowledge and concerns about broader outcomes, including safety, quality, and social responsibility.

Summary

A network's biggest benefit—flexibility—may open up the possibilities of achieving high levels of sustainable effectiveness. The network structure depends on exchange for its success, and especially exchange among partners who have invested heavily to achieve trust. Achieving the trust and capacity to reconfigure people, budgets, and priorities may look like creating slack resources to someone trained and rewarded for cutting costs. Applying tight integration requirements in the name of efficiency to the flexible relationships in a network structure is a fundamental conflict between the SMO style and the CCO assumptions. If the issue of power is not addressed, traditional leadership behaviors and CCO goals not only can negate the network structure's advantages, they can result in failure.

Conclusion

An organization's structure can make an important contribution to its sustainable effectiveness. Structures focus attention and resources on the activities, issues, and decisions that an organization must make to be successful. If those activities, issues, and decisions include financial performance, social benefits, and ecological health, then the traditional functional organization must be modified in ways that increase surface area, collaboration, transparency, and flexibility in resource allocation decisions. Ambidextrous and network structures accomplish these objectives and challenge traditional ways of thinking about structuring organizations.

Assessment Questions

1. What is your organization's surface area like?

   a. Most managers spend their days talking only to other internal managers; talking to customers or external stakeholders is rare except for a few roles.

   b. There's a strong customer focus here—we listen to both internal and external customers.

   c. We naturally have a strongly external focus due to our structure (for example, small business units), processes, or culture.

   Here is what the answers imply:

   a. It's normal for organizations to become more and more inward looking, but it is a disease.

   b. Many organizations have realized how important customers are, but they are only one stakeholder.

c. Everything you need to do to be sustainable will come more easily if most employees are close to the external world of customers, competitors, external stakeholders, and global forces.

2. How interested is your organization in an innovative structure?

a. There is little interest in structural innovation; we are content with our traditional structure.

b. Management is sufficiently committed to innovation that they would pursue an ambidextrous structure if they understood how to do it.

c. The culture is inclined toward a network model, and people will embrace it if management leads the way.

Here is what the answers imply:

a. The only "wrong" answer is "a." An organization won't be able to sustain any notable success with traditional structures. It's not clear what the "right" model is, or even if there is a right model, but organizations moving toward some form of ambidextrous or network structure are more likely to find their way to a structure that works.

CHAPTER SEVEN

| Sustainable Work Systems

HP's acquisition of Compaq in 2001 was one of the largest, most complex, and most expensive mergers in history. The two organizations had redundant product lines, overlapping customers and distribution channels, but radically different cultures. Along with Web McKinney, who headed up the integration team from the HP side, Stu Winby was at the center of the integration action. As the merger was being implemented, Winby kept running into the problem of critical initiatives and projects that were behind schedule. What he needed was a way to accelerate decision making, problem solving, and innovation.

Earlier in his career, Winby had worked with a type of organization development intervention known as large-group interventions (LGIs).[1] In an LGI, all the relevant stakeholders are brought together in one place over two to three days. The assumption is that if you can get the stakeholders in the same room at one time, you will have all the knowledge needed to make inclusive and sustainable decisions. By using a structured process to bring out the different perspectives, LGIs not only speed up and improve the quality of decision making, they create energy and commitment to a course of action.

In his work at HP, Winby challenged the assumption that the major stakeholders possessed all of the knowledge necessary to address most problems and issues. While Winby believed that a multi-stakeholder group could bring a great deal of knowledge to an LGI discussion, he argued that in many situations the discussion would be much more informed if it was able to access a broader range of information. As a result, he augmented the knowledge of the stakeholders with an information system tied into HP's and Compaq's intranets as well as the global Internet. He called this innovation a "decision accelerator"—or DA for short—and used it to inform and speed up the integration process.

In its original incarnation, a dedicated room at HP headquarters was established, and any time a critical decision in the merger integration plan went "yellow" or "red" in status for two meetings in a row, the issue was diverted to the DA. A staff under Winby's direction looked at the problem and designed a work process to bring all of the relevant parties together—face-to-face—to describe the problem, generate alternative solutions, explore the options, and decide on a course of action. If the players in the room—anywhere between twenty and seventy people—could not come up with a solution, then an executive was brought in to break the tie. This was an embarrassing situation that no one wanted. In fact, the DA process worked so well, the tiebreaker was only needed once.

But Winby saw . . . a much larger opportunity. He thought the DA process could help organizations vision the future, create innovative strategies, accelerate the development of action plans, and even actually accelerate the implementation of those plans. He saw in the DA a new way to do work.

Thanks in large part to the DA process, the HP-Compaq merger integration process not only met most integration milestones and cost-saving projections, it is still widely regarded as a best practice. But Winby saw more. He saw a much larger opportunity. He thought the DA process could help organizations vision the future, create innovative strategies, accelerate the development of action plans, and even actually accelerate the implementation of those plans. He saw in the DA a new way to do work, a way that we think supports the way SMOs should operate.

The purpose of this chapter is to describe the work system of an SMO. In Chapter Six, we identified the structural forms of ambidexterity and networks that are likely to characterize SMOs. The ambidextrous structure provides a means to achieve both efficiency and innovation. Network organizations are a flexible way to reconfigure around projects and tasks to deliver products and services reliably. Both structures support innovation—figuring out how to change products and services for new or emerging markets—as well as finding better ways to do routine work.

Most organizations are familiar with traditional work design and processes of continuous improvement, such as total quality management or six-sigma. Much less is known about the innovation process and very little is known about designing work systems that make innovation a capability. SMOs need to go beyond the simple policy statements of Google and 3M that say "spend 15 to 20 percent of your time thinking about new ideas"; they need to create work systems in which innovation is a continuous process.

The Evolution of a New Work System

One of Winby's early experiments in the development of a new work system using DAs was at Alegent Health in Omaha, Nebraska.[2] In 2004, following a bitter series of confrontations with local physicians, a new CEO was appointed. He challenged the organization to build an innovation capability that would propel the health care system to "world class" status.

To support its commitment to change, Alegent Health dedicated a whole floor—about three thousand square feet—of its headquarters office to the DA process, which was branded as "Right Track." The workspace consisted of a large open area with moveable chairs, tables, whiteboards, and flip chart easels that could be easily configured and reconfigured. The space also had a dedicated area with Internet-enabled computers, printers, copiers, office supplies, small private meeting rooms, a kitchen and room for eating, and audiovisual support. Alegent even went so far as to prepare the walls with a special paint. When participants in a DA—or anyone else for that matter—wanted to have spontaneous conversations about solutions or innovative ideas, they could draw figures or put notes on the walls as if they were a whiteboard.

Winby and his colleague Joel Fadem orchestrated six DAs. They were done to vision the strategies for the health system's six clinical service lines and to build the innovation capability.

Over an eight-week period, the cardiology, behavioral health, oncology, women's and children, orthopedics, and neurology service lines each pulled together a large group of about sixty to seventy physicians, administrators, hospital presidents, nursing managers, community members, regulators, patients, and other stakeholders. They spent two-and-a-half days thinking about what it meant to be "world class," considering what the vision of the service line should be, and staking out a set of implementation milestones or indicators of progress for a fifteen-year period.

Typical DA designs break the large group into small, multi-stakeholder teams of seven or eight people. Each team receives a set of data—an article, case, table or figure, or scenario—and discusses several questions. For example, to help the health care system think about the implications of being a "world class" organization, the teams read short articles about Disney, Nordstrom, and Ritz-Carlton and discussed, "How does this example reflect 'world class'?"

The small groups report out to the large group, and common themes are discussed and debated. Using the combined traits of a world-class organization, the large group breaks up into different multi-stakeholder teams with the question, "How should we apply these criteria to our situation?"

Alternatively, the small groups might be asked, "How would stakeholder X view this criteria?" with X replaced with any number of different stakeholders, including patients, health care industry regulators, and physicians. This iterative process—take some ideas or data, discuss and improve on them, and report back to the large group (what innovation people call "rapid prototyping")—continues until a vision or strategy or solution or action plan emerges.

The original six DAs exposed people to a new way of doing work and propelled innovation and action in the system. Soon afterward, other DAs were convened to address clinical quality across the health care system, implement an electronic medical records system, develop a primary health care strategy, and tackle issues of access and working with underserved populations.

Over the next two years, Alegent Health ran more than a hundred DAs and involved nearly every one of its members in some form of multi-stakeholder decision-making process. Inspired by the DA recommendations, Alegent's board approved a $350 million capital improvement plan. In June 2008, Alegent was recognized by the Network for Regional Healthcare Improvement as the number one health care organization in the nation because of high-quality clinical outcomes and patient satisfaction.

Alegent also used the DA to develop its sustainability approach. In combination with its clinical quality and social responsibility efforts, Alegent developed the Eco-Alegent program and began making changes in the carbon footprint of its hospitals, clinics, and other locations. Alegent's vision is to extend its sustainability operations to the supply chain and begin working with medical device suppliers, pharmaceutical companies, and other vendors.

Yes, Alegent still does traditional patient care and no, it is not done through a DA. They admit patients, do surgeries, deliver babies, handle emergencies, and discharge people. That is the regular work of a health care system, and the organization is always working to make it more efficient and effective. However, even this work is influenced by the DA philosophy.

Nurses, environmental services staff, and cafeteria workers routinely call together the stakeholders who will be involved in a change to think about the work and the implications of change and find a solution that works. The vocabulary in the organization has changed. "Accelerated decisions," "rapid prototyping," and "multi-stakeholder decisions" are frequently used terms that can be traced directly back to the original DAs.

The Natural Occurrence of New Work Systems

Alegent Health's use of the DA reflects a big step away from thinking about the LGIs as an isolated change intervention and a big step away from traditional views of how work is structured and done. It defines a new way of adding value and innovating that can support sustainable effectiveness.

The same work systems characteristics that were developed at Alegent can emerge naturally. Consider the case of Aisin Seiki.[3] Aisin Seiki is a member of the Toyota Production System (TPS) network. It produces P-valves, a part that helps to prevent skidding by controlling the pressure on the rear brakes.

Alegent Health's use of the DA reflects a big step away from thinking about the LGIs as an isolated change intervention and a big step away from traditional views of how work is structured and done.

The fist-sized P-valves are not complicated, but require precision manufacturing in specialized facilities using custom-designed drills and gauges because their role is so critical to safety. In 1997, Aisin was producing all but 1 percent of the P-valves for Toyota's twenty plants because of its efficiency, low costs, and high quality. Aisin's only P-valve manufacturing factory, the Kariya plant, produced 32,500 valves a day.

Because of the success of their just-in-time manufacturing system, Toyota held between four hours and two days' worth of P-valves in stock. Production at the Kariya plant was, therefore, a critical element of Toyota's supply chain. Toyota's production control manager conceded that depending on a single source and holding essentially no inventory was a calculated risk, but it also kept Toyota's production lean.

On Saturday, February 1, 1997, the Kariya plant burned down, and by Wednesday, February 5, all production at Toyota had come to a halt. Economists estimated that the shutdown would damage Japan's annual industrial output by 0.1 percentage point each day. Toyota estimated that more than two weeks would be needed just to restore a few milling machines to partial production, and six months to obtain new machines. By Thursday, February 6, however, two of Toyota's plants had reopened, and by the following Monday, little more than a week after the crisis begun, production of almost fourteen thousand cars a day had been restored. A week after that, the daily production volume was back to its pre-disaster level. How could this happen?

Aisin managers realized immediately that the recovery task was beyond their capabilities as an individual firm and beyond the capabilities of their immediate suppliers. A much broader effort would be required; one over which they would have little direct control. Before the fire was out, Aisin officials organized a committee to assess the damage, notify customers and labor unions, and order over 300 cell phones, 230 extra phone lines, and several dozen sleeping bags.

At 8:00 A.M., Aisin asked Toyota to help. Kosuke Ikebuchi, a Toyota senior managing director, set up a "war room" at Toyota headquarters to direct the damage-control operation. Toyota also sent more than four hundred engineers to Aisin. Later that morning, having set up an emergency response headquarters, Aisin sent out a distress call to other keiretsu members, defining the problem broadly and asking for help. Within hours, they began making blueprints for the valve, improvising tooling systems, and setting up makeshift production lines.

On Saturday afternoon, Toyota and Aisin invited some of their major parts suppliers to a second war room, at Aisin headquarters. It quickly became a hectic scene because the firms involved in the recovery effort lacked the tools and expertise specific to P-valve production; Aisin's expertise rested largely with its own processes. As a result, small groups of people from different organizations with different technical backgrounds were forced to invent novel manufacturing procedures in real time, and to solve both design and production problems simultaneously.

The capacity of this initial group of suppliers was not sufficient. So Toyota purchasing officials called more parts makers to a Sunday afternoon meeting. Masakazu Ishikawa, a former Toyota manager whose division had designed Toyota P-valves, was now executive vice president of Somic Ishikawa Inc., a supplier of brake parts and suspension joints. Somic's efforts represent one of several concurrent processes with other organizations and demonstrate this emerging type of work system.

Mr. Ishikawa called Somic's top production engineers and asked them to meet at 8:00 P.M. Sunday. They met until after midnight plotting to contract out some of their current factory work to free up machines to make the Toyota parts. By 6:00 A.M. Monday, Somic's four designers had begun an eight-stage design process. Staying up for forty hours, the engineers designed jigs, and then they called in some favors from Somic's chain of suppliers. Somic got a machine-tool maker, Meiko Machinery Co., to turn down other orders and put thirty workers on round-the-clock shifts to make the jigs it needed. Somic drafted technical and administrative staffers to help man the machines. On February 6, Somic delivered its first P-valves to Toyota.

The Aisin case describes how one organization recombined the resources of many firms in multiple distinct and original configurations to produce an equivalent output of P-valves. All of this happened without a formal hierarchy, without job descriptions, without central direction, and without a budget, and all of it happened in just three days.

The Characteristics of Sustainable Work Systems

The Alegent Health and Aisin cases—two very different situations, industries, and technologies—have much in common. They both describe a very different way to think about work. Drawing on these two cases and the structural characteristics we described in Chapter Six, we suggest that work systems in SMOs should be

1. Based on activities, not jobs
2. Guided by shared goals
3. Performed by multiple stakeholder teams (they can be virtual)
4. Temporary and iterative
5. Supported by the physical space and technology
6. Managed strategically

Work Is Based on Activities, Not Jobs

CCOs are all about stability, predictability, and efficiency, and their fundamental building block is the job. Job descriptions are the result of breaking down work into its component tasks and then grouping them together into a logical set, which is called a job.

A job description states what an individual is supposed to do, in some cases the kind of skills needed, and how performance can be measured. People are given fixed jobs with detailed job descriptions and clear reporting relationships. They are usually grouped together on the basis of functions, such as sales, marketing, production, and accounting, or the part of the function they perform (such as phone centers or product assembly). They report up a hierarchy that is managed by individuals in their function.

Individuals typically are not encouraged to explore or consider how work might be organized to better promote social, ecological, and economic gain. Sometimes, individuals do participate in continuous improvement and six-sigma activities that focus on how to make their work more efficient, stable, and predictable.

CCOs are all about stability, predictability, and efficiency, and their fundamental building block is the job.

A job-based approach to work design makes a lot of sense when the primary objective is economic performance, the work is not likely to change, and there are minimal social and ecological consequences resulting from the operation. But change is rampant in today's workplace, and as a result this approach is woefully outdated. Most employees readily acknowledge that much of the time they are performing "other duties as assigned," not what is actually in their job description. Instead of worrying about this and trying to keep job descriptions up to date, we believe SMOs should simply abandon the fiction that fixed jobs and job descriptions are a good thing.

The alternative to a job-based, hierarchical structure is one that is characterized by the dynamic work assignments and relationships that are characteristic of network organizations. In the context of a clear identity and integrated goals around financial performance, social value, and ecological health, work assignments are created. In the DA work at Alegent Health, work is defined by the objective—a new sustainability strategy, a better clinical process, or a more effective community outreach program—not some presupposed set of tasks. This is a much more flexible way of working.

With this type of structure, most individuals do not have fixed jobs or typical boss-subordinate reporting relationships. Instead, they ask, "What needs to get done?" HIOs have this as a core design feature, and we often see this kind of structure in consulting firms and other professional service organizations.

Individuals continually are moved from project to project, with a different project lead for each assignment.

What occurs in a DA depends on the kind of projects and tasks that need to be done to achieve the goals and strategies of the organization. The projects and tasks change depending on what is happening with a particular customer, product, or stakeholder. As a result of being in a work system that is designed to change, individuals are comfortable with continuous change. They are not led to expect, nor do they experience, changing group memberships, new tasks, or fluid agendas as a disruption of their lives. Instead, it is the way the organization does business, and it provides a fine-grained picture of how work gets done in a network. They do not fear change, they embrace it.

The Aisin recovery story describes a different kind of work system with SMO characteristics. Like the DA, there were no jobs, just novel activities that needed to be created in real time so that economic and social safety nets could be reestablished. Because everyone knew this, Aisin only needed to define the critical output details for the P-valve, allowing potential suppliers the greatest possible latitude in deciding how to proceed. Even more important, while the particular situation was unfamiliar, the idea of cooperating was not.

Because many of the firms involved in the recovery effort had previously exchanged personnel and technical information with Aisin, Toyota, and each other, they could use lines of communication, information resources, and social ties that were already established. They understood and trusted each other, an arrangement that facilitated transparent information flows and the flexible allocation of resources, two critical structural features that were described in Chapter Six. The work defined what people did, not some archaic notion of a job.

This is exactly what happens in the work teams at Cisco. The councils set the broad strategies and bargain for the right resources. The boards take particular slices of the strategies and the work teams carry out the specific projects and disband when the task is over, ready for the next priority.

At Gore, novel ideas are championed by associates who draw together a team interested in making the innovation work. If it does, the product is funded and an organization created. If not, the team disbands and the people are available for another task assignment. There is no need for job descriptions; if they did exist, they would probably read, "Go find a way to contribute."

Work Is Guided by Shared Goals

When work is organized according to functions, an individual's goals are often at odds with the goals of other functions. In alignment with their job descriptions, the people running the manufacturing plant are interested in efficiency, the sales and service organization is interested in pleasing the customer, and the legal function is concerned with risk management. Since nobody's job is concerned with mitigating environmental harm, it either doesn't get done or a new group has to be created to convince everyone that it should.

Unless there is an overarching, shared view of an organization's purpose and identity, groups in different functions all too often work at cross-purposes. McDonald's recently struggled with this dilemma. To increase sales, it offered toys from recent movies with its meal deals. The operations people purchased the toys from low-cost manufacturing sources and ensured that the toys were not hazardous to kids. Meanwhile, the legal organization and public relations functions ended up battling with NGOs who claimed that by offering toys, McDonalds was contributing to childhood obesity.

The work described in the Alegent and Aisin cases has a very different goal structure. Instead of goals being set independently, goal setting was approached from a multi-stakeholder perspective from the very beginning. In a DA, the framing of the opportunity, problem, or issue is critical. It has to be substantive enough to attract the interest and commitment of relevant stakeholders. As a result of understanding the opportunity issue from multiple perspectives, goal clarity and goal commitment are achieved. As the DA concludes with an action agenda, there is energy and momentum for change.

In the Aisin case, the goal was clear and shared—get quality P-valves designed and manufactured as quickly as possible. All the companies involved understood the problem to be solved and were committed to getting it done. Achievement of the goal had clear economic and social consequences that bound everyone together.

Work is motivating when it is designed right.[4] First, people need to see their work in its context—not just as one part or piece of what is done. Second, they need to see how their work has an impact on customers, vendors, and the larger system. Third, goals should be set collaboratively, and at a challenging but achievable level. As will be discussed in the next chapter, having an effective performance management process is the best way to set motivating goals.

Goals that are set by multi-stakeholder groups are more likely to encompass a sustainable performance focus. In the Alegent case, for example, involving representatives from the business, the community, and the natural environment in goal setting led to a comprehensive and integrated set of goals.

Work Is Performed by Multiple Stakeholder Teams and Can Be Virtual

A crucial difference between CCOs and SMOs is that in the latter, work often is done by groups. In CCOs, work is performed by individuals because much of the interdependency among them is managed by either the hierarchy or the technology. Where managerial oversight or the technology cannot handle the complexity of independent work, sometimes teams are formed, although the individuals on the team often have little discretion and narrow skill sets. The teams have little interaction with specialists from other functions, let alone external stakeholders.

HIOs have a more systemic view of work than do CCOs. In HIOs, cross-functional teams are common. They may have major customer interfaces, but they are rarely asked to juggle social and environmental concerns along with economic ones.

As the Alegent Health and Aisin cases suggest, we have passed the point in time when organizations can be considered freestanding. No single organization is completely in charge of its own destiny. An organization's performance and effectiveness must be seen in terms of the interactions and relationships among a range of stakeholders—often in tacit coordination (or opposition!).

The DA form of work suggests that instead of acting independently of each other, stakeholders should intentionally coordinate their behaviors to achieve all of their respective goals. In a DA, the large group is deliberately composed of multiple stakeholders. In the small breakout groups, there is a conscious effort to put representatives from different stakeholder groups into conversation and debate over a problem, opportunity, or action plan. Work, by definition, is done by multi-stakeholder groups. Using the DA as a metaphor, we are suggesting that SMOs make this a routine way of doing work.

Working in multi-stakeholder teams is a lot like working in a cross-functional team. Each member of the team brings a different perspective to the work and decision-making process. The members of the different groups in the Aisin case came not only from different companies but from different technological orientations. Early in a group's life cycle, this can be frustrating and slow as people listen to each other's views. But research and experience suggest that with patience and persistence, better decisions and higher performance result.

Decision making in a multi-stakeholder group is complex. Typically group members are not from the same organization and are seeking to optimize the performance of the organization in different ways. They may be much more interested in the welfare of the community or the health of the environment than in the organization's financial performance. As a result, a lot of effort needs to be invested in helping multi-stakeholder teams operate effectively and make good decisions.

The Alegent case provides a good example of how a multi-stakeholder decision-making process can result in sustainable effectiveness. Creating a DA around sustainability gave the organization an opportunity to bring carbon footprint issues together with concerns about community responsibility, health care access, and clinical quality. Alegent was able to quickly pull together interested parties. Internally, a blast email asking for volunteers to attend the DA received so many responses they had to institute a lottery. Their external invitations to participants were almost universally accepted, and the DA facility was pressed to its maximum capacity. Alegent generated a highly integrated strategy and operational plan in three days, and the plan's implementation began almost immediately.

Although the Alegent and Aisin work took place in face-to-face settings, the increasingly available capability to connect employees and others through technology means that organization work can and will increasingly be done by teams whose members are scattered. Using their own WebEx and Telepresence technology, Cisco's councils, boards, and work teams are good examples: they are collaborating and innovating in an increasingly virtual system of meetings that supports agility, a smaller carbon footprint, a better work-life balance, and lower costs.

Work Is Temporary and Iterative

To be agile, SMOs need temporary and iterative work systems. This is contrary to the work systems of CCOs and HIOs. When the focus of an organization is stability and economic performance, the logic of scale and leverage dominates. Product runs are scheduled to be as long as possible because experience curves suggest that the longer individuals, groups, and plants engage in the same task, the more efficient they become.

There is strong pressure on designers to keep product features the same over time. This avoids the need for new manufacturing practices, mitigates changeovers in manufacturing plants, and allows customer service processes to be designed for reproducibility. Change in any task is seen as a distraction, a waste, and a threat to the organization's financial performance. For any current product that is not designed and manufactured with sustainable effectiveness in mind, CCOs and HIOs continue to embrace economic outcomes at the expense of positive social and environmental results.

Because SMOs eschew the idea of a sustainable competitive advantage, they drive revenue as best they can under a particular strategic intent until change is necessary, but change is expected. Thus any work system is temporary; it will change when it is not contributing to the goals of economic performance, positive social outcomes, or ecological health. In the Aisin case, multistakeholder teams from Aisin, Toyota, and other firms formed around the work that needed to be done, and when they completed the work, the teams disbanded.

The movie industry—in Hollywood, Bollywood, and else-where—moves around the globe for location filming, hiring a variety of support work—catering, equipment, transportation, technical advice, or government assistance—on a project basis. When the movie or project is over, the resources are freed up to reconfigure. The work in an SMO is similar; issues are identified, the work is designed, the stakeholders are gathered, decisions are made, actions organized, and the resources are freed.

Because SMOs eschew the idea of a sustainable competitive advantage, they drive revenue as best they can under a particular strategic intent until change is necessary. . . . Thus any work system is temporary; it will change when it is not contributing to the goals of economic performance, positive social outcomes, or ecological health.

Some work, of course, cannot be temporary. Car manufactur-ers have to produce cars in large numbers to precise standards; drug companies must produce pills over a long period of time; and no one goes to the supermarket for a unique experience. There is nothing in the SMO style that negates doing routine work well, and SMOs can still innovate their work processes. The way cars are made today is not the way they will be made tomorrow. The best way to improve how they are made is to involve multiple stakehold-ers in the change process and then start the process over again.

Thus, in addition to being temporary, some SMO work is iterative. That is, productivity is achieved and sustainable effective-ness supported through small and frequent improvements in the product or service. This is one of the key features of innovation in the world of hardware, machines, automobiles, aircraft, and the cyberworld of software design. Innovation in these businesses is fostered by the creation of a prototype. Creating a working model or physical representation of an idea allows engineers to see things that cannot be seen when an idea is an equation or concept. This is no less true for strategies, solutions, or action plans. Creating an initial "product," such as a list of criteria or a proposal for action, makes abstract ideas concrete and allows them to quickly pass the "common sense" test of practicality.

In a DA, a small group creates products in the form of models, lists, or ideas that are presented to the large group, where they are tested and refined. They are then iterated and improved on in the next round of small-group discussions. But the process doesn't have to be structured as a DA; it can occur naturally, as it did in the Aisin case. The different teams had to combine their particular skills and experiences to generate a method for manufacturing P-valves. The sooner a proposed idea could be tested, the sooner they could find out if it worked. If it didn't work, new information was generated that guided the process to completion. Iterative work systems allow an organization to change and to design its work and products to support an integrated set of sustainable outcomes.

Work Is Supported by the Physical Space and Technology

One of the key features of work systems that support sustainable effectiveness is the creation of a space that complements the way the work is done. Much of the work in a DA happens in a physical setting constructed for that purpose. The Aisin war rooms were created in response to a crisis. In addition, the work was supported by appropriate applications of information technology.

Capital One's Future of Work project shows how technology and the physical setting of a DA can be extended into the workplace.[5] Like other financial service organizations, Capital One adopted the flexible, low-walled cubicle as an efficient way to maximize the use of expensive real estate and provide associates with a semi-private work space. With few exceptions, the concept has not worked well, leaving us with Dilbert-ian stories of emails being sent to the person in the next cubicle and other "humorous" results.

What got Capital One interested in changing its "cube farm" was the observation that 40 percent of the cubicles in a building were empty 60 percent of the time. Much of the work at Capital One, outside of the call center operations, involves visiting customers, collaborating with colleagues on future products or improvements to existing ones, working from home, or any number of activities that removed Capital One associates from their desks. The physical arrangements did not match the way people were working and did not take advantage of advancements in technology.

Beginning with the goals of using space more efficiently, increasing employee satisfaction and work-life balance, and increasing personal productivity, Capital One created a variety of different "neighborhoods" or "activity settings." Desk-sharing neighborhoods were created where anyone who is in an office can park their stuff and use available computers, phones, and supplies.

Vice presidents and executives work in what are known as the "executive digs." They have long workstations designed like a kitchen table that allow them to sit close to one another and have easy access to associates. "Director digs" are highly visible spaces in centrally located areas where managers and supervisors are given relatively permanent places. Other neighborhoods include "quiet zones" with comfortable furniture (phones and conversations are not allowed); "backyards" for informal gatherings; "lounges" to sit, converse, and have a cup of coffee; and "huddle rooms" for impromptu meetings. With the exception of the huddle rooms, there are no walls or partitions.

The Capital One design saves real estate costs, lowers its carbon footprint (because their people are traveling less), improves the quality of work life, and increases customer contact (maximum surface area), all of which result in higher sustainable effectiveness.

The groups whose offices were converted to neighborhoods were provided with technical support and training. Each person, for example, was given a laptop computer and mobile phone. The teams were trained in using different applications, such as email, instant messaging, video-conferencing, the company's intranet portals, and other multimedia software.

Notably, the teams went through a process in which "norms" of communication were established. For example, teams agreed on how quickly everyone is expected to respond to emails and voicemail messages, and on the appropriate use of instant messaging.

The Capital One design saves real estate costs, lowers its carbon footprint (because their people are traveling less), improves the quality of work life, and increases customer contact (maximum surface area), all of which result in higher sustainable effectiveness. Capital One has found that 87 percent of the people do not want to move back to the old way and satisfaction with the workplace has increased from 57 percent to 80 percent. Although there are still some bugs to be worked out—many people report that time is wasted looking for available space—there is strong agreement among the Capital One workforce that the new work arrangements fit the way they work. It also fits the way SMOs work.

Work Is Managed Strategically

The traditional functions of management, including planning, leading, organizing, and controlling, generally describe how managers add value and get work done through others.[6] Supervisors and managers in CCOs rely on stable business environments, static job descriptions, and a goal of profit maximization; they hold the decision-making power and control information concerning when and how work gets done. In addition, they are responsible for ensuring that workers have the training they need to perform their tasks, and they reward behavior in line with job descriptions and performance. HIOs accomplish the managerial tasks of planning, leading, organizing, and controlling by giving some power to employees, providing them with access to more information, supporting their developing knowledge and skills, and letting them influence operational decisions.

The Alegent and Aisin cases demonstrate a different way of accomplishing the traditional functions of management. In the Alegent case, the work people do changes a lot. A nurse may be delivering routine patient care one day and then working in a DA to design a sustainability strategy the next. In the Aisin case, the focus was always on a particular kind of work—figuring out how to get P-valves produced—but in both cases, it was the manager's job to plan, organize, lead, and control the work when the conditions were anything but stable, static, and simple.

When work is defined in terms of temporary and iterative activities, shared goals, and multi-stakeholder processes, the traditional functions of planning, leading, organizing, and controlling must be carried out in a strategic way. Managers must link the activities they sanction to the organization's strategic intent. It is a manager's job in an SMO to think about the most important areas for innovation and ensure that processes are in place to address them. They need to bring the right stakeholders together and design a sequence of small- and large-group discussions—to figure out the sequence of prototypes to develop—that will produce the right products, whether that's a strategy, a process, a decision, or an action plan.

Extending the metaphor of "work as DA" further, it doesn't matter if the work is in a formal DA. Work in an organization—whether it is routine patient care, installing a P-valve in a car, designing software, or running a printing press—can be thought of in terms of the characteristics of a DA. Management's job is to think about creating processes in which the right people are involved and the right sequence of tasks is carried out. As will be discussed more in Chapter Eleven, this often involves creating shared leadership and being a good follower.

Conclusion

Work systems are an important contributor to an organization's achieving agility and sustainable effectiveness. The work systems of SMOs need to shorten cycle times, improve decision-making quality, increase productivity, and increase commitment to courses of action. Multi-stakeholder and team-based work systems that consider the voice of the community, the natural environment, and the business in important decisions are the best way to create sustainably effective organizations.

Assessment Questions

1. What is management's attitude toward large-group interventions (LGIs) like the DA process?

   a. They believe any large group would be too chaotic to achieve anything; why air our dirty laundry in front of others?

b. There have been a few experiments, like "all hands" meetings, but it's still seen as an odd way to get things done.

c. It's a tool that has been adopted and is deployed when the need is there.

Here is what the answers imply:

a. Large-group interventions are a relatively new technique and a counterintuitive one, but organizations that dismiss them as "unworkable" are not paying attention to the progress that has been made in running these processes.

b. If LGIs have been tried but are not readily available as a tool then management needs to invest in building this capability.

c. Congratulations, you've got a powerful organizational device most competitors likely are missing.

2. Is designing work around activities not jobs possible in your organization?

a. To a large extent we already do so; it's about time we stop pretending we had jobs, since that concept has been largely obsolete here for years.

b. There are a few places were this could work, but not in most of the organization.

c. Well-defined jobs are so much a part of how we do things that suggesting an alternative isn't worth doing.

Here is what the answers imply:

a. People in fast-moving work environments may have adopted an activity-based structure while feeling they were doing something wrong in not keeping job descriptions up to date. Understanding that what you are doing is the right thing can be very liberating.

b. The best way to become comfortable with an activity-based approach is to try it, so adopt it where it is most likely to take hold.

c. A rigid adherence to a job-centric approach will act as a continual drag on the organization's success; it's like having hundreds of little anchors slowing down your ship at a time when you need speed and maneuverability.

PART THREE

The Way People Are Treated

| Managing Performance

We have studied, seen, designed, been subject to, and heard about a lot of performance management systems. Every large organization we have ever studied has had one. They have all been different in important ways: some used rating scales, others didn't, some forced the managers to assign a certain percentage of employees to a performance category (for example, exceeds expectations), others didn't, some were hard-wired to pay, rewards, and dismissal, others weren't. The one thing they all produced was a pretty high level of "user" dissatisfaction. We believe a degree of user dissatisfaction is inevitable because most performance management systems involve the appraisal of performance. It is difficult to do well and in certain cases must involve messages that some managers don't like to send and most people don't like to receive.

The "how to" of performance management has been the subject of innumerable books, articles, speeches, and research studies. The research evidence shows that appraisals are usually poorly done and, in most organizations, are dreaded both by the individuals doing them and the individuals being reviewed.[1] As a result, the failure rate is high, as is the resistance to doing them.

It is tempting to say, and some indeed have said, that the appraisal part of the performance review process wastes more time and causes more problems than it is worth. Done poorly, appraisals of performance cause alienation, disruption, dissatisfaction, misdirected behavior, poor superior-subordinate relationships, and, in some cases, poor peer relationships. In addition, they are often the subject of lawsuits charging organizations with doing inaccurate appraisals that have an adverse impact on older employees, minorities, and women. In short, they often become a time-consuming, destructive annual event that is dreaded by everyone. As a result it is reasonable to say that unless they are done well, they should not be done at all.

Indeed, an increasing number of books and articles go further and argue that there is no use even trying to do them right.[2] The appraisal piece of performance reviews simply cannot be done well. It is a nice thing to do, but impossible to do well.

The message of inevitable failure undoubtedly gives some comfort to those who have failed appraisal systems, but it doesn't seem to be leading to very many organizations not doing appraisals. Indeed, our data show that the recession has led to most companies putting more focus on doing appraisals. We think this is the right response and that it is particularly important for SMOs to do appraisals.

Not only should SMOs do performance appraisals, we think that it is more important that they do them—and do them well—than it is for CCOs and HIOs. We will explain why appraisals are so important in SMOs but first, there is one performance management system that we have been intrigued by for years because we believe it includes most of the "right" practices. Let's take a look at it.

Doing Performance Management Right

In the late 1990s, Siebel Systems was the leading provider of customer relationship management (CRM) software. Unlike other large enterprise resource system providers such as PeopleSoft and SAP that provided a broad array of information systems applications, Seibel focused on specialized customer relationship niches. At the time there was a concern among Seibel's top management that the way they managed workforce performance was no longer adequate. Despite considerable success, they thought Seibel needed a system that would enable the company to better execute its strategy across all its global locations. CEO Tom Siebel was afraid that the "strategy execution" gap—the difference between what people knew they should do and what they were actually doing—was too big.

Leveraging their industry-leading capabilities in CRM software, they developed an "employee relationship management" (ERM) system called "*my*Siebel." Deployed in December 2000, *my*Siebel provided planning and performance management, training, content management, workforce collaboration, and employee support. It streamlined many processes within the company, including performance evaluation, communication of objectives, and expense reporting. Siebel's executives credited the implementation of *my*Siebel with a substantial improvement in employee satisfaction and corporate performance. Here's how the process worked.

At the end of each quarter, the executive committee—the top fifteen senior managers—spent three days (Thursday, Friday, and Saturday) in a retreat analyzing the results of the prior quarter and establishing objectives for the upcoming months. Corporate quarterly objectives were discussed and agreed to during the meeting. Then, by the seventh calendar day of the month following the offsite, Tom Siebel's personal objectives and those of his direct reports were posted on the performance management module of *my*Siebel. By the fifteenth, these objectives had been translated into objectives for the functions and business units that reported to the VPs and posted on *my*Siebel. By the twenty-first of the month, every employee had posted and received feedback on their individual quarterly objectives. The objectives served as the key metrics that would be used to evaluate their performance over the next three months.

CEO Tom Siebel was afraid that the "strategy execution" gap—the difference between what people knew they should do and what they were actually doing—was too big.

Through *my*Siebel, all employees could view the objectives of any other employee, including those of Tom Siebel himself and other members of the executive committee. This allowed people to understand how others were allocating their time and attention.

Commensurate with Siebel's core values, customer satisfaction was a shared objective for everyone. There was also a clear understanding among all employees that if some activity was not on their list of objectives, they should not be doing it. Employees all the way up to the executives were encouraged to be clear about what they would NOT be doing.

The individual performance evaluation process ran parallel to an objective-setting process. Each manager was responsible for evaluating his or her direct subordinates by the fifteenth of the first month of each new quarter. The review and feedback had to be posted to the *my*Siebel performance management module. But unlike the posting of objectives, which were accessible to everyone inside the company, performance evaluations were visible only to the managers to whom the employee reported. Accordingly, only Tom Siebel, as CEO, could access everybody's performance evaluations.

Bonuses were tied to the achievement of quarterly objectives. For people involved in delivery projects, a large part of their objectives and compensation were tied to sales targets and customer satisfaction scores. For salespeople, part of the bonus was held back and paid out over the course of a year on the basis of quarterly customer satisfaction scores. The salesperson could lose some bonus if the implementation got poor scores. The bonuses could be as much as 40 percent of salary.

The company encouraged employee stock ownership. Employees owned 40 percent of the company (including the 15 percent that Tom Siebel owned). As part of its workforce improvement initiative, in a policy that was similar to General Electric's at this time, Siebel Systems had a policy of discharging the bottom 5 percent of employees every six months.

The process of performance management was part of and was supported by Seibel's information system architecture. The information system both pushed information to employees and allowed them to pull the information they needed. After logging on, each employee had their own "home page" that contained a different corporate announcement or story every day. This pushed current communications and corporate agenda items to the employee. It also contained an area that suggested training opportunities for work and career paths.

Each employee was expected to complete five web-based training modules per quarter. The system also allowed employees to pull corporate data and information; detailed information about corporate strategies, products, and customer information; performance data; and competitor and market information. It provided real-time access to any project in the company. The type of system Siebel developed in-house in 2000 is now available from several talent management vendors.

Need for Effective Performance Management

Before discussing in detail what it means to do performance management well, we are going to review why we believe it is so important to do it well in an SMO. The reasons for doing it well tell us more about SMOs and provide important guidance concerning what a performance management system should look like in an SMO.

- The absence of traditional job descriptions in SMOs means that one of the crutches organizations use to make up for the lack of an effective performance management system is gone. Individuals cannot look at a job description and use it as a guide to how they spend their time and what work they should do, nor can managers use it as a basis for directing what people do. An effective substitute is needed for the absence of job descriptions, and arguably the best one is a performance management system that effectively sets goals and appraises the performance of individuals against those goals.
- Budgets provide a crutch in organizations that do poor performance reviews. They provide some data and feedback to individuals about their performance and provide management with a tool they can use to evaluate and direct behavior. Because they are absent in SMOs, a good performance review process is needed that sets goals, encourages ongoing feedback to individuals from their manager(s) about how they are performing, and allows for informed judgments about the performance of key contributors.
- In SMOs, some or many of the management relationships may be virtual. Or, if they are not virtual, they are of such a nature that managers cannot see employees performing; they only see the results of their work and even that may be on a sporadic

basis. In addition, it may be hard for them to judge how well work is being done until there is an end product. This is particularly true when the major work in an organization is knowledge work and the individuals doing the work know more than their managers know about the technical elements of the work process. In this situation, managers need a substitute for direct observation of an employee's performance. The best substitute is goals and data about accomplishments that are gathered through a performance review process.

- As already suggested, as work becomes more complex and more discretionary in its content and performance, it is often difficult for managers to assess how well individuals are actually performing their jobs. The effectiveness of their performance only becomes obvious when they reach or fail to reach key completion goals. The implication of this for SMOs is that they need to have a performance review system that sets goals and holds individuals accountable for reaching them.

- How work is done is an important determinant of what kind of impact organizations have on both employees and customers. But it is difficult to measure in many sales, service, and knowledge work organizations. In traditional organizations, the frequent failure of their performance management systems is one of the many reasons why they often don't emphasize how work is done and typically do not reward individuals on the basis of it. In an SMO, this is unacceptable. Individuals need to be measured and rewarded on how they do their work as well as on what they accomplish. This is particularly true for managers. Negative behavior by them (such as being abusive) can have a very negative effect on their subordinates and on customers.

- Change and innovation are at the core of what makes for an effective SMO. They are achievable only if an organization provides the right resources to individuals and defines what types of change and innovation are needed. Part of the secret to making an organization good at innovation and change is the strategizing process that was discussed earlier, but it certainly is not the only key. An organization needs to be able to recognize innovation and reward it, and it needs to be able to provide individuals with a sense of direction, goals, and desired accomplishments when it comes to change. This requires a performance review process that can set change goals, support innovation, and reward change when it occurs.

- Effective talent management is a key element in SMOs. To have effective talent management, an organization needs to know the skills, competencies, learning capabilities, and performance of its workforce. Of course, it is desirable to have this in any organization, but it is particularly critical to the success of SMOs. Thus, it is especially important that SMOs have a performance management system that gathers valid data on the condition of its talent and that can influence the skills individuals develop.

- SMOs need individuals to perform in ways that lead their organization to be sustainably effective. This means considering the financial, social, and natural environment effects of their behavior. Often tough trade-offs and balanced decisions need to be made in order for an individual's performance to support his or her organization's strategy. An effective performance management system is the best way to accomplish this. In a CCO with only one bottom line, financial performance, having a performance management system balance decisions may not be critical, but it is for organizations that are committed to sustainable effectiveness.

Keys to Success

Given the importance of having an effective performance management system, SMOs must use a system that is different—and much more effective—than the flawed performance appraisal systems that are used in CCOs. They can't simply tell managers to do a better job of judging performance and provide a software program to make it less cumbersome and faster. They cannot tell managers to identify the worst 10 percent of their direct reports like GE did when Jack Welch was the CEO. They have to elevate the importance of performance management so that it is a key element of the organization's management strategy, and they have to design a system that is not just an appraisal tool—it must truly be a performance management system.

Only when performance management systems are well designed and well implemented can the kinds of accountability and performance direction that are critical to an SMO's success be realized. Given the number of pieces that have to be in the right place, and the difficulty of doing it in the kind of culture that exists in CCOs, it is hardly surprising that performance management systems usually fail in them. But, failure in CCOs does not mean that performance management systems can't operate effectively in SMOs.

Universal Performance Management Principles

There are eight number of principles concerning performance management effectiveness that CCOs, HIOs, and SMOs should follow. We are not saying that most or all organizations do follow them, we are saying that they should! We will review them first and then turn to six principles that are not a good fit for all organizations but are key to the effectiveness of performance management systems in SMOs.

Universal Performance Management Principle 1: Start at the Top

The starting point for an effective performance management process should be the business strategy of the organization. As is the case in Siebel, it should guide a goal-setting process that leads to individuals, teams, and business units having transparent goals and objectives that are directly tied to the strategy of the business. For this process to be effective, the goal setting has to begin at the top of the organization and cascade down. As a part of the process, there should be agreement on what will be accomplished, how it will be accomplished, and which measurement processes will be used to assess whether the goals were accomplished and whether they were accomplished in the correct manner.

In SMOs, the performance management system must start with, be led by, and be committed to by senior management and the board. As we pointed out in our discussion of governance, the board needs to appraise itself, its members, and the CEO. The CEO needs to appraise his or her direct reports, and the appraisal process has to cascade down the organization so that every level experiences it.

It is not an overstatement to say that if the senior management of an organization is not fully committed to the performance management process, it is simply better not to have a performance management system. Committed in this case means not just giving lip service to having an effective process but being part of the performance management system themselves and being a role model to the individuals who report to them. All too often in CCOs, support for the appraisal program consists of "the top telling the middle to do it to the bottom."

It is not an overstatement to say that if the senior management of an organization is not fully committed to the performance management process, it is simply better not to have a performance management system.

Universal Performance Management Principle 2: HR Should Support, Not Own, the System

In all too many organizations, the human resource department is the owner of, and the implementer of, the performance management system. For a number of reasons, this is the wrong way to position and manage the system. There is nothing wrong with the HR function handling the logistics, but it should not be their system. They should not be the ones who act as the conscience of the organization and the piece of the organization that drives and sells it.

Our research shows that the success of the performance management system is closely tied to the degree to which it is seen to be a senior management program.[3] Having strong HR department leadership is not a predictor of the success of the performance review system—having strong senior management leadership is!

Universal Performance Management Principle 3: Set Measurable Goals

The appraisal system needs to be based on measurable goals.[4] All too often appraisals are based on personality traits (for example, reliable, trustworthy), on vague and unmeasurable goals, and on a host of poorly defined attributes and outcomes. Measurable goals need to be set and individuals assessed against them. This applies to the skills and competencies individuals are expected to possess or need to develop as well as to their performance deliverables—the how and the outcomes of it.

A word of caution is in order here about the mistakes that organizations often make when using goal-driven performance management systems. The effectiveness of goals as motivators is very much influenced by their difficulty, particularly how difficult they are seen to be by the individual who has the goal.[5] Easy-to-achieve goals are poor motivators because there is a tendency for individuals to work at a level that will lead them to reach the goal, not at their maximum performance level. Overly difficult goals, or as they are sometimes called, "stretch goals," are dysfunctional.

When individuals feel that they cannot reach a very difficult goal, there are essentially two things they can do. They can simply give up and decide it is not worth trying because the goal and reward that is attached to it are not reachable. The second is to try to figure out how to "beat the system" in order to reach the goal.

Individuals are particularly likely to try to beat the system when there are large financial rewards attached to achieving goals that look virtually impossible to achieve. Time after time in fraud cases (such as Enron) in which managers have broken the rules and done things the wrong way, it is because a large reward was offered. But it wasn't just offered, it was offered for reaching a goal that was essentially unreachable without individuals cheating or ignoring the environmental and social impacts of their actions.

Some of the biggest financial scandals of the past decade had their root in excessive incentives being offered for behavior that could only be achieved by highly risky or unethical means. Faced with this situation, many individuals decided to "game" the system and create ways around the risk management systems of banks, brokerage firms, and other financial institutions. Safety short-cuts, such as those that led to the BP Gulf of Mexico oil disaster, also are often the results of "stretch goals."

A less serious mistake, but one that also has a negative impact on motivation, is to tell employees in great detail how they are to achieve their goals. This approach makes a lot of sense in a CCO, but it does not fit an SMO. It doesn't fit with the kind of work systems discussed in Chapter Seven. It also tends to be a significant reducer of motivation for individuals who see themselves as intelligent, knowledgeable, and capable of problem solving and using their expertise to figure out how to get things done. The reason for this is clear: when there is no discretion in how they perform a job, they do not feel responsible for successful performance!

We are not arguing that individuals should be given free rein as to how they get things done. We are arguing strongly against carefully prescribed methods that take the problem-solving autonomy and creativity out of the work individuals do and ruin the sense of achievement that they feel when they reach a goal.

Universal Performance Management Principle 4: Rate Outcomes, Rate Performance, but Don't Rank People

An effective assessment of how and how well goals are accomplished should be relatively easy if good goals exist and good agreement exists on how goal accomplishment will be measured. CCOs, in keeping with their stability-oriented, bureaucratic structures and micromanagement practices, tend to use evaluation systems with performance metrics that go way beyond the precision that is necessary and possible. For example, some organizations (such as Exxon-Mobil) rank-order hundreds, or in some cases thousands, of people from first to last; they number them from one to whatever the total number of individuals is in the part of the organization where performance is being appraised. This effort is like trying to measure the length of an object to the closest thousandth of an inch using an ordinary straight ruler; the information needed to compare people so precisely just isn't available and cannot be developed.

Not only does ranking create bad data, it sends a negative (although sometimes accurate) message about how much an organization values its talent. Instead of showing a concern for individuals and fairness in assessing them, it sends the message that the organization values structure and rules. This is clearly unacceptable in SMOs because they are committed to fair treatment.

Another seriously flawed rating practice is forced distributions.[6] Some organizations (for example, GE, EDS, and Accenture) require their managers to identify a certain percentage of employees who are failing, often 5 to 10 percent, and a certain percentage who are doing particularly well, often 15 to 20 percent. The forced-distribution approach ignores the reality that some work areas have no poor performers and others have no good performers. It causes managers to disown the appraisal event and say essentially, "I was just following the rules" when they talk to a "poorly" performing employee.

Instead of employees asking how they can improve organizational performance, the method fosters internal competition and survival of the luckiest or most political. It also can lead to the departure of valuable human capital that does not want to live in a competitive environment or that is evaluated as performing poorly simply because it is part of a group of high-performing individuals, and as a result, gets a low rating. In a *Wall Street Journal* interview, Steve Bennett (who left GE to become CEO of Intuit) provides the best summary evaluation of the GE forced-ranking system: "I think that's really dumb. I would never do forced rankings."[7]

Given the problems, why do companies use the forced-distribution approach? The answer is simple but not particularly flattering to its users. It represents an easy way to solve a classic problem: rating inflation. Just as some university professors tend to give high grades to everyone, some managers find it easier to be generous with high ratings, and, as a result, many organizations suffer from top-heavy performance appraisal scores.

Instead of dealing with the problem as a failure of leadership judgment, some companies adopt a dysfunctional bureaucratic solution, mandating a result they think is "good." In other words they try to solve a problem that is caused by the control management approach with another command and control action. Because it is a leadership problem, the best solution rests in creating effective leadership, not in ordering a predetermined result.

Forced distributions speak loudly to people; they tell them they are not trusted to make good judgments about the individuals who work for them. Instead of allowing them to exercise their judgment, they are told what form their judgment should take. It ignores leadership behavior as a way to influence the behavior of others and relies strictly on a traditional management approach—giving an order. It is a leadership failure that is being "corrected" by a managerial edict or order. GE did it for years under Jack Welch, and he continues to recommend it as a good practice. However, GE has moved away from it for innumerable reasons including resistance on the part of managers and the competitive environment that it creates within the organization.

One final note on forced distributions: they tend to be particularly dysfunctional when there are automatic reward system consequences attached to individuals falling in different areas of the distribution. Particularly dysfunctional are programs that state that the bottom 10 percent or so of the distribution will be fired each year.

Numerous studies that we have done show that forced firing produces a great deal of "gaming" behavior on the part of the individuals making the ratings.[8] They do everything they can to be sure that they are not faced with having to fire individuals who simply should not be fired. For example, they sometimes transfer them to protect them and, even more dysfunctional, they hire individuals who they think will be poor performers so they will have them available to fire when it comes time for forced distributions appraisals to be made.

As was mentioned earlier, another unacceptable approach to measuring performance is rating individuals on poorly defined general traits or personality dimensions such as reliability, communication skills, customer focus, and leadership. These traits are difficult to judge and almost always lead to communication breakdowns and misunderstandings between appraisers and the individuals being appraised. They also fail to provide the type of assessment required for the organization to have valid metrics concerning the condition of its talent and its performance.

Organizations need to adopt a balanced scorecard of behavior- and outcome-based measures that quantify, or at least clearly identify, what performance and behavior are being judged. For example, rather than assessing the general dimension of reliability, the appraisal should focus on whether critical work was completed on time and whether preset goals were met.

Universal Performance Management Principle 5: Appraise the Appraisers

Given the importance of performance appraisals, appraising how well managers do appraisals is a logical and important part of the entire appraisal process. A good manager simply needs to do good appraisals. Goals need to be set, progress checked, feedback given, the right competencies developed, and, of course, performance assessed correctly and rewards distributed accordingly. To motivate managers to do these activities well, it is important that they be appraised and rewarded on how well they do them. Failure to appraise and reward managers for the appraisals they do speaks volumes about the low priority given to these activities.

Managers need to be held accountable for the ratings they produce. It has to be clear to them that ratings must be justified by operating results that are correspondingly high. It often helps to set up cross-organizational meetings in which managers have to justify their ratings to their peers and top executives. Capital One and Intel call these "cross-calibration" meetings. Both companies have used them effectively to control rating inflation and to develop consistency in how managers use their rating scales.

Universal Performance Management Principle 6: Train Managers and Employees to Do Performance Management

It is critical that organizations train everyone on how their performance management system works. It is surprising how many organizations do not do this, given the importance of the system and the fact that it is a relatively complex process that involves behaviors (goal setting and feedback) that many people are not skilled at. The training that is needed is not just a matter of explaining how the system works and what its purpose is.

All too often, organizations fail to provide any training to the managers who are expected to execute a performance management system.

Individuals need to develop the interpersonal and feedback skills to lead effective review sessions. All too often, organizations fail to provide any training to the managers who are expected to execute a performance management system. This is true despite the fact that one of the hardest things for many individuals to do is to give negative feedback to others and to handle difficult interpersonal interactions in a constructive way.

While we are on the topic of training, it is important to point out that training is not needed just for the individuals who are appraising someone else. It is also needed for the individuals being appraised as well. Getting feedback about performance and being part of the performance management system is not a comfortable situation for most people and not something that they have the skills to handle well. Thus the most effective performance management training systems train both the appraiser and the appraisee. A good way to do this is to have them role play a feedback situation before they go "live" with the actual appraisal of the individual. This is clearly an area in which individual coaching can help and is often needed.

Universal Performance Management Principle 7: Link Rewards to Performance and Discuss Development Separately

An important feature of a performance management system is the degree to which it affects the reward system; in other words, the degree to which it leads to pay increases, bonuses, stock options, and promotions. Over the years, there have been articles and books which have claimed that performance review processes should separate the review of performance from discussions about salary increases and promotions.[9] This may indeed make some of the discussions easier, but it is not the way to make money and other tangible rewards effective motivators.

Given the potential importance of goals and money as motivators, it is definitely not appropriate to have a review process that separates the discussion of performance from the discussion of financial rewards. They need to be discussed together and tied together so that individuals see a clear connection between how well they perform and how well they are rewarded. Yes, it's true that some individuals work simply for the feeling of accomplishment of a goal and, of course, to further the purpose of the organization. But for others, the relationship between pay and performance is critical to their motivation. The research on this clearly shows that pay is a strong motivator when there is a direct and immediate tie between performance and significant pay changes.

What should be separated from the discussion of financial rewards is the development needs of individuals. Research shows that discussing training and development at the same time as performance and rewards doesn't work. The discussion of performance and rewards dominates the meeting and prevents a meaningful discussion of development activities. Development activities need to be paired with a forward-looking goal-setting discussion, not with a backward look at past performance. The key here is combining two forward-looking events, future performance objectives and what it takes to reach those objectives, rather than matching a retrospective event with a forward-looking event.

Universal Performance Management Principle 8: Use 360-Degree Appraisals but Not for Rewards

Using 360-degree reviews has become increasingly popular over the past decade. In many respects they make sense because peers, subordinates, and customers often see elements of someone's behavior that cannot be seen by their boss. The problem with 360-degree reviews is that raters, particularly peers, may not give valid data about how someone is performing. If the raters know that the data will be used to determine pay increases, promotions, or educational opportunities, it can be very difficult for them to make an "objective assessment" of somebody's performance. They are in essence being asked to rate their competitor knowing that if they score somebody highly they may very well lose part of their bonus or a promotion.

What is the right answer? We believe it is to use peer and subordinate ratings primarily for developmental purposes. The results should go directly and only to the individuals being appraised so that they can use them for their own development. If an organization is determined to use peer and subordinate ratings for reward system purposes, there are some things they can do to limit the problems this creates. For example, Goldman Sachs for a long time has done a careful analysis of its peer ratings to see if it can detect a self-interest bias in the ratings and has actually corrected its ratings for these biases. This is a possible alternative, but we still come down on the side of 360-degree reviews being done primarily for developmental purposes and being fed back only to the individual who is being rated.

One possible alternative is to have an initial rating with results going only to the individuals being evaluated. This gives them a chance to improve their behavior before future ratings are used to make decisions about raises, promotions, and so on. This still leaves in place the bias factor once the results are used for reward decisions, but it at least eliminates the problem of individuals feeling they were blindsided by the ratings coming from their peers and subordinates. They get an early warning as to what they are going to be like and a chance to correct their behavior.

SMO Performance Management Principles

SMOs require performance management systems that fit their structures, work designs, and objectives. They need to follow the eight universal principles, but following them is not enough. There are six more principles they need to follow in order to have an effective system that avoids the well-deserved criticisms that are heaped upon most performance management systems. These principles when combined with the universal ones will produce a performance management system that supports sustainable effectiveness. It will do this by directing and motivating change, innovation, and sustainable effectiveness.

SMO Performance Management Principle 1: Establish a Balanced Scorecard

The goals that are set in an SMO should include social and environmental goals. Measures of goal accomplishment need to be specific to a person's work area, and they should always cover more than just financial performance and productivity. Unlike the goals in CCOs they should include diversity, social impact, environmental impact, and employee impact goals.

SMO Performance Management Principle 2: Set Talent Development Objectives

The performance management process should not just establish what performance goals are to be accomplished, it also should deal with the skills and competencies individuals and teams need to accomplish them. It should assess their development needs, plan for development, and support their acquiring the skills they need to accomplish their goals.

Individuals should be assessed on their skills and competencies. This is critical because they determine what an individual's value is in the market and therefore what their compensation level should be. It is also a critical input to the organization's strategic planning around the competencies and capabilities that it has and can develop.

Development activities that are not related to enabling current goal accomplishment may be part of the performance management process but, as will be discussed in the next chapter, because of the employment relationship that exists in SMOs they should not be the main focus. The number one objective should be to see that individuals have the skills they need to accomplish their immediate performance goals.

SMO Performance Management Principle 3: Don't Assume an Annual Appraisal Is Often Enough

There is no right frequency with which the performance management process should take place in all organizations. Historically, in most organizations, performance appraisals have been done on an annual basis. For some organizations, that probably is a reasonable frequency, but for most SMOs, it is likely to be too infrequent.

Given the speed with which the world is changing and the needs that organizations have to update their strategic intent, it is likely that SMO organizations need to go through new goal-setting and performance review processes on a semiannual or, like Siebel, on a quarterly basis. Those organizations that engage in a quarterly review may not do a full review every quarter, but at the very least need to update their goals, get a reading on how performance is proceeding against those goals, and make the necessary adjustments and changes.

Organizations that are focused on projects or assignments, as many professional services firms are, should do a brief review at the end of each assignment. If the performance review process is not done frequently enough, it runs the risk of ending up the way job descriptions usually end up, woefully out of date and not particularly useful. SMOs rely on goals to guide and motivate behavior; they cannot afford to have out-of-date performance reviews.

SMO Performance Management Principle 4:
Use Web-Enabled Technology

All too often in organizations the performance management process is paper intensive and slow. This not only doesn't need to be true in any organization, it should never be true in an SMO. The performance management process in SMOs should be web-enabled, just as at Siebel.

The best talent management systems have powerful and easy-to-use performance management modules. These systems take the administrative burden of performance management off of HR and make it easier for managers by putting information and advice at their fingertips. These systems also make it easy for employees and managers to capture information relevant to performance over the course of the year.

Finally, as was true in Siebel, both transparency and cascading goals are enabled by these systems. Just as you would never ask an accountant to add up accounts by hand, an organization should not neglect implementing performance management technology. Many of the key features SMOs must have in their performance management systems (speed, frequency, cascading goals, transparency) are enabled by web-based technology.

SMO Performance Management Principle 5:
Appraise Team Performance

In CCOs, a strong emphasis is always placed on assessing the performance of individuals, as it should be. Their work needs to be well defined, and they need to be held accountable for what they do. The implications of this for the appraisal process are clear. It needs to assess their individual performance on what usually are relatively simple and straightforward tasks.

The situation is much less clear in HIOs. They are often populated with self-managing teams and groups that have temporary project and problem-solving activities. In these cases, a strong argument can be made for appraising and in fact rewarding groups and teams.

In some cases, the work in SMOs is so complex and interdependent that holding teams at least partially accountable for performance is a key to success. In these situations, there needs to be a process in place that appraises the group. This may be combined with an individual appraisal process that is run by the team leader, or the appraisal process may simply make a judgment about how well the team as a whole has performed.

In many cases, if the team is highly motivated and committed to performing well, it will naturally give feedback to its members and deal with them outside of the formal reward system and feedback programs of the organization. In essence, as we will discuss in Chapter Eleven, what is happening here is that some of the shared leadership that is present in SMOs comes to the forefront. This kind of intra-team feedback points out to individual members of work teams and groups what they need to do to contribute to the success of the group and assesses how they have performed in the past. In many respects, it is an effective substitute for the hierarchy that exists in CCOs, and it contributes to effective team performance. When teams are assessed, it may well make sense—as will be discussed in the next chapter—to reward teams as a whole, or even for that matter, to reward divisions and the organization as whole on the basis of their sustainable effectiveness.

SMO Performance Management Principle 6: Have Review Discussions Online

The traditional approach to appraisals calls for face-to-face discussions between the appraiser and the appraisee. This is true in CCOs and especially true in HIOs. There are a number of reasons why it is said to be important to have a face-to-face discussion, including the perception that it is likely to lead to better feedback and more meaningful discussions about how performance can improve. That said, there are a number of problems with face-to-face discussions.

There is research which shows that individuals are very anxious before and during performance reviews.[10] They often don't hear quite a bit of what is said to them during appraisals. Either their minds shut down or they are still thinking about something that was said at the beginning of the discussion that they are trying to evaluate and decide how to react to. In short, face-to-face meetings rarely produce good communication between the manager and the individual being appraised.

One way to improve face-to-face appraisals is to give individuals a look at the paper version of the appraisal and then have the discussion. This allows them to get over the shock that occurs when they first see the appraisal and for them to decide what questions and issues they want to raise. It also allows them to correct any factual mistakes in the appraisal. It is not uncommon when goals are set and when goal performance is being measured for bad data to creep in and for an individual to correctly point out there has been a mistake. Obviously it leads to a better discussion if these data validity and credibility issues can be resolved before a face-to-face discussion.

There is research which shows that individuals are very anxious before and during performance reviews. They often don't hear quite a bit of what is said to them during appraisals.

Organizations should also ask the people who are being appraised to provide appraisal data at the end of the performance appraisal period. They should be able to present their version of how well they have performed their work assignments against their preset goals. Our research supports the value of giving people this opportunity before their appraiser reaches a final performance judgment.[11] It leads to more accurate appraisals and to individuals believing they have been fairly appraised.

Let's move to another level. Does there really need to be a face-to-face discussion at all? In today's world, where we interact so comfortably and frequently on the Internet (at least some of us do), it seems quite reasonable and in fact potentially more functional to have performance appraisals done online. It gives individuals a chance to think a bit before they make their responses and provides for an opportunity to check appraisals for accuracy and meaningfulness.

Giving people a choice with respect to how a performance review meeting takes place is one more way to meaningfully individualize the way people are treated in an SMO. In SMOs, it may even be best to have all appraisals done on a virtual basis. It fits well with the type of work that is usually done in SMOs and with the idea of people being more self-managing and interacting virtually on a regular basis. It also creates the opportunity to do group appraisals of individuals. With multiple reporting relationships, it can be difficult to schedule face-to-face discussions with all the individuals who need to be involved in appraising an individual or for that matter a team. When travel is necessary in order to hold face-to-face appraisal meetings, online meetings not only save travel costs, they have an environmental benefit.

Conclusion

Perhaps the best way to summarize and conclude our discussion of performance management is to say that those who argue for abandoning it may well be right when it comes to CCOs. We don't think they are, but we are willing to admit it often is difficult to do appraisals in them and doing them is of limited value. In the case of HIOs, and certainly in the case of SMOs, the right answer definitely is not to abandon performance management systems. They are simply too important. It is necessary, however, to reinvent them—both from a purpose point of view and from a process point of view—if they are to be used by SMOs. The way performance reviews have been done in most organizations simply cannot produce the results that are needed in an SMO. As we stressed earlier, having effective performance reviews is critical to the effectiveness of an SMO. It is time to rethink the technology of performance reviews as well as to improve them in terms of their accuracy, validity, and centrality.

Assessment Questions

1. Looking back over the six SMO Performance Management Principles, how many would you say your organization currently meets?

    a. 1–2

    b. 3–4

    c. 5–6

Here is what the answers imply:

a. 1–2 is not unusual, but it means the performance management system is likely doing more harm than good, particularly if you do not meet all or most of the Universal Principles.

b. 3–4 is a good score, but pick the next principles you can put in place to improve the system and be sure you have the Universal Principles in place.

c. 5–6 indicates an excellent system.

2. What does the top management team see as the purpose of performance management?

a. A means for deciding on merit increments and bonuses; other outcomes are secondary.

b. A core HR process for talent management with important talent development, reward, and work planning outcomes.

c. A business process for managing sustainably effective performance.

Here is what the answers imply:

a. Many performance management processes are run as if this is the intent. If it is, then it may not be worth the effort it takes to do it.

b. There is value in a well-run performance management process, but SMOs need more.

c. It's a wonder that the title "performance management" has not been a clue that the purpose of the process is to manage performance. Organizations that see this as a business tool rather than an HR tool can use it to strategically guide sustainable effectiveness.

| Reward Systems

Manchester United is one of the most successful sports teams in the world, with fans from Manchester to Malaysia to Madagascar. Manchester United doesn't provide annual merit increments, doesn't pay people doing the same job (for example, goal tender) even remotely the same, and ignores hierarchy by paying the boss (the coach) less than many players. To what extent should an organization model its reward system on the basis of how Manchester United rewards its players?

A soccer (football) team is a very different kettle of fish than a complex global corporation, but the Manchester United approach to rewards shows that organizations can break away from the entrenched traditions of pay that exist in most organizations and be successful. So what about SMOs? We believe that like Manchester United they require reward systems different from what either CCOs or HIOs have because they are structured differently and have different employment relationships.

A major reward system design challenge exists because of the employment relationship that SMOs operate with. They need to create a reward system that motivates and attracts individuals even though, as we discuss in the next chapter, they do not have a secure long-term employment relationship. SMOs need individuals to commit to their long-term success while not promising them that they can spend their careers working for them.

The situation with respect to rewards is further complicated by the diverse workforce that SMOs employ. It is clear that individuals in different stages of their careers value different kinds of rewards, people in different countries view rewards quite differently, and different types of work designs require different approaches to rewards.[1] One of the traditional design principles of reward systems is to treat people the same, yet this desire for similar treatment is incompatible with the diversity that today's organizations face and must deal with. In SMOs, the absence of traditional job descriptions, more flexible work assignments, and rapid organization change create additional challenges and opportunities that their reward systems must take into account.

Can the challenges that are present in SMOs be handled effectively? We believe the answer is yes, but not without throwing out many traditional reward principles and practices. Like Manchester United they must pay much more attention to the individual value a player contributes and count on employees' enthusiasm for the purpose of the work they do and the rewards they can earn to drive excellent performance. We will review twelve principles that when followed will lead to effective reward systems for SMOs. But before going into detail about the type of reward system practices that fit SMO organizations, we need to consider the basic principles of individual motivation and satisfaction that must guide the design of reward systems for SMOs.

How Rewards Affect Behavior

In discussing motivation it is important to distinguish among three kinds of rewards. The first type of rewards are tangible extrinsic rewards that have significant economic value. They include money in its many forms: bonuses, merit increases, stock options, promotions, fringe benefits, perquisites, and so on; they are the major focus of this chapter.

The second kind of rewards involve recognition and personal relationships. They may take a tangible form such as plaques, titles, or formal recognition ceremonies. Recognition may also be informal, for example, praise from a boss, customer, or team member. Often just a thank-you for a job well done when it comes from someone who is respected is an important reward.

Patty McCord, the head of HR for Netflix, whom we will get to know better in the next chapter, says there is something special about going to the local farmer's market in a Netflix t-shirt and being mobbed by enthusiastic customers—now that is meaningful recognition! You can imagine, too, the reaction someone from Médecins Sans Frontières (Doctors Without Borders) gets when someone asks, "Where do you work?" Recognition can be a powerful source of reward that identity- and mission-driven SMOs are well positioned to tap into.

The third type of reward is intrinsic. They are the rewards that individuals experience when they or their team accomplish something significant, something that they wanted to accomplish, something that they value. It can be successfully completing a project, closing a sale, learning a skill, or a plethora of other types of positive experiences. Intrinsic rewards cannot be given by others; they are self-generated, which is why they are called intrinsic. Because intrinsic rewards are internally given, organizations cannot directly influence their reception and tie their reception to the kind of performance the organization needs. But what organizations can do is create situations in which individuals will experience them when they perform well.

The literature on rewards is dominated by articles and books that assert a certain type of reward is what really matters to employees.[2] Indeed, there seems to be a whole book publishing sweet spot having to do with saying one kind of reward is more important than all others. One says it is money, another says it is interesting work, another says it is contributing to an important mission, and so on. The reality is they are all right and they are all wrong. The research evidence shows that there are large individual differences in how much individuals value different rewards.[3] For some people it is making a contribution to a mission that is of utmost importance, for others it is money, for others it is job security, and for others it is recognition.

Once we recognize that there are major differences in what people value, it is natural to ask what the characteristics are of individuals who value one type of reward more than another. There is no shortage of books and articles that try to answer this question. There are studies that show when it comes to reward importance there are regional and geographic differences, gender differences, and education-level differences. Recently, a great amount of attention has focused on generational differences, among gen-x, gen-y, millennials, the five generations that are in the workplace today, and so on.[4]

Current events can affect what is important to members of the workforce. For example, surveys of the U.S. workforce a year before the 2008 recession found that job security was not rated as very important. Surveys during the recession showed it rated as much more important.

The key issue is not what is most or least important to different groups but how SMOs should manage rewards given the differences and changes in importance that exist. One choice is to feature one type of reward and to recruit a workforce for which it is very important. Another is to focus on and to design policies and practices that assume all three types of rewards are important to most of the workforce.

Our view is that most SMOs should take the latter approach for two reasons. The first is that it is very difficult to create and maintain a workforce that is homogenous, and doing this has a number of downsides. Perhaps the most important downside is creating a workforce that doesn't bring different viewpoints to bear on business and social issues. The second is that rewards have a cumulative effect; even if an individual values one type of reward more than another, as long as they both are valued, combining them will have a bigger impact than using just the most important one.

Rewards and Performance Motivation

What determines employee motivation is relatively straightforward, but that doesn't mean it is easy to manage. Employees are motivated to perform well when they anticipate receiving rewards that they value as a result of their performance. There are two keys here: rewards that are valued and rewards that are tied to performance.[5] What doesn't drive motivation is job satisfaction—it determines turnover. A happy workforce is not necessarily a productive one, but it is likely to "stick around."

While much has been written about how a carrot-and-stick approach to motivation can actually demotivate employees, the research evidence shows that rewards based on performance do motivate people to excel. What's important to understand is that the nature of the reward is critical—as is the way in which the reward is related to performance.

Offer the wrong carrot, and employees will feel insulted, misunderstood, or just apathetic. Motivation requires offering to individuals rewards they value and that are clearly tied to their performance.

While much has been written about how a carrot-and-stick approach to motivation can actually demotivate employees, the research evidence shows that rewards based on performance do motivate people to excel.

SMOs need to do everything they can to make sure that the receipt of both the internal and external rewards that are valued by their employees are directly related to how well they and their organization perform. This, of course, is where the performance management system comes into play. As was stressed in the previous chapter, it needs to be designed so that individuals can be rewarded according to their performance.

Clear measurable performance goals need to be established.[6] Establishing them has a positive effect on both intrinsic motivation (people reward themselves when they accomplish goals) and extrinsic motivation when rewards are tied to goal accomplishment. Also critical are the design of work and the identity and purpose of the organization, since they too can be important in determining whether individuals receive intrinsic rewards as a result of performing well.[7]

Diversity makes it difficult to create reward systems that motivate everyone but not impossible. A diverse workforce requires offering a variety of rewards and delivering rewards that are based on what individuals value. Tying rewards to performance can also be complicated because in the kind of knowledge work done in SMOs performance can be difficult to measure, hence the need for an effective performance management system.

Attraction, Retention, and Satisfaction

It is well known and obvious that individuals are attracted to organizations that offer rewards they value.[8] All organizations have a brand as an employer. Some are very well developed and sharply tuned to attract the kind of individuals that fit the organization; other organizations do not have a recognized brand. At one extreme are the Apples, Googles, and Microsofts of the world; at the other extreme are local organizations that have little, if any, visibility.

The key for any organization is presenting an employer brand that it can deliver on and that will attract and retain the right type of employees. In the case of SMOs, the right type of employees are individuals with skill sets that fit the type of work they do and who have values and desires that are aligned to sustainable effectiveness so that they will be motivated to perform at a high level.

What retains employees follows directly from what attracts them. Attraction is based on the expectation of receiving valued rewards; retention is based on actually receiving them and expecting that they will continue to be received. Basically, rewards drive job satisfaction, and high levels of job satisfaction cause employees to maintain employment with an organization. If organizations do not provide valued rewards, job dissatisfaction and turnover are inevitable, as is low performance motivation. Turnover occurs because people don't receive rewards they value, and low motivation occurs because the rewards that they value are not tied to their performance. From an SMO point of view, the best of all worlds is a situation in which the company offers rewards to individuals that attract, retain, and motivate them for as long as they are "needed."

Designing a Reward System

Given that business strategies differ, there is no right reward system for all SMOs, but there are some general design principles that are always right. We will focus on twelve principles that are the key to how SMOs should design their reward systems. We will begin by considering five "Universal Reward Principles" that are important guides to how all organizations should manage rewards and as a result should be followed by SMOs. Then we will consider seven principles that should be particularly important in guiding how SMOs design their reward systems even though they may not be principles that should guide CCOs and HIOs.

Taken together these twelve principles provide a comprehensive basis for the design of an SMO reward system.

Universal Reward Principle 1: Create Rewarding Work Assignments

The nature of the work that individuals do has a major impact on intrinsic motivation. When individuals use skills they value, feel responsible for producing a whole or meaningful part of a product or service, and receive performance feedback, their work is motivating because they reward themselves for their good performance.[9]

Often the results of someone's performance are obvious (the Manchester United striker can see whether or not he scores a goal), but in some cases workers can see the results of their behavior only if the measurement processes of the organization provide relevant feedback. This is one of many reasons why performance reviews are so important and why it is important for individuals to be in contact with the external world. One advantage of external contact is that it helps ensure that individuals will receive feedback concerning how well they are performing.

Having work that is motivating and satisfying is perhaps the major feature of an HIO. The beginning of the high involvement management approach can be traced back to experiments in manufacturing plants that created motivating work. To improve the work in their plants, Volvo began using "self managing" teams in the 1960s. In the United States, General Foods, Procter & Gamble, TRW, and a number of other companies created high involvement "green field" (new) plants that were structured around self-managing teams. The teams produced complete products and as a result got feedback, a sense of doing a whole piece of work and using their skills.

The enrichment of individual jobs is a second approach to creating motivating work that is core to high involvement management.[10] Instead of focusing on teams it focuses on creating meaningful work assignments for individuals that lead to their producing whole products or offering complete services to customers so that they get feedback and customer contact.

The major stimulus for the development of both the job-enrichment approach and the self-managing teams approach was the negative impact of command and control management. The jobs it creates are simple, repetitive, and boring. Because of their failure to generate meaningful intrinsic rewards, they lead to high turnover and absenteeism, poor-quality products and services, and low productivity. Who can feel a sense of accomplishment and competence as a result of doing the same simple task every thirty seconds? It was clear in the 1950s that an alternative approach to work design was needed. Many organizations have recognized the need to design motivating work, and more and more have created jobs that are more rewarding than repetitive assembly-line-type work.

Teams and enriched work should be an important part of the SMOs. They are needed to attract, motivate, and retain a talented workforce. In this respect, HIOs and SMOs are similar; both need to provide rewarding work experiences. Where they differ is in the permanency of the work assignments. In HIOs they tend to take the form of "permanent" job assignments. As we pointed out in Chapter Seven, in SMOs, they are more likely to be the result of a changing combination of task assignments—some done by teams, others by individuals—that have clear deliverables and require individuals to use their valued skills and abilities.

Universal Reward Principle 2: Forget Merit Increases, Give Bonuses

Most CCOs use merit salary increases as a vehicle for rewarding performance and motivating individuals. This approach to rewarding performance does not work well in today's world, and there are many reasons to believe it is even less likely to work well in the future.[11]

Reward systems have to involve more than just a salary increase that becomes an annuity. Merit increases end up creating a highly paid group of employees who are highly paid primarily because they have been with the organization for a long period— their salaries don't reflect the value of their current skills or their performance.

For a pay raise to be a meaningful reward, it must be large enough to be important. A great deal of research shows that the typical merit increase plan, which may give anywhere from a 2 to 8 percent raise in good economic times, simply does not provide large enough pay increases to motivate performance. The solution is not to increase the size of merit increases; it is to use bonuses or some other form of variable pay as a means for rewarding performance.

How much variable pay is used needs to be very much dependent on the type of work individuals do and the situation of the organization. A good rule of thumb is that there should be at least a 10 percent cash difference between what the best-performing individual receives and what the least-performing individual receives. In other words, the incentive opportunity should be at least 10 percent, but that often is not a sufficient amount for individuals in more senior management positions. There the opportunity may need to be 20 to 30 percent.

In case you haven't already figured it out, we are about to argue for the use of variable pay plans that reward either individuals and or collections of individuals on the basis of their performance. There are numerous advantages to giving bonuses based on collective performance. The advantages of bonuses that are driven by corporate or business unit performance include the fact that they automatically adjust to the ability of the organization to give pay increases and can focus attention on sustainable effectiveness.

Reward systems have to involve more than just a salary increase that becomes an annuity.

In tough times, such as a recession, bonuses can be eliminated or significantly limited. In addition, they can reflect the fact that sometimes there are large differences between the performance of the best employees and the performance of poor employees. Instead of the best employees getting an increase a few percentage points larger than that of the rest of the workforce, they can get a 15, 20, or 30 percent larger bonus while the worst employees get none. This not only positions the best performers high in the market where they should be, it creates a powerful incentive for them to continue to perform well and for others to perform well.

Bonuses make it possible to adjust the pay of individuals to reflect their current performance level because they don't have to be paid for performance that took place years ago. This is a particularly important feature, given the need for SMOs to reward innovation and change. In essence, it creates a truly meaningful pay-for-performance system that has a real impact on total compensation. This is just what is needed to make pay a powerful motivator of sustainable effectiveness.

Universal Reward Principle 3: Pay for Team Performance

When we talk about rewards, we usually fall into thinking about how individuals are rewarded, but there are good reasons to emphasize team rewards. It is true that there are a lot of advantages to rewarding individual performance. It can establish a clear line of sight between performance and pay. It is also the best way to align an individual's compensation with his or her market value. But rewarding individual performance is not always easy or even possible.

We have already noted that a good performance management system and skilled managers are needed, but that is not enough. Also required is work that lends itself to measures of individual performance. Complex work is often the result of a team effort in a way that makes it difficult to untangle the contribution of individual members, and as a result, rewarding the team as a whole makes sense.

Sometimes, particularly in SMOs that are team-based and do complex, highly independent projects, good measures of performance can only be obtained for group performance or perhaps multi-group performance. This is why, in our discussion of performance management, we argued for assessing the performance of teams.

In the case of interdependent work, giving large bonuses or any other reward on the basis of individual performance can be counterproductive. In American football, players often have individual incentives that reward them for such things as touchdowns scored. All too often, this can lead to conflict among members of a team over who should get the ball when they are near the goal line. Not only does rewarding individuals cause competition among employees, it can lead to money being misspent and to reductions in motivation and satisfaction.

Sports provides clear examples of different kinds of work. Soccer is an example of a highly interdependent sport. In the case of Manchester United, even though there are large salary differences, it makes sense to give equal bonuses to team members on the basis of the team's performance. The same is not true of less interdependent sports such as the Ryder Cup in golf or track and field (except for the relays).

Particularly in highly interdependent work situations, good measures of individual performance simply cannot be developed. The results of performance can be measured only at the collective level. Rewarding individual performance in such situations has the dysfunctional effect of causing individuals to try to optimize their performance, which in many cases leads to suboptimal collective performance.

One approach to mitigating the negative effect of rewarding individuals is to measure them on the degree to which they cooperate and behave as good team members. This may be a solution when there is not a high level of interdependence, but it has its problems. In essence, it creates a situation in which individuals are competing to be the best team member (most cooperative) in order to get a reward or recognition rather than focusing on what they need to do to make the team successful. It is a subtle difference, but can be a critical one in highly interdependent work situations.

When there is truly a group project, the best solution usually is to reward the group as a whole. This can to some degree blur the connection between an individual's performance and reward and as a result reduce the line of sight from behavior to reward. However, this is a small cost to pay in return for establishing a connection between the performance the organization needs and the rewards individuals get. Building this connection ensures that all individuals will be motivated to accomplish the goals of their organization.

Universal Reward Principle 4: Give People a Piece of the Action

In some cases rewards that are based on organizational performance should play a major role in SMOs just as they often do in CCOs and HIOs. Stock options, profit-sharing plans, and stock-grant plans are all examples of compensation vehicles that reward individuals according to the performance of their organization. These approaches to rewarding individuals are particularly appropriate in small organizations and when there is a strong desire to motivate individuals to make a commitment to the organization's success rather than or in addition to their individual or their team's success. In large organizations, these compensation approaches often are weak motivators of individual performance because of the poor line of sight they create between individual behaviors and measures of overall corporate performance such as corporate profitability and shareholder value increases.

In CCOs and HIOs, organization-wide bonus plans are usually driven solely by financial performance. Good profits lead to large bonuses. SMOs need to take a different approach. The idea of a corporate-wide bonus makes sense, but it should be based on an SMO's sustainable effectiveness. Profits yes, but also social and natural environment performance. Even though the line of sight may be weak for many organization members, it is important to measure and reward sustainable effectiveness in order to create an identity and culture of attention to it.

The one exception with respect to weak motivation is the situation of the very senior executives who are responsible for corporate performance. It makes a great deal of sense to reward them for the long-term sustainable performance of their company. When part of an executive's compensation is based on sustainable effectiveness, it says that senior management is not driven solely by their self-interest at the expense of other stakeholders in the organization.

Universal Reward Principle 5: Don't Be Satisfied with a Once-a-Year Reward Cycle

The frequency with which rewards are given is a critical determinant of how effective they are. In most organizations there is an annual cycle that determines when individuals can receive salary increases and other extrinsic rewards. In some companies and particularly in relatively slow-changing organizations this may be an appropriate time schedule. But as we saw in the case of Siebel, the reality is that in many organizations change is much more rapid than this, and as result a much shorter reward cycle is needed.

Organizations over a period of a year may have two or three changes in tactics and perhaps in strategy that require new skills, new performance goals, and new rewards to support them. This is particularly likely in SMOs because of their heavy reliance on innovation and change in order to be successful. It is one reason that Siebel used a three-month cycle in its approach to pay and goal setting.

The timing of pay for performance systems needs to balance two issues: the desirability of rewarding performance as soon as it happens in order to establish a clear line of sight and the need to be sure that the true effectiveness of the performance being rewarded can be fairly judged. All too often organizations give short-term-focused rewards that ultimately turn out to have rewarded performance that has a damaging effect on the organization's longer-term performance.

A quarterly or semiannual performance reward cycle is likely to be the best fit for many SMOs or at least for many parts of SMOs. Paying bonuses or giving other rewards on a quarterly basis creates a close relationship between performance and reward and fits what often is an appropriate schedule for setting new performance goals and targets. We mentioned this in the chapter on performance management and argued there that more frequent performance reviews may be needed and that reviews should be tied to rewards. In some cases what may be the best combination is a series of quarterly cycles that involve goals, performance measures, feedback, and bonuses, as well as an annual bonus that is based on the sustainable effectiveness of the total organization.

It's rare to find one group of managers or professionals being paid on a different cycle from that of others according to the nature of the work they do. Why is an R&D manager paid on the same twelve-month reward cycle as the marketing manager?

The best overall approach to timing is to design a system that is customized to the type of work being done. Short-cycle work should be rewarded frequently whereas long-cycle work should have a much longer measurement-and-reward cycle. This sounds obvious, but it's rare to find one group of managers or professionals being paid on a different cycle from that of others according to the nature of the work they do. Why is an R&D manager paid on the same twelve-month reward cycle as the marketing manager?

With an emphasis on sustainable performance and organizations taking reasonable risks, particularly at the senior level, SMOs need to focus rewards on measures that evaluate the long-term impact of key management decisions. In other areas, for example in sales and production jobs, it often does make sense to have relatively frequent rewards that are based on operating results.

Finally, in some cases it makes sense to reward individuals on the basis of both short-term and long-term measures of performance. As we mentioned earlier, this is particularly true at the senior management level, but may also be true in research and development units, knowledge-creation work situations, and a host of others in which some results are immediately obvious but others cannot be judged for several years.

Designing an SMO Reward System

Now that we have stated five universal reward system practices that should be followed by all organizations, we can turn to reward system design principles that may not fit CCOs and HIOs but are key to the sustainable effectiveness of SMOs. All of these seven principles need to be followed by SMOs. They are an integrated set, not a set from which SMOs can pick and choose.

SMO Reward Principle 1: Pay the Person, Not the Job

An important determinant of the kind and amount of reward an individual receives in an SMO should be the skills and competencies that he or she has and can use in the workplace. This requires management to identify the skills and competencies that they need individuals to have and to determine who has them. This is one of many reasons why it is important that SMOs have an effective performance management system. The ability to develop an effective pay-for-competency system depends on having an effective performance management system that accurately documents the competencies that individuals have and helps them identify which competencies they need to develop.

CCOs base their salaries mostly on the types of work that individuals do and on salary survey data that say what individuals in other organizations are paid for doing that kind of work. As a result, the pay rates for individuals are largely based on jobs rather than competencies. The job-based approach offers some advantages in determining what the market pay rate for any individual is when organizations have well-defined jobs. But SMOs don't have traditional jobs and as a result shouldn't adopt traditional pay practices. In fact, the opportunity exists for them to gain a competitive talent advantage by focusing more on skills and competencies in determining salaries and reward packages.

They can give salary increases as a reward for learning additional competencies and in this way encourage individuals to develop the skills and knowledge that are needed by the organization. This has the additional advantage of attracting and retaining just the kind of individuals they want: those that have the skills and knowledge that are needed to perform their work and that are interested in continuing to develop their skills.

High involvement organizations often use one type of pay for skill systems in many of their manufacturing and service delivery operations. In their skill- and competency-based pay systems, individuals are paid for both the kind of skills they have and the number of skills they have.[12] This encourages individuals to learn how to do multiple steps in a production or service process. It has been shown to have a number of advantages, including making individuals more product knowledgeable, helping them get a good understanding of how the total product is produced, and giving them contact with customers and other stakeholders.

Some parts of most SMOs should base pay partly on the number of skills someone has, but in others it may be more important to reward the amount of depth knowledge that individuals have in a particular competency. This is particularly likely to be true in areas that are the basis of an organization's core competencies and key organizational capabilities. The important point is to move as far away as possible from rewarding people for what they are told to do by a job description and to get as close as possible to rewarding them for being good at doing what the organization needs them to be able to do in order for it to be sustainably effective.

Effectively paying for skills and competencies depends on being able to get salary market data that show how much individuals with key competencies are paid. Although this can be difficult, in many cases it is easy to do since many technical skill areas such as engineering and finance have well-established salary survey data that clearly show how much individuals with different skill sets and different amounts of experience are paid. In some cases, interpretation of salary survey data that are based on jobs may be needed in order to figure out how much some individuals should be paid.

The simple reality is that jobs do not have a market value, individuals do. Job-based salary surveys are simply a convenient way for CCOs to share data about what they pay individuals and to set their pay rates. It reflects their way of thinking about people and organizations. SMOs need to look at the world differently. They need to focus on the value of individuals, their most important asset!

SMO Reward Principle 2: Define Fairness Strategically and Ethically

All organizations should set their pay levels according to the external market; a high involvement organization, for example, might choose to pay everyone above the market since HIOs intend to compete through talent. On the other hand, a CCO pursuing a low-cost strategy might choose to pay below the market for most jobs as a way to achieve a cost advantage. Whatever the compensation strategy of an organization is, it usually sets the same pay "market position" target for everyone (for example, at market, below market)—that is what is said to be "fair."

The right policy for SMOs is different. It needs a reward approach that pays above the market for people in the most critical positions or with the most critical skills. The reason for this is simple; replacing them can be extremely costly and disruptive. Paying them another 10 or 15 percent in salary or whatever might be needed in order to get them significantly above the market is a small cost compared to replacing them. In the case of recruiting, it may be what it takes to get them to say yes and is a small amount compared to the performance improvement they can produce. If Manchester United was in desperate need of a world-class striker, it wouldn't hesitate to pay above the market for the right individual.

Just because it makes sense to pay some individuals above market does not mean that everyone in the organization has to be paid above or even at the market. There often are some work assignments that simply are not that pivotal to the success of the organization for one or more reasons.[13] They just are not closely related to the core competencies of the organization. In other cases, the work can be easily outsourced, transferred to a web-based system, or done by a contractor or temporary employee.

In the case of nonpivotal work, the approach for an SMO should be to pay the individuals doing this work at a rate that is at or perhaps slightly below the market. For example, Boeing needs to pay engineers with expertise in composite engineering more relative to the market than it needs to pay an equivalently skilled interior designer, since its success depends more on the 787 composite airframe than the look of the cabin. It needs to be best in the world in composite airframes, whereas being average in interior design is good enough.

Fairness in SMOs should be based on the strategic value delivered to the organization and what is socially responsible. If someone has hard-to-replace critical skills, then it is fair and strategically important to pay them more. If they do not have critical skills it is okay to pay them less, but there should be a limit to how much less.

SMOs need to keep in mind the importance of being socially responsible in dealing with their employees. They need to provide cash compensation and benefits that are responsible; in most cases this means rates that are at or near the market rate. However, in some cases it may mean paying above the market because the market rate is lower than a reasonable wage. This can occur in developing countries—when it does, SMOs need to pay a living wage in order to meet their social responsibilities.

SMO Reward Principle 3: Individualize Rewards

There is no doubt that for a reward to be motivating it has to be significant to the individual. The importance of a reward varies considerably, not only according to its size but according to its nature and to the needs and values of individuals.

As we noted earlier, in a highly diverse workforce there are large differences in what individuals value. Some individuals are more concerned about financial rewards, others about status rewards, and still others about the social impact of their work and that of the organization. Public recognition is valued greatly by some individuals, but actually disliked by others. Some individuals simply are uncomfortable with any form of recognition, particularly highly visible public recognition.

An important feature of SMOs should be recognizing that there are differences in what individuals value and giving them choices concerning what they do, where they work, and how they are rewarded.[14] In CCOs, individuals have very little choice with respect to rewards. They are told what the pay-for-performance system is; they are told that they are paid on the basis of their job; and they are given a standard benefits package, recognition opportunities, and so on. This approach may fit CCOs and some HIOs. It does not fit an SMO.

When possible, it makes sense to give individuals choices with respect to how they are rewarded.

Given the large individual differences that exist in people's reward, career, and work preferences, in SMOs an individualized and differentiated reward approach is needed. So far in this chapter we have already mentioned some reward areas in which individuals can and should be treated in an individualized way. At this point however, we would like to go beyond that and establish that a major feature of the reward system in an SMO should be individualization and choice.

When possible, it makes sense to give individuals choices with respect to how they are rewarded. This is the best way to ensure that individuals receive only rewards that they value and that SMOs do not waste their resources on rewards that are not valued.

Organizations can give individuals choices in terms of what type of incentive rewards they might receive, for example, cash or stock, and indeed what kind of incentive plan they are on (a lot of or little pay at risk). Incentive plan choices are intriguing, but to some degree limited because of the importance of designing pay for performance plans that fit the work situations individuals are in. More broadly applicable is giving individuals choices with respect to the fringe benefits that they receive and, as will be discussed later, in their work arrangements and working conditions.

For a number of years many organizations have given individuals some choices with respect to their benefits. They offer a number of health care plans, variations in vacation plans, choices among retirement plans, and so on. This approach has a number of advantages, the main one being to ensure that individuals get only the rewards that are important to them.

In SMOs the best approach is to accelerate the growing trend toward benefits being flexible. Whenever possible, individuals should be given the freedom to choose which benefits they receive and whether they receive cash instead of a benefit (such as holidays or life insurance). It may also make sense to give them a choice of whether they receive a cash award or stock. Doing this fits well with the increased diversity in the workforce and with giving individuals greater choices about where they work, how they work, and how long they work.

SMO Reward Principle 4: Don't Base Rewards on Hierarchy

In CCOs, hierarchy is the major driver of the rewards that individuals receive. As one moves up the management hierarchy, virtually everything about the reward system changes. Rewards get larger, they are more variable, and they are more visible. As a result, many individuals are very focused on getting promoted and working their way up the hierarchy. This approach certainly fits the CCOs, but it does not fit an SMO.

We are not arguing that the type of work an individual does and his or her level in the organization are irrelevant to how someone should be rewarded. What SMOs do not need, however, given their relatively flat and networked structures and their approach to leadership, is a very hierarchical reward program. Such programs simply do not fit well. They create a culture of differentiation that decreases flexibility and focuses leadership at the top levels of an organization.

Hierarchical reward systems are poor motivators because the promotions and the rewards that go with upward mobility are rarely available. Many organizations depend on growth to provide this reward, but as we have seen, SMOs are unlikely to grow rapidly. They also do not have very hierarchical structures. Thus there are not that many promotions an individual can get in an SMO. As a result of their limited availability, promotions are a poor incentive. Overall, it is simply much better to base rewards on competencies than on hierarchy.

Particularly inappropriate for SMOs are the many status symbols that CCOs use to reinforce hierarchy and make promotion attractive. Large offices, special parking places, and so on tend to separate senior executives from the rest of the organization and certainly discourage the kind of shared leadership that should be practiced in SMOs. It makes it all too obvious that there are a few leaders rather than an organization of leaders.

Just to be clear, we are not arguing that there should be no reward differences based on hierarchy. What we are arguing is that the differences should reflect the type of work individuals are doing and the relatively flat dynamic structure that exists in an SMO. This means that individuals at higher levels may have different kinds of rewards and perhaps in some cases be rewarded by different types of reward programs (for example, stock option plans), but it is not because they are at level 4 in the organization versus level 2. It is, for example, because the kind of work they are doing has a time span and market for individuals who can do it that fits a particular approach to bonuses and stock rewards. In other words, it's a natural outcome of the type of design principles that we advocate for creating a reward-for-performance system in an SMO.

A pay-for-skills-and-competencies system will produce some hierarchical pay differences. The simple fact is that markets tend to reward some skills more highly than others, and in particular they tend to reward skills that are associated with senior management positions very highly. Thus in an SMO individuals with more senior management responsibilities will in fact be paid significantly more than others in their organization. However, it is important that they not receive the kind of executive compensation levels that make headlines in the *Wall Street Journal* and *Financial Times*. Instead of a ratio of 500 to 1 from top to bottom in organizations, a ratio of 50 to 1 or so makes a great deal more sense for SMOs. It says that there are not huge reward differences, "just" large ones.

SMO Reward Principle 5: Don't Base Rewards on Seniority

Most CCOs and HIOs base rewards on the length of time someone is employed by them. As an employee's tenure increases, so do such benefits as company-funded retirements, medical coverage, number of vacation days, and a variety of other benefits and perquisites. In addition, CCOs and HIOs often give anniversary recognition (service) rewards when people have been with them for five, ten, fifteen, twenty, twenty-five, or more years.

Often the service rewards that are given by CCOs and HIOs are not meaningful. We were recently talking to someone who had been with her CCO employer for twenty-five years and had gotten an email thanking her for twenty-five years of dedicated service. It began "Dear Employee #7421XXX . . ." (number is incomplete to "protect" the identity of the employee who provided the story). The one positive was that it offered her a choice among rewards (none worth more than $100). Very different is how service rewards are handled in CCOs and HIOs that take them seriously. In one construction firm we studied, the twenty-five-year awards were given out at a company-wide meeting. There was no choice of award—everyone got a gold Rolex watch. In their company the reward was "meaningful," but that doesn't mean it was money well spent.

Organizations speak out of both sides of their mouths when they reward length of service but downsize or "right size" their workforces on a regular basis. This is particularly cynical when downsizing is done without taking seniority into account. Even if done well, service-based rewards do not fit SMOs for a very clear reason. They "reward" something that SMOs do not necessarily want: long-term employees. As will be discussed further in the next chapter, the career model in SMOs does not assume long tenure is always a good thing.

SMO Reward Principle 6: Be Transparent

In many organizations the pay of hourly employees and top managers is public. Publicly traded firms have to report on executive compensation. With respect to the hourly employees, the organization has to share pay information if it has a union. But when there is a choice, most CCOs try very hard to keep pay levels secret. Some HIOs, including Whole Foods, make pay levels public, but many do not.

In response to individuals making their pay public, some CCOs have installed policies which state that employees who discuss their salaries will be fired. Not only is this a dysfunctional policy even in a CCO, it is illegal in the United States according to the National Labor Relations Act.

Secrecy about pay and rewards simply does not fit an SMO organization. It gets in the way of accountability, informed judgments on the part of individuals, and what makes for effective pay for performance systems.

In many organizations the pay of hourly employees
and top managers is public.

The most common argument against making reward system information public, particularly individual pay, is that it leads to employee dissatisfaction. This is certainly possible, but it does not mean that the situation will be worse with public pay than it is with pay secrecy; in fact, it is likely better because the dissatisfaction will be data-based and addressable. With pay secrecy there is often great dissatisfaction because of individuals misperceiving what others are paid.[15] In some organizations very-well-designed pay systems don't get the credit they deserve because individuals cannot see they are in fact equitable and rational. They also cannot see the degree to which good performance is rewarded, and as a result don't see as clear a connection as they should between rewards and performance.

Perhaps what is more insidious is that with secrecy, organizations don't hear valid complaints about the reward system and as a result don't take the kind of corrective action that would make their pay plans more effective. All too often we hear organizations say, "Give us a few years to straighten out the pay system and we will make it public." Of course, what happens in most organizations is that it is never straightened out and never made public.

We don't think it is an overstatement to say that if decision makers knew that their reward system decisions would face public scrutiny they would be more careful and more effective when making them. Knowing that they will not be publicly accountable all too often leads managers to do things that simply are not defensible.

Finally, in discussing the importance of making the reward system data public we can't help but to note that with the Internet and all the other communication technology currently available, it is highly unlikely that reward system information can remain "secret." Individuals certainly can and do share their pay information on a number of websites (such as Glass Door). The problem with this approach to making reward information public is that there is no guarantee that it is accurate, and inaccurate information usually causes many more headaches than valid data.

With the amount of hacking that goes on, organizations should expect that more and more of their reward system data will in fact become public whether they want it to be or not. What's the best answer for SMOs? Sure, greater data security is possible, but on balance we feel strongly that the best solution is to simply be public about pay in SMOs. Put the pay of everyone in the public domain. Create a culture of transparency and accountability.

SMO Reward Principle 7: Use Identity and Purpose as Rewards

The soccer players for Manchester United get paid very well, but you find amateur Olympic athletes working incredibly hard simply because they believe in representing their country and being the best they can be. We've already mentioned the reaction someone from Médecin Sans Frontières is likely to get at a cocktail party. It underlines the point that purpose- and identity-driven organizations can offer rewards that attract and motivate employees. If they pursue true sustainable performance objectives, caring for planet and people, then being a member can be an important reward employees receive. This is one area where SMOs can have a major advantage that CCOs and HIOs do not when it comes to recruiting and retaining talent.

But, and it is a big but, SMOs must do more than say they are a triple-bottom-line company. They must establish an employer brand as a sustainable management organization. This requires publicizing what they do so that it is well known that they are walking the talk. For example, their sustainable effectiveness performance should be a part of their advertising, their annual reports, their metrics systems, and their products and services. Patagonia has done an excellent job at this, and PepsiCo has moved aggressively to do it.

JM Eagle is an example of a company that walks the talk and publicizes it. The company is the world's largest manufacturer of plastic pipe, much of which is used for water systems. The first page of its website highlights its commitment to social responsibility and its effort to provide clean water to communities in developing countries. Recently it donated 277 miles of pipe to improve water access for 110,000 people in multiple African countries.

But what about purpose and identity as motivators of performance? It depends on individuals believing that they make a difference in the sustainable effectiveness of their organization. This condition is much easier to create in a small charity than it is in a large corporation like Whole Foods or Wal-Mart, but it is not impossible. It requires a clear purpose and a high level of transparency with respect to how successful the organization is in achieving it. Also necessary are work designs that allow individuals to experience how their performance affects organizational performance. In other words, they need surface area work that has the same features we mentioned earlier when we discussed intrinsic motivation: autonomy, use of skills, feedback, and a meaningful task.

Conclusion

SMOs need to create reward systems that are very different from those of CCOs and HIOs. Here are some examples. They should be performance- and competency-based in order to motivate individuals to develop and perform. Individuals should be able to choose how they are rewarded. The reward systems should define what is just in terms of the market and what is a socially responsible level of pay. Pay should be public so that everyone can see who and what is being rewarded. These reward system practices are right for SMOs because they fit and support their overall design.

Assessment Questions

1. How open is the organization to innovative approaches to reward?

   a. Anything that threatens the status quo (for example, not rewarding for hierarchy and seniority, or rewarding teams instead of individual performance) is strongly resisted.

b. There is a sense that the pay system is not effective, so there is room for change.

c. There is already a wide range of custom deals, so there are opportunities to change how we handle pay including pay for competencies and special bonus plans.

d. There is a willingness to change.

Here is what the answers imply:

Reward is one of the areas likely to generate the most serious resistance to change. Thinking through where your organization sits in terms of attitudes to innovative rewards practice will help you focus your change efforts.

2. How would your organization react to transparent pay?

a. The idea would be rejected out of hand.

b. It would create many problems.

c. People would soon get used to it.

Here is what the answers imply:

a. Since transparency is a principle SMOs broadly embrace, the inability even to consider the idea shows a cultural barrier to becoming sustainably effective.

b. If transparent pay would create many problems then it probably indicates the pay system is badly run and won't stand up under scrutiny. The big concern should not be avoiding scrutiny by keeping things secret, but making the fixes so that the pay system is not an embarrassment.

c. This is probably an accurate view. The experience of organizations that have gone transparent with pay is that usually it is far less of a deal than everyone expects.

CHAPTER TEN

Managing Talent

The talent management approach of an SMO must establish an attraction, selection, development, and work assignment process that gets the right people into key jobs. This, of course, is much easier to say than to do. It requires the effective operation and integration of a number of systems, including those for recruiting and selection, pay, performance management, and development and career management. Together they should lead to talent management decisions that are made with the same rigor, logic, and strategic attention as are decisions about financial investments, consumers, products, services, and technology.

One of the major differences among CCOs, HIOs, and SMOs is how important talent is to their success and how it should be managed. Although it is common for the CEOs and other senior executives in all kinds of organizations to say employees are their company's most important asset, they often do not behave like this is the case. This may be acceptable in CCOs, but it certainly is not in SMOs.

One piece of "evidence" that many senior executives do not treat talent decisions in the same way as they treat investment, technology, and other business decisions arrives on many doorsteps every Sunday morning. The business section of the *New York Times* has an interview with a senior executive that includes a question about how his or her organization makes hiring decisions. To say the least, many of the answers would not get even a C in a course on talent management. Here are a few answers we would say show a lack of knowledge about how decisions should be made.

- "I see how they treat the receptionist. I always get feedback from them."
- "I ask very boring questions, and see if they get agitated."
- "I like to ask, 'What makes you howl at the moon?'"
- "I like to take them out to dinner and watch how they eat."
- "There are five animals—a lion, a cow, a horse, a monkey, and a rabbit. If you were asked to leave one behind, which one would it be? If you picked the horse, the conversation would end. I wouldn't hire you."

Of course, some CEOs do know something about the research on selection or at least do what the research says is most effective.

- "We do 'critical behavior interviewing.' It's based on the premise that past behavior is the best predictor of future behavior."
- "First I ask, 'Tell me about your results.' I also ask about how they achieved them."

Talent Management Approaches

In the case of CCOs, most employees simply aren't a critically important asset or stakeholder and should not be treated as such. CCOs are designed so that most employees are not and cannot be a source of competitive advantage, the exception being senior executives, knowledge leaders, and those in a few key positions. For CCOs to successfully implement their strategy, most employees need to perform at an adequate level; they are not expected to be difference makers.

Employees clearly are a very important asset in both HIOs and SMOs. They are expected to perform at a high level and to be a source of competitive advantage. Both HIOs and SMOs treat employees as important stakeholders. The major difference between HIOs and SMOs lies in how talent is expected to contribute to their organization's competitive advantage and therefore in how talent is managed.

HIOs focus on having a long-term relationship with people and make a commitment to job stability and career development in an effort to develop a committed and involved workforce.[1] This commitment-to-development approach leads to a stable, involved workforce and has a number of advantages: low turnover costs, stable customer interfaces, and a workforce that knows the company and each other. The major downside of this approach is that it produces inflexibility in terms of the cost and capabilities of the workforce. It also can lead to an egalitarian approach to rewards that makes it impossible to establish strategic reward and career practices that support change and target pivotal individuals and work.

The talent management practices of SMOs need to contribute to the strategic competitive advantage gained from SMOs' superior ability to perform in a sustainably effective manner. They also need to create an organization that is agile and innovative. Accomplishing this requires an approach to talent management that enables relatively rapid changes in the workforce's areas of expertise, and as a result, in the organization's core competencies and organizational capabilities. It also requires an organization that can deal flexibly with individuals and create different relationships with its diverse workforce. A "one size fits all" approach to employment and employee relationships clearly does not fit an SMO. What does fit is a travel-light talent management approach that allows an organization to perform in a sustainably effective way.

Virtual employment, temporary employment, outsourcing, and contingent employment are travel-light talent management approaches that may be used by SMOs. They are needed to create the kind of flexible overall talent pool that an SMO needs in order to be effective in rapidly changing knowledge work businesses.

Often, SMOs can't wait for internal development programs to move the organization's competencies to new areas, and they can't wait for natural attrition and other forces to change the nature of the workforce. They have to be proactive and disciplined in making staffing changes. The need to do this means that many of the employment "deals" that are offered by SMOs need to be significantly different from those offered by HIOs.

The challenge that SMOs face is getting a high level of performance and commitment from their talent while at the same time being flexible and adaptive when it comes to the talent that is hired and retained by the organization. Perhaps the best way to describe what SMOs need is a deep committed relationship with the right kind of talent for as long as it needs them. They need relationships that can be rapidly changed (often ended) when there isn't a good fit between the individual and the organization. When they do end relationships, they have to provide a "soft landing" so that the SMO lives up to its commitment to treating people fairly and well.

The reason for using a "travel light" approach to talent management is clear; it is expensive and slow to change the skills and competencies of individuals.[2] As a result, often it is better to change who is employed than to change existing employees. Hiring someone who already has the needed skills often is cheaper and less risky than trying to develop such skills in an existing employee.

The reason for using a "travel light" approach to talent management is clear; it is expensive and slow to change the skills and competencies of individuals. As a result, often it is better to change who is employed than to change existing employees.

With the relentless pressure that exists to improve shareholder value, it is unlikely that SMOs can afford the amount of slack and expense that is needed to train and develop a large percentage of its employees. This is one situation in which difficult sustainable effectiveness trade-offs have to be made. Secure employment is a big positive for most and, as a result, by not delivering it to all or most employees SMOs are not maximizing the overall social value they are creating. Still, as we shall see, the travel-light approach can provide an employment deal that is attractive and fair to most individuals.

Even though the travel-light approach is used with most employees, other approaches may be used when it does not fit the type of work that needs to be done or the labor market. For example, management and leadership skills are always in short supply, and how people are led is a key source of competitive advantage. So even a travel-light organization may have little choice but to have a core group of leaders that the organization is committed to developing and are there for the long term.

In addition, travel-light organizations may simply not be able to find the technical and knowledge talent they need because there are few people in the labor market who have the necessary skills. This is particularly likely to happen to organizations that are technology leaders, such as Intel, Google, and Applied Materials. These organizations often have no choice—they have to train and develop their employees because the skilled individuals they need do not exist in the labor market.

If the most advanced knowledge in software programming is already in Apple, why go outside for talent? It makes a great deal more sense to invest in transferring the knowledge Apple has to its employees and to pay more to individuals who have it.

But if the talent an SMO needs is an available commodity, it makes economic sense to simply hire individuals and pay them very well for as long as they are useful to the organization. In almost all cases, it is cheaper to hire people with the right knowledge than it is to train and develop people internally.

Finally, one additional consideration: the travel-light policy calls for employing people only as long as they can meet the current needs of the organization. This means there may be large recruiting and orientation costs because of workforce churn. It also can lead to a workforce that is not loyal. Thus the direct and indirect costs of workforce turnover may make travel light a poor choice in parts of an SMO or in some cases almost everywhere in an SMO.

Travel Light in Action

Let's look at a company that uses the travel-light approach. It has worked well there because it fits the company's business model and its need to change quickly.

Netflix is well-known for pioneering the model in which consumers rent DVDs by mail or downloading them rather than picking them up at the local video store. What is less known is Netflix's travel-light approach to talent management. Salary is just a small slice of its total costs; the big cost elements are in content, postage, information technology, and marketing. These costs outweigh salaries by a large amount. Netflix serves over seventeen million customers, and in 2010 it streamed more than three hundred million videos. It earns a couple of billion dollars in revenue with just five hundred exempt employees. These five hundred professionals need to be extremely good at what they do.

Patty McCord, chief talent officer at Netflix, said in a recent interview with the authors, "We are very focused so we don't need a lot of people; we just need very talented people to solve the problem at hand."

Netflix cares a lot about its talented professionals, but that does not mean they intend employees to stay around for the long term nor do they worry about retention. The essence of the employment deal is that as long as it works that's great, and as soon as it doesn't work, then it's time to part ways. The motto is "Adequate performance gets you a good severance package," and the theme of the deal is that employment is a one-year renewable contract. The idea that everyone is on a one-year renewable contract does not describe a formal process, it describes a philosophy.

"We hire very senior people and pay them very well. We give them a lot of freedom and then they either pull it off or they don't," McCord explained. "If they don't—or if the business changes—then the employee won't be kept around."

Change is, of course, very much a part of the business. Netflix has always believed that one day sending DVDs by mail would be displaced by online delivery of movies, and that transformation is in fact well under way. This significant change in their business led to the need for new skills and conversely the obsolescence of old ones.

McCord recalled, "I had a person in the other day saying that the troops weren't happy, that things are changing, that things are not like they used to be. I said, 'Of course it's changing!' We are successful. It's not a small company anymore. I know we need to be constantly evolving, I want to knock something down every year." Of course, this means that having someone leave, voluntarily or otherwise, can't be a traumatic event. When someone leaves to go to a better job, Netflix will celebrate their accomplishment. When Netflix asks someone to leave, it's done with dignity.

"The traditional HR person who needs to terminate some-one will give them three warnings to prove they're incompetent (which they are not, it's just a bad fit), which takes at least a couple of months. I don't want to spend the next two months making someone feel horrible. I just tell them it's not working, and adults can handle that. They get a solid severance. There is no shame in having something not work out. We have a great alumni group."

Not only does the travel-light approach mean that the company does not hesitate to terminate people when the fit is no longer there, they also don't focus on long-term development.

"Our current thinking is that we have high performance people in each slot. For us it's not about grooming your not-so-great quarterback into a great quarterback, we go out and buy someone who is amazing."

In Netflix we see a company that's very talent-focused but not concerned about retention or long-term development. It's not a model that would work for everyone; it's an approach that supports their business.

In Netflix we see a company that's very people-focused but not concerned about retention or long-term development. It's not a model that would work for everyone; it's an approach that supports their business.

Looking at the long term, they have seventeen million cus-tomers in the United States, and there are a hundred million people who have cable, so they have lots of market share waiting to be tapped. But they are not sitting on a long-term competitive advantage. Their ability to sustain success will depend on adapt-ability, innovation, and the talent practices that support them.

McCord concludes, "I don't think we'll come up with the answer and then stick to it. Our ability to invent and morph is what will allow us to survive."

Talent Management Principles

Now that we have given a general overview of how talent should be managed in an SMO, we need to explore in more depth at what practices are needed. We will look at nine principles that should be particularly powerful drivers of the way talent is managed in SMOs.

SMO Talent Principle 1: Use Competencies to Drive Talent Management

One approach to deciding what kind of talent is needed and what kinds of skills and competencies employees need to have is to use job descriptions. This approach, however, does not fit the SMO style nor is it a particularly good fit for most CCOs and HIOs. In the case of SMOs, the absence of job descriptions and the need to have a flexible adaptive organization argues against having job descriptions and using traditional approaches to talent management. Instead, a more talent-focused approach is needed.

The key to creating an SMO talent management approach is to start with the organization's competencies and capabilities. The major focus should be on those that provide a source of competitive advantage in terms of the organization's business strategy and sustainable effectiveness.[3]

The competencies and capabilities that the strategy calls for need to drive the talent management model. Managers need to develop descriptions of the kinds of skills necessary to establish the important organizational competencies and capabilities. Once these have been developed, managers then need to determine how prevalent the different skills should be and what the most logical combinations of them are. The results of this analysis should be person descriptions that are the foundation for the talent-staffing and development model of the organization.

When possible, the needed skills should be hired from the outside because of the general orientation of SMOs in favor of buying rather than building skills. Those that cannot be found in the labor market should be part of the talent development processes. Developing the right organization profile of skills and competencies is the foundation upon which the system needs to rest, because it provides the guidelines for staffing, recruiting, development, and rewards, and should be an important input to the strategizing activities of the organization.

SMO Talent Principle 2: Use Targeted Talent Management

Both CCOs and HIOs tend to have a single approach to how people are treated once they join the organization. Of course, there are differences based on hierarchical level (particularly in the case of CCOs) and legal mandates, but fundamentally these differences are driven by the structure of the organization and the needs of certain technical specialties. What is not taken into account is the importance of the work that individuals are doing to the performance of the organization. In SMOs as well as in some CCOs and most HIOs this is a critical issue.[4] When combined with the variation in the work performance of people, it should lead to individuals being treated differently on the basis of whether their work is pivotal to the organization's success.

If the work is such that significant variance in the performance of individuals exists and the variation significantly affects the organization's performance, special attention needs to be paid to these individuals and their jobs. As a general rule, some jobs are so simple and repetitive that many people when well managed can do them at an acceptable level. Further, often in CCOs, how well such jobs are performed does not have a critical impact on the sustainable performance of the organization. Many low-level service jobs and manufacturing jobs in CCOs very much fit in this category.

At the other extreme are software programmers. Microsoft has told the authors that their "top software developers are more productive than average software developers not by a factor of 10 or 100 times, or even 1,000 times, but by 10,000 times." This may be a bit of an overstatement. It is certainly true that few jobs exhibit the enormous variation of performance cited by Microsoft. But significant differences appear all over the place in knowledge work. It is true with university professors and their research publications, it's true in financial analyst services, and so on.

In addition to focusing on how much variation there is in performance, organizations need to identify the impact of performance variation on organizational effectiveness. It's one thing to know that individuals vary greatly in their ability to perform a task; it's another to determine whether this really makes a difference in the performance of an organization. Only when individuals are in jobs that have both performance variation associated with them and a significant impact on the operating results of the company should they be singled out as critical contributors. Given the sustainable performance demands that exist in SMOs they are particularly likely to have a large number of individuals who are critical contributors.

Work that has significant variation in the performance of individuals and that has an impact on organizational performance is exactly where organizations should focus their talent management efforts. When staffing these jobs, extra time should be taken in the selection process. We have heard this referred to as hiring "hard." Individuals who are effective in pivotal jobs should be particularly well compensated. Performance management systems should identify who the best individuals are at doing pivotal work and, of course, who the individuals are that need to be replaced. Often these jobs are ones for which the knowledge needed to perform them well is continually changing. As a result, new graduates and experienced individuals from other organizations should always be on a company's hiring radar so that it can upgrade the existing workforce or add to it.

When a work situation is identified as critical to the organization's performance, there can be no slack with respect to tolerating poor performance and filling jobs. These are jobs for which organizations simply cannot tolerate "okay" performance. They must constantly strive to upgrade the workforce—either through internal development or external hiring. It is because SMOs have a lot of pivotal work that they need to take the travel-light approach.

Sometimes positions appear as pivotal or critical in organizations that are a bit surprising. It is not surprising, for example, that Microsoft considers its software development engineers pivotal employees. They basically create the organization's product, and there is a large variation in how well individuals do the work.

On the other hand, it is a bit surprising that in FedEx and UPS, the package pickup and delivery drivers are among their most pivotal or critical employees. It turns out to be a relatively complicated job that involves making a lot of decisions about routes, how to handle delays, whether to respond to customer demands for them to wait to pick up a package versus getting packages to the airport to meet a departure time. And, of course, there is the pleasantness of the interaction with customers, which ultimately can determine whether repeat business occurs.

SMO Talent Principle 3: Use Contract Labor

Using contract labor is a logical way to operate an SMO that takes the travel-light approach to talent management. It clearly represents a "buy" rather than a "build" strategy. Often contract labor is easily obtained and, as a result, fits very well into situations in which SMOs have changing needs for labor and skills. It makes workforce reductions relatively easy to manage and can be used to react to surges in the need for labor.

Clearly, the contract labor approach does not fit work that is close to the core competency of the organization and is a critical determinant of the performance of the organization. However, it does fit in the support tasks that are relatively low in impact on organizational performance and for which adequate contract labor is available.

It is common to think of contract labor and temporary labor as filling only relatively simple jobs, but this needn't be true. In some situations, SMOs can profit from hiring contract labor to do skilled tasks that require specialized knowledge.[5]

The key to using contract labor successfully is establishing an employment deal that will prove to be attractive to skilled individuals and is consistent with respect to treating people fairly. It turns out that many high-skilled individuals in areas such as software engineering, architecture, and other professions prefer to work as contractors rather than as regular employees. It gives them an opportunity to earn a good wage for a period of time without getting involved in company politics. They also often find it a chance to do work that is new and challenging, thus adding to their resume and, to some degree, their skill set.

SMO Talent Principle 4: Outsource Nonpivotal Work

As is the case with contract labor, using outsourcing fits well when the work is not a critical determinant of organizational performance and it can be performed adequately by a third party.

The big advantage of outsourcing for an SMO is that it makes adaptability much easier. Resources deployed to the SMO can be added and subtracted by the outsourcing vendor as the workload changes without the kind of disruptions that would occur if the individuals were full-time regular employees of the SMO. For many kinds of work (such as seasonal or non-core) outsourcing to a responsible organization can be more sustainably effective than having the work be done by employees.

Outsourcing can make it easier for an organization to have a diverse workforce. Instead of having individuals inside the organization with different employment deals, contractors can be used who have the right kind of deal for the work that needs to be done. This reduces the number and complexity of the talent management systems that an organization needs while at the same time enables it to get work done by people who have the right kind of employment deals. A number of areas are prime candidates for outsourcing. They include HR administration, information technology management, accounting, and advertising. In this respect, what SMOs need to do is not new and radical—CCO and HIO firms outsource. What may be new and radical is the total amount that is outsourced by an SMO.

SMO Talent Principle 5: Create Career Diversity

In SMOs, diversity in careers and work arrangements should be the "normal" approach. This is a very effective response to the large individual differences that exist in the workforce with respect to career objectives, work-life balance preferences, and career state. Without career diversity, workforce diversity is unlikely to exist; with it, workforce diversity is not only possible, it is part of an organization's identity.

There are a variety of workload options that organizations can offer: sabbatical leaves, part-time employment, family leaves, job sharing, and others that can attract and retain key contributors. They can also offer virtual work arrangements and a variety of career "tracks" that can range from an emphasis on upward mobility to an emphasis on in-depth knowledge.[6]

As we pointed out at the beginning of this chapter, most SMOs are likely to have some work areas where the travel-light approach is used and others where a long-term development approach is used. This means that two significantly different career options are going to be available. But in most SMOs the choices should not end with two. A variety of career tracks should exist: one for upwardly mobile executives, one for technical specialists who want a career that is based on being subject matter experts, one that has a balanced career-family orientation, and one that is focused on the purpose of the organization.

CCOs and HIOs typically don't individualize careers because they fear it will lead to too much "complexity" and widespread feelings of unfairness. This goes in the face of an ever-increasing amount of diversity in the workforce (in terms of age, national origin, family situation, and so on). When all is said and done, it simply doesn't make sense to think of a one-size-fits-all deal for employees.

In SMOs, diversity in careers and work arrangements should be the "normal" approach.

Because of the great amount of research on generational differences (by our count there are at least five generations in the workforce now), one way to individualize work is to design employment deals that fit different generations. We do not have a problem with this, but we think it is very important that this doesn't lead to "age profiling" or for that matter any kind of profiling. Yes, there are generational differences, but within each generation there are enormous individual differences.

The solution, of course, is to give individuals the chance to choose an employment deal that fits them. For example, when it comes to business travel, Unilever found that it was limiting its diversity efforts. Women with children found it to be a problem. The company responded by adding a TelePresence option to its meeting program. Given the choice, men and women of all ages choose to use it. In addition to being socially responsible, the option reduced travel costs and Unilever's carbon footprint. It was clearly an improvement in sustainable effectiveness.

SMO Talent Principle 6: Build a Sustainable Management Brand

To attract the right individuals, organizations need an employer brand that fits their purpose, identity, and strategic intent. In many respects, attracting the right employees is no different from attracting the right customers. Employees seek to work for organizations just as customers seek to do business with them when they feel that the organization offers what they desire.

The major reason for developing an employer brand is to help employees make a good decision about whether there is a fit between them and the organization. Just as there are good and bad potential customers, there are good and bad applicants for jobs. Good applicants are ones who are the type of individual an organization can motivate; who can do, or learn to do, the work of the organization; and who fit the identity of the organization.

A number of organizations have done a good job of developing their brand as employers. Who, for example, doesn't know what it is like to be a U.S. Marine? Nordstrom's has a clear brand for its salespeople, with the result that they are called "Nordies" because of the distinct relationship they have with the department store. Abercrombie & Fitch; Starbucks; and, in California, In-N-Out Burger have all developed the distinct brand of being a "cool" place to work. Netflix has developed its employer brand by posting on the Web a PowerPoint presentation about their employment deal. Patagonia has done a great job of developing an employer brand as a sustainable effectiveness company. Individuals who care about the natural environment and social issues are attracted to Patagonia.

Basic to having an accurate, and therefore effective, employer brand is a statement of the organization's employment deal or deals. An effective deal identifies both what the individual is expected to do and what the individual will get in return for being an effective employee.

Well-stated deals aid in the recruitment process by reinforcing an organization's value proposition and contributing to a realistic job preview. After people are hired, contracts establish the ground rules for performance and rewards and serve as a fairness touchstone for the organization and the individual throughout their relationship.

Each organization needs to fine-tune its employment deal to fit the type of rewards it can offer and the type of skills it needs employees to have. Because of its focus on change, sustainable effectiveness, and multiple employment relationships, the employer brand of SMOs must be significantly different from those of CCOs and HIOs.

SMO employment contracts are not "loyalty" deals that offer job security and a career employment relationship for everyone. What should the employment value proposition of SMOs be? The answer is obvious: it should offer a sustainable management brand that includes frequent change and stresses the variety of employment deals that are offered. The latter is an important feature because the acceptance of an organization having multiple employment deals depends on transparency and knowing at the time of joining that it is the way the organization operates. The brand should also stress the purpose and identity of the organization and its commitment to sustainable effectiveness.

Research shows that the right employment contracts can be a significant enabler of an organization's ability to change.[7] Organizations such as Netflix that clearly link skill development with employment security—and rewards with performance—execute change more effectively than others. They create "mobile" human capital, that is, people who realize that they must continue to learn, develop, and perform to maintain their positions and careers.

Once an organization has established its employer brand, its next challenge is to use it effectively. For an organization to recruit effectively, its brand needs to be known and understood. One way to ensure this is to feature it in all communications about job openings. In the case of some companies, it makes sense to feature the brand in ads for products and services. Southwest Airlines does this in its TV commercials, which attract the "right" employees and customers simultaneously. The brand also should be featured on the company's website, with videos that show employees talking about what it is like to work for the organization and what the brand means to them.

When individuals actually apply for a job in an SMO, either online or in person, they should be given an introduction that emphasizes what life will be like if they join the SMO. It should be a realistic preview that tells it like it is. This type of preview not only can help set realistic expectations but can drive away individuals who are not a good fit and if hired would not stay long. Decades of research show that realistic job previews reduce turnover because they set realistic expectations and drive away individuals who are not good fits.[8]

Google, as part of its effort to attract the right type of software engineer, has worked hard to establish its brand as an employer. One of the more interesting things it has done is place ads in a number of technology journals and magazines that feature its GLAT (Google Lab Aptitude Test).

The GLAT contains questions that, over the years, Google has found useful in predicting who will be a good engineer. By putting the GLAT into the public domain, Google allows individuals to self-assess and see whether they are a good fit for the organization. In essence, it is a different kind of realistic job preview and a way to brand Google as an employer. What kind of questions are on the GLAT? Here is a sample: *What number comes next in this sequence: 10, 9, 60, 90, 70, 66, . . . ?* Sorry, we don't know the answer, but if you do, contact Google. You may be right for them!

SMOs should reject job applicants who are not a good fit very early in the hiring process. Organizations often spend far too much time interviewing and processing applications from people who are simply not a good fit. Much of this time can be saved if SMOs develop a clear employer brand that features sustainable effectiveness and make a strong effort to acquaint individuals with it.

In addition to discouraging bad applicants, having a strong brand can serve to attract individuals who otherwise wouldn't apply for a job. Given an unclear image of what working for an organization is like, individuals who in fact would be a terrific fit may not be interested enough to go through the application process. A strong brand that makes it clear what working for the firm is like can significantly help in creating an applicant pool that is an excellent fit for the organization. It also is the socially responsible thing to do.

SMO Talent Principle 7: Make Career Management the Individual's Responsibility

One of the major differences in how SMOs manage talent concerns how careers are managed. HIOs and CCOs typically take a considerable amount of responsibility for the careers of their employees, providing them with coaching, career paths, training, and development as needed. Indeed, one of the most attractive features of HIOs is that they provide career help to individuals and promise employment security and stability.

In the case of SMOs, career management is not the responsibility of the organization. It is the responsibility of each individual. Still, because of their commitment to treating people fairly, SMOs should help individuals manage their careers by providing information and development opportunities. It is the fair and just thing to do.

Movement of individuals from one work assignment to another can be self-managed only when an organization has a well-developed posting system for openings and a willingness to support internal transfers.

There are a number of reasons why SMOs should not manage the careers of most individuals. Perhaps the major one is the unpredictability of the organization's needs for employees and the recognition that rapid technological and environmental change may quickly make any advice, no matter how well intended, obsolete in a short period of time.

What an SMO can do, and should do, is provide business transparency and job trend information to its employees so that they can make career decisions that are based on valid and pertinent data. Organizations can also facilitate individual's work assignment changes. This can be advantageous to both individuals and SMOs.

Movement of individuals from one work assignment to another can be self-managed only when an organization has a well-developed posting system for openings and a willingness to support internal transfers. Many of the new human resource information systems (HRISs) that organizations are adopting do include postings. However, it is not enough just to post work openings; the posting needs to include a great deal of information about the characteristics of the work, including the skills and competencies needed and what the application process involves.

A number of companies, including IBM and other professional service firms, have developed sophisticated web-based systems that provide job information to employees. They also allow managers to search the organization and identify people with the right skill sets. Web-based systems make it possible for the internal movement of employees to be dynamic and interactive and as a result be a positive for both individuals and financial performance.

Current employees provide profiles of their background, interests, and skills, which are then stored in the system. When jobs open, their characteristics are matched to the database of profiles, allowing the technology to make a first determination about whether someone might be a good fit. Push technology can then be used to inform individuals of the job opening. This has the obvious advantage of providing current employees with a strong assurance that their skills and experience are important. It also sends a message to employees that the organization takes talent utilization and the concerns of individuals seriously.

Web-based systems also can help meet the staffing challenges of managers who must fill open jobs. They can use the technology to search the profiles of skills and competencies and identify employees who fit a job opening they need to fill. This is a quick and efficient way for the people doing staffing to obtain a list of qualified internal candidates.

The willingness of organizations to let individuals make internal moves and workload changes is the last and sometimes most difficult piece that needs to be put in place so that individuals can reasonably self-manage their careers in SMOs. There are a number of reasons why it is difficult for individuals to make internal moves, but often a major factor is the lack of management support. The transfer of a valuable employee inconveniences the manager in whose work area the individual currently works; as a result, managers sometimes hide their most talented people or go out of their way to discourage movement.

SMOs must find ways to overcome the natural tendency of individual managers to horde talent. The simplest way is to keep track of how much talent a manager "exports" to other parts of the organization and make that part of the manager's performance appraisal, so that it affects his or her rewards. Just as financial capital has to be used effectively, human capital has to be put to its best use and people need to be given the chance to learn, develop, and grow—it is key to their being treated fairly in a travel-light organization.

Overall, web-based systems can help organizations know what talent is available internally, and they can help individuals with their career planning because it makes them aware of where the organization needs talent. They also give individuals a chance to seek out and compete for jobs that fit their needs. Finally, web-based systems are a nice complement to having multiple employment "deals" for individuals. If someone does not like the one under which they are working, they can apply to work in areas where there is a deal they prefer.

SMO Talent Principle 8: Make Executives the Primary Talent Managers

The top executives of an SMO need to take primary responsibility for the talent management decisions that are made. Senior executives need to be actively involved in succession planning and work assignment decisions. They need to contribute to the design and operation of the talent management systems in the organization and see that they are aligned with the organization's other systems and strategy. This means that a lot of their calendar will be filled with talent management issues. Twenty-five percent is not out of line—indeed in some businesses, it may require significantly more.

Let's look first at what executives' role should be in making talent management decisions and how they should be involved in things ranging from who's hired to how much individuals are paid. Managers in SMOs need to be knowledgeable and informed about what good talent management involves. As already noted, unfortunately, all too often they are not. Perhaps this reflects the reality that most organizations are not managed in an SMO or HIO style and, as a result, there is little pressure on managers to make high-quality human capital management decisions.

Trying to get by with managers who don't have good knowledge of human behavior and decision science principles about human capital may work in a CCO but it won't work in an SMO. Talent decisions, both at the strategy level and at the tactical level, are simply too critical to the sustainable effectiveness of an SMO to be made by poorly educated managers. The implications of this point are many and involve both who gets to be managers and the role of the HR function.

Let's look first at the issue of who gets to be managers and how they get to managerial positions. In most organizations today, managers don't get to senior decision-making positions unless they have a good understanding of finance; operations; and perhaps such specialty areas as marketing, sales, and information systems. But many do get to senior positions without ever having worked in or been trained in talent management and sustainable effectiveness.

It often seems that everyone thinks they understand people and can make good decisions about talent. Of course, nothing could be further from the truth. A great number of research studies have shown that most managers have a poor understanding of what determines individual behavior and what should be done in organizations to be sure that human capital is well managed and effectively utilized.[9]

Our research shows that as a result of the kind of career tracks that most senior managers are on in U.S. corporations, they have inferior knowledge when it comes to human capital management. Ratings by them as well as by HR executives show that their knowledge of key principles concerning human capital management is much lower than it is with respect to key principles in other important areas of business (such as finance, marketing, and sales).[10]

At the strategic level, there is a serious need for the managers in an SMO to understand how work designs, talent management systems, information systems, and organization structures affect human behavior and influence the competencies and capabilities that an organization has. Knowledge of these connections is precisely what managers need to know in order to make decisions that lead to sustainable effectiveness.

Executives need to understand how their decisions will affect each of the sustainable effectiveness areas and how they can develop individuals who can make decisions that increase sustainable effectiveness. They should be actively involved in decisions about talent with respect to pay, promotion, and work assignments.

They should also be responsible for decisions concerning the fundamental design and architecture of the organization from a human capital point of view. Decisions about what to outsource, what to do online, what positions to fill with the existing talent, what to do through contract labor, and so on should all be made by senior managers who have a good understanding of human capital management principles and how these decisions affect sustainable performance.

The need for senior managers to have good knowledge of human capital in SMOs should be reflected in the kinds of career tracks they follow. Typically, managers in CCOs rotate from function to function as they develop their careers. Unfortunately, in most U.S. organizations, that rotation does not involve spending time in the human resource function. This is a serious oversight in terms of preparing managers for senior positions in SMOs. Given that talent is such a critical resource in SMOs, it is certainly as important that managers spend time in a human capital position as it is that they spend time in operations, marketing, or finance.

Overall, talent management must be the responsibility of managers throughout an SMO. It cannot be handed off to HR. It needs to be a high priority and constantly in the forefront of the thinking of managers throughout the organization. First- and second-level managers need to be skilled at making tactical decisions in the talent management area. At the very top of an SMO there is no substitute for having executives who both take a leadership role in human capital management and are able to contribute to key strategic human capital decisions. This is the minimum that should be expected of individuals leading organizations that depend on human capital for competitive advantage.

SMO Talent Principle 9: The HR Function Plays a Strategic Role

In many CCOs, the human resource function does not play a strategic role, nor is it designed to. It is largely an administrative function that services the needs of employees for fringe benefits, training, and a host of support services.[11] In many respects, this is neither surprising nor dysfunctional. HR does not need to be a strategic partner adding great value in CCOs. It does in HIOs, particularly from the point of view of organization design, training, and development, and it certainly does in SMOs because it can make a substantial contribution to sustainable effectiveness. Let's explore how.

In SMOs, HR does not just need to be at the table when it comes to strategic decision making, it needs to set the table. It needs to bring to the table relevant business data about the talent in the organization so that informed decisions can be made about the feasibility and attractiveness of different business strategies and different initiatives. Because of the importance of human capital, its condition and capabilities are critical in determining what services and products the organizations offers and how they should be produced and delivered.

In SMOs, there is simply no substitute for having a human resource function that plays a true strategic role. This will only happen if SMOs treat the human resource function as equally important to or more important than the other staff groups. Unfortunately, HR often is a backwater that offers careers within a silo and relatively low pay. It clearly is not seen as a stop individuals must make before they reach a senior management position.

In SMOs, there is simply no substitute for having a human resource function that plays a true strategic role. This will only happen if SMOs treat the human resource function as equally important to or more important than the other staff groups.

In an SMO, where so much depends on an organization's governance, structure, and talent management, the human resource function needs to be an important career stop for anyone and everyone who aspires to reach senior management. They need to understand what good human resource management systems and practice look like and acquire expertise in the talent management that allows them to lead an SMO that is constantly changing and sustainably effective.

What about the administrative role of HR? In most cases, the administrative role of HR can be handled either by creating an internal information technology service group or by outsourcing. There are now a number of firms that are quite expert at providing outsourcing services in the HR administration field. They provide call centers and information technology that can take most of the administrative work out of the HR function, leaving behind an organization that is focused on talent management and organizational change and that can support sustainable effectiveness.

In SMOs, the best design may be one that transforms the HR function into an organizational effectiveness staff group. In addition to having responsibility for HR, the organizational effectiveness function should have responsibility for organization design, change management, and strategizing. These functions all are highly interdependent and critical to the development of an SMO. Most of the decisions in one area strongly affect decisions in the others, and sustainable effectiveness can only truly be achieved by developing an integrated set of practices. The organization effectiveness group needs to be headed by one of the top four or five executives in a corporation, and that leader should have extensive experience in human capital management and organization design.

Conclusion

Talent management in SMOs must fit their unique needs. What is right for CCOs and HIOs simply is not what is needed for SMOs. They need an employment deal that allows for change and attracts individuals who can perform in ways that contribute to sustainable effectiveness and who care about it. Accomplishing this requires an integrated approach to attraction, selection, development, and careers.

Assessment Questions

1. How does the top team approach talent management?

   a. They feel comfortable with their intuitive approach to making talent decisions.

   b. They seek out the specialized know-how and the processes that the human resource function brings to the subject.

   c. They have built an advanced capability that includes analytics and metrics, and it leads to good talent decisions.

Here is what the answers imply:

a. Managers can have good intuitions about talent just as they may have good intuitions about marketing or inventory management, but treating talent like that is not good enough in an SMO.

b. It is encouraging that HR expertise is valued, but most HR functions are not sophisticated enough to meet the demanding needs of an SMO.

c. There is a huge opportunity to differentiate the organization by developing superior talent management systems.

2. How close is your organization to a "travel-light" approach?

a. It is contrary to our view that we want to retain and develop employees in the long term.

b. We often act in a travel-light manner when it comes to layoffs, but we've not crafted a deal with employees so that they know it is part of our employment deal and have bought in.

c. The culture supports a travel-light approach, and employees feel a bit like free agents already. They work with us as long as it makes sense and are okay about parting ways when it isn't.

Here is what the answers imply:

a. The appealing HIO view is that employees are valued and hence have secure jobs. However, an SMO, while valuing employees, realizes that job security is not something it can offer to most or all employees so it offers a "travel-light" approach.

b. The worst approach is to pretend you intend to retain employees long term when that is not actually the strategy. It's better to be explicit about the travel-light philosophy and get buy-in.

c. Being travel light is a big step toward having the flexibility SMOs require and treating people fairly.

PART FOUR

The Way Behavior Is Guided

CHAPTER ELEVEN

Leading, Managing, and Following

Leadership is one of the most—perhaps the most—important determinants of an SMO's sustainable effectiveness. There are millions of books and articles about what makes leaders effective. Thousands of new books appear every year. They all stress how important leadership is, but few call for an approach to leadership that is right for SMOs. Leaders in SMOs need to do four things that are not expected of leaders in either CCOs or HIOs:

1. Compensate for the lack of structure
2. Focus on the importance of sustainable effectiveness
3. Both lead and accommodate the changes and innovations that SMOs need to make continuously
4. Lead and encourage a culture in which hierarchy is minimized and leadership is shared

We think leaders in SMOs must do all of these; if they fail to do one or more, SMOs will not be able to sustain their performance any better than other organizations. Because these actions are not expected of leaders in most organizations, SMOs face a special challenge in developing leaders who can deliver them. But before discussing how SMOs can meet this challenge, we need to consider in more detail what leaders in SMOs need to do.

Compensate for the Lack of Structure

SMOs are built to change, so they do not have stabilizing elements such as job descriptions, detailed operating procedures and structures, and annual budgets. SMOs value adaptability, so they adopt fluid organizational forms, such as networks and ambidextrous structures. Furthermore, they lack the simplicity that is created by the single goal of financial performance.

A CCO models itself after a machine; in a CCO you hear managers complaining they are just a cog in that machine, but CCOs do make management simpler. Certainly managing in a hierarchical, rule-bound organization is a well-developed role that is familiar to almost everyone who has held a job. Managing in an HIO is closer to doing it in an SMO than to doing it in a CCO. HIOs have fixed structures and budgets but usually lack detailed job descriptions and hierarchical structures. Managing in an SMO feels more like canoeing down a fast-moving river than being part of a machine.

Leaders and Managers

Much of the writing on leadership makes a distinction between managers and leaders. Although there is not a consensus view on what precisely differentiates a manager from a leader, the distinction generally rests on how much an individual does the basic blocking and tackling of organizing (assigning tasks, monitoring the work of others) versus providing a sense of meaning, direction, motivation, and inspiration.

When behavior is more oriented toward providing feedback to individuals on their performance, setting standards, and maintaining a well-organized workflow, an individual is generally considered to be managing. When behavior is focused more on providing employees with a sense of mission and inspiration—when it involves helping employees find and understand their niche within the company—an individual is considered to be leading. The difference between leaders and managers is often characterized by a Warren Bennis point: managers do things right; leaders do the right things.[1]

To be sustainably effective, SMOs require leadership because they do not have the structures and job descriptions that substitute for the lack of leadership in CCOs. In addition, more often than not, there are not the clearly established work methods and work procedures that exist in most CCOs. As a result, leadership is needed to ensure that individuals know what to do, know how to do it, and are motivated to do it.

The adulation of leadership and the dismissal of managing can lead to the wrong conclusion when it comes to SMOs: that they don't need managers. Yes they need effective leaders, but they also need good managers. Management is about getting work done through others. Effective leadership can contribute to getting work done by others, but it is not all that is required in order for that work to support the way an organization creates value.

Organizations can be overled and undermanaged and as a result perform poorly. Effective leadership does not necessarily lead to the adoption of the best work methods, organization designs, and communication patterns. Managers in an SMO should not abandon most of the nitty-gritty of management, but only doing it is not enough. They also must provide context and direction in an organization that is trying to achieve something more than just acceptable financial performance. The objective of sustainable effectiveness is uncommon enough that it may not be obvious what needs to be done to achieve it, hence the need for managers who are skilled at both leading and managing.

The right approach to management in an SMO is to balance leadership and management. It is not about directing individuals but about ensuring they are committed to the purpose of their SMO and have the information they need to figure out what they need to do.

Effective Attention Management

If you want to get a feeling for a setting in which there is little structure, few established procedures, and no job descriptions, take a look at startups. Successful startups are in a constant state of flux as they try to find a niche and continually adapt as they grow. In a startup, the founder must exhort everyone to run as fast as they can without necessarily being able to tell them precisely where to run or how to surmount any obstacles they face.

They need to keep control of limited resources while trusting that employees can figure things out on their own.

If you want to get a feeling for a setting in which there is little structure, few established procedures, and no job descriptions, take a look at startups.

We can envisage managers in SMOs working in a fluid world that in some ways is reminiscent of a startup. They don't manage by making sure everyone is in their place doing what they are told to do; they lead by making sure everyone knows where the organization needs to go and what they need to do to get it there.

A manager in an SMO should ask, "Am I focusing the attention of the organization—and that includes not just my direct reports but all those I interact with—on the really critical issues that determine sustainable effectiveness?" With direct reports, a big part of this is communicating to them directly and effectively about the organization's purpose, identity, and strategy.

Perhaps the most common mistake that top executives make in all types of organizations is not recognizing the importance of communicating directly and effectively with employees about where the organization is going. It is the key to effective attention management. The constant demand of the day-to-day details of doing business distracts managers and employees alike from paying attention to critical issues that need to be their organization's focus.

Effective SMO managers deal with the day to day, but they are also constantly asking about and focusing on their short list of things that truly determine sustainable effectiveness. Are key costs under control? Is the market changing? What impact are we having on the environment? Can we do things in ways that are less expensive and more environmentally friendly? Are we treating people fairly?

They stay on message and return to this short list again and again; doing so is a job responsibility that is built into their behavior and recognized in performance reviews. It is particularly important that leaders in SMOs do this so that the behavior of everyone will be focused on sustainable performance.

One CEO that does recognize the importance of attention management is Tim McNerney, the CEO of Boeing. Boeing has a global workforce of over 160,000 employees, so communicating with everyone is not a simple task. When asked by a reporter soon after he became CEO if he was going to spend more time with customers and stock analysts, McNerney's response was that it was more important for him to spend time with Boeing's employees than to spend it on increasing his profile and his visibility in the press. According to him, employees "have got to know that working with them is more important to me than public forums where I'm making big speeches."[2]

In customer-service-oriented SMOs, a dramatic way for managers to get to know employees and the organization is to do a "front-line job." This communicates to employees that what they do is important to the leadership of the organization and educates the executives. Key executives at Southwest Airlines and Jet Blue have done this for decades, while DaVita expects its managers to do front-line customer service jobs as a part of their development.

Limits on the Sharing of Power

Attention management is one way for leaders to influence sustainable performance in a low-structure setting, but it's not all they need to do. Like leaders in HIOs they must share power in ways that build commitment and motivation. However, they can be less concerned with power sharing than are managers in HIOs. Leaders in HIOs need to be sure that individuals at all levels are given the kind of information and training that will allow them to be full participants in the business and as a result identify with its successes and failures.[3] This is crucial to their willingness and ability to self-manage and to creating a culture in which there is a high level of commitment to the firm's success.

In the case of SMOs a significant amount of power sharing is appropriate, but it does not need to be a defining feature of the company's culture. For example, some power sharing is needed so that the work people do is motivating and rewarding, but it may not involve the kind of power sharing that includes most employees in shaping their organization's business model and strategy.

We stressed in Chapter Eight that managers in SMOs need to be particularly skilled at setting reasonable goals and doing performance management. An important reason for this is the nature of the travel-light employment contract. It is likely that some individuals will not be highly committed to the organization and focused on what they can do to make the organization successful. Individuals who have travel-light deals are much more likely to be concerned with the rewards they can control and receive in the short term. Thus performance contracts and rewards based on their performance are an important part of their relationship to both the organization and their manager.

Overall, SMOs need leaders at all levels who are willing and able to translate the organization's strategy into practices that support and reward individuals who do the right things and that correct individuals who do the wrong things! Leaders in SMOs need to use their behavior to demonstrate what it means to be committed to the goals and objectives of the organization, and they need to be willing to call to account individuals who don't do the right things. They also need to support, by effectively managing the knowledge and skill development of the individuals they manage, the development of organizational capabilities that are strategy driven. In short, they need to not just be role models but also be active definers of what constitutes effective behavior.

Focus on the Importance of Sustainable Effectiveness

We can get a sense of what it is like to lead in an organization where simultaneously achieving multiple outcomes is paramount by stepping into the shoes of Sandy Davis. Sandy is the regional director general of Parks Canada with responsibility for eighteen parks and a staff of 2,200 people. Davis was one of the managers studied in Henry Mintzberg's book *Managing*. We draw our comments from Mintzberg's research notes.[4]

Consider the sort of issues Davis confronts on a typical day:

1. A protest in one park that could turn violent (community stakeholders)

2. Complaints about a trail closure in a park due to expected bear activity (customer stakeholders)
3. Links with the Heritage Department in Vancouver (other departments as stakeholders)
4. Construction of a new facility, with the expenditure occurring just before an election (political stakeholders)
5. Intense conflict between environmentalists and developers over a parking lot desired by developers but opposed by environmentalists (economic and ecological stakeholders)
6. Announcing an agreement between the government and a native band on a new wilderness site (government and native stakeholders)

This is just one day.

While leaders in an SMO may not face the same bewildering array of diverse stakeholder issues as Davis does in Parks Canada, they certainly will not have the simple reassurance that hitting the budget numbers is going to be enough. Leaders in SMOs focus on people, profit, and planet and are on the lookout for actions that will serve all three; in SMOs this balancing act is central to the job. Simply pleasing one's immediate boss or bulldozing things through to hit a single metric is not acceptable in an SMO. When Mintzberg noted how attuned Davis was to the political dimension and to overlaying that on the administrative process, she replied, "That's my value added."

In terms of the actual mechanisms Davis uses to handle this kind of leadership challenge there is nothing novel: conference calls, meetings with direct reports, walking around, and so on. The methods for dealing with ski hills and grizzly bears are not too different from dealing with grandé frappuccinos and café patrons. The difference is that a Starbucks branch manager might focus more exclusively on revenues than on community involvement whereas a Parks Canada manager needs constant awareness of the interests of a broad range of stakeholders.

SMO managers in all organizations must be intensely aware of the three competing dimensions of sustainable effectiveness. In some ways their jobs are more like a politician who practices the art of the possible rather than an engineer who optimizes an equation.

Lead and Accommodate Continuous Change

An important feature of an SMO organization is its ability to respond to rapidly changing circumstances with the right innovations and strategic changes. As a result, SMOs need employees at all levels who are committed to innovating and changing. Often the best way to produce this commitment is through all members of an organization sharing a common sense of purpose, identity, and commitment. Effective leadership is the key to developing this shared sense.

Leaders are needed not just to articulate what an organization's goals and mission are, but to translate them into meaningful work and information flows. This allows organizational members to see how their work is relevant to the organization's mission and that they are contributing to its success. They also need an effective, accurate, and challenging view of what is going on in the external environment. They are sure to get some of this because of the SMOs' future-focused capabilities and external-facing nature, but often they need more than just their experiences. SMOs need leaders who can describe what is happening in the business world, how their organization will be affected by it, and what the organization needs to do to respond to it.

A key issue for SMOs is the balance between optimizing decisions and getting things done in time to respond to the rate of change. Patty McCord from Netflix tells a story about this balance in their business. One engineer who had experience in the semiconductor industry kept missing his deadlines. When she spoke to him about this, he explained that his desire to architect better long-term solutions was holding up some of the projects. McCord emphasized that there were weekly deadlines that needed to be met, and his response was that maybe they needed to hire a couple of engineers to work on the short term while he worked out the longer-term answer—that's how they would do it in semiconductors. McCord's answer was, "That's not how we are going to do it here."

At first glance it looks like Netflix is focusing on the short term at the expense of the long term—hardly the kind of behavior we think fits a sustainable organization. Yet it's better understood as valuing agility over efficiency. The longer-term solution would be more efficient in a stable world, but Netflix's world is one of constant change—more so than the semiconductor industry, in which billion-dollar investments in physical infrastructure require companies to impose a certain amount of stability despite the rapid pace of technological change.

Leaders in SMOs need to do more than just create substitutes for the CCO management systems that managers in other organizations have. Yes, they need to create substitutes for the control systems that are missing in SMOs, but they also need to provide a type of leadership that creates organizations which love change and innovation, encourage self-management, and motivate individuals through a sense of commitment to their mission. Leadership needs to be the glue that holds their organization's design elements together and causes them to create sustainable effectiveness.

Create and Encourage a Culture in Which Leadership Is Shared

Without question, senior executive leadership is very important to the effectiveness of all organizations. The leadership of an organization's CEO and the leadership practiced by those who hold senior executive positions clearly affect financial performance and the motivation and satisfaction of employees. But the quality of senior leadership is only one of the determinants of how effectively an organization is led.

Many studies show that the key determinant of most employee behavior is not the leadership that is provided by the CEO or the senior executives but the behavior of managers throughout the organization. These are the individuals who must provide the day-to-day motivation and sense of direction to most employees. These are the people who possess—and pass along—the technical and organizational knowledge when it comes to strategy implementation, change management, and work processes. They are also the ones who set the culture for employees; their behaviors shape the culture in a much more tangible way than the behavior of the senior executives.

Because too much importance is ascribed to how the very top executives lead, all too often organizations focus too little attention and too few resources on the way in which individuals in management positions throughout the organization behave, and the impact of their behavior. In SMOs, this focus needs to change. As Paul Polman, the CEO of Unilever, has argued, "If you positively influence someone, you are a leader."[5] Leadership opportunities are always present throughout SMOs, and they need to be taken advantage of. Any employee can create a leadership moment by encouraging someone, being a role model, explaining a corporate policy or business decision, and, yes, by expressing disapproval of what someone does or doesn't do.

Many studies show that the key determinant of most employee behavior is not the leadership that is provided by the CEO or the senior executives but the behavior of managers throughout the organization.

The financial scandals of the 1990s and 2000s, starting with Enron, show just how much harm a few senior executives can do. Bad leadership at the top can bring down a company in today's highly competitive, high-risk environment. However, a single leader cannot make a company great; it takes a company of leaders. Individuals don't have to be managers in order to be leaders. Individuals who are not in managerial jobs can and should act as leaders in SMOs. Simply stated, all managers should be leaders, but all leaders do not have to have management jobs. Leadership in SMOs should not respect titles and hierarchy.

Have No Imperial CEOs

There has always been a tendency for CEOs to adopt a model of leadership we will call the "imperial" model. They make decisions and develop strategies on their own with little input and discussion. Their decisions are above criticism and challenge. They adopt lifestyles that make them celebrities, and their companies become vehicles that make them "rock stars." They are supported by technology that keeps them in touch 24/7. But in reality, most imperial CEOs are dangerously out of touch with the people they lead, particularly when it comes to the issues of culture, strategy implementation, and organization development.

The automobile industry bailout in 2009 helped show just how out of touch some CEOs are: the U.S. auto CEOs flew to the congressional hearings on corporate jets to ask for government money. Not surprisingly, they were met with public outrage. This kind of out-of-touch behavior is not limited to just this incident. Managers in the auto industry get new cars every few months. They are parked in special garages where they are washed and serviced every day. Further, when the cars are manufactured they get "special attention" so they will be "defect" free. Given this treatment, it is hardly surprising that the executives may not understand what it is like to own one of their cars and why their companies have lost market share for decades. Executives who earn millions of dollars a year and fly on corporate jets are rarely in touch with what it is like to work in their organization or buy their products.

Strategies and business plans in SMOs are likely to be successfully implemented only if the individuals who have to implement them know that they are listened to. Even if a brilliant CEO or senior leader can craft a successful strategy without input, the issue of how it is going to be implemented remains. Without individuals throughout the organization understanding what is in a strategy and agreeing that it is the right strategy, it's highly unlikely they will want to and be able to implement it. The following comment by Sam Palmisano, the CEO of IBM, captures the importance of people having a say: "There's no way to optimize IBM through organizational structure or by management dictate; you have to empower people."[6]

In an SMO the gap between leader and led should never be large. It is simply too important for leaders to gather information from others and receive feedback about their performance. Leaders need to be approachable. They need to be told when they do something wrong or have made a mistake, and they need to be able to hear it. Only if they are understood by the critical capital in the organization, which is the talent that works there, will they be able to create and lead an SMO.

Senior executives need to demonstrate visibly that they value employees. When cost-cutting is needed, they should explore alternatives before cutting staff. When it is necessary, they should be sure it is executed in a way that is just and fits their SMO employer brand. When leadership training is done, they should take part. When it is time for talent reviews, they should lead the process.

Jeff Immelt, GE's CEO, stated what CEOs need to do in GE's 2005 annual report: "Developing and motivating people is the most important part of my job. I spend one-third of my time on people. We invest $1 billion annually in training to make them better. . . . I spend most of my time on the top 600 leaders in the company. This is how you create a culture. These people all get selected and paid by me."[7]

Sergio Marchionne, the CEO of Fiat, makes the same point when he describes the most important thing he does as CEO: "My job as CEO is not to make business decisions—it's to push managers to be leaders."[8]

Some firings of CEOs suggest that corporate boards are recognizing that imperial CEOs may not be the best CEOs. Hank Greenberg, who has been described as the prototype "imperial CEO," was forced out at American International Group after three decades. Perhaps the most visible case was the firing of Bob Nardelli by Home Depot following his dreadful decision to have his board of directors not attend Home Depot's annual meeting!

In a speech at West Point in 2009, Jeff Immelt was particularly critical of business leaders like Greenberg and Nardelli: "I think we are at the end of a difficult generation of business leadership, and maybe leadership in general. Tough-mindedness—a good trait—was replaced by meanness and greed—both terrible traits. Rewards became perverted. The richest people made the most mistakes with the least accountability. In too many situations, leaders divided us instead of bringing us together."[9]

When Frank Blake became the new CEO of Home Depot, he recognized the importance of moving away from the imperial leadership style of his predecessor. In addition to taking a much lower salary he discontinued the catered executive luncheons that the company's top management team enjoyed under Bob Nardelli and "suggested" that the members of senior management eat in the cafeteria with the other employees. This act sent a clear message to the employees that he intended to be a different kind of leader.

Sergio Marchionne is now trying to change the leadership style of Chrysler. Just after Fiat took over Chrysler, he arrived at Chrysler's headquarters in Michigan and settled into an office there. Instead of taking up residence in the top floor of the executive office building where his predecessor had his offices, he chose a fourth floor office near the technical center so he would be close to the people who run the company.

Be a Good Leader and a Good Follower

Everyone in an SMO organization needs to be a good follower. This, of course, is also true in a CCO for everyone except the CEO, but the situation is different in SMOs. In SMOs, people need to be good followers and good leaders. At one point in time in SMOs, individuals will be followers of someone and at other times they will be leading them. This is the result of the use of project teams, collaborative work arrangements, and internal entrepreneurial ventures. For example, it is not unusual for an individual to be leading a venture that has a team member who is actually leading another venture the individual is part of. Hence the necessity to be both a good leader and follower.

------

*Everyone in an SMO organization needs to
be a good follower.*

In Cisco's "councils and boards" structure that we discussed in Chapter Six, a functional executive might be the leader of a segment council with all the responsibilities and accountabilities associated with developing and implementing a plan. At the same time, that executive may be a member of another council or board and be required to support the leadership of another executive.

It takes just as much strength and skill to be a good follower as it does to be a good leader. The skill sets are different, but are not necessarily in conflict. Individuals who do not need to always be in control and who have a high level of self-esteem can be both.

What Leaders Who Are Managers Should Do

We have set a very high bar in this chapter and the ones that preceded it for what managers should be like in SMOs in order for them to be effective. Here is an overview of what they should know and be able to do:

- *Have expertise in performance management.* They need to be effective coaches and committed to making it possible for people to perform effectively. Nothing they do in their job is more important than this. They need to own performance management and employee development as their number one priority.
- *Have expertise in human behavior and organization effectiveness.* They should make talent decisions with rigor equal to the decisions they make concerning financial resources and operations. In short, they need to have a decision science approach to their management of human capital.
- *Look to the future.* They need to help the organization and its members develop a sense of what the critical future challenges of the organization are likely to be and constantly encourage their organization to develop the kind of competencies and capabilities it needs to meet them.
- *Understand the vision, values, and identity of the organization.* Managers should be able to understand and articulate the links between values, identity, and the operation of the organization.
- *Create truth telling and open communication with individuals throughout the organization.* They need to minimize the social distance and maximize the communication between themselves and those who work for them.
- *Know how to "walk the talk."* Discrepancies between what managers say and what they do are all too obvious and very damaging. Managers must know how to walk their talk.
- *Balance the interests of multiple stakeholders.* Managers are constantly faced with decisions about what trade-offs to make and where to invest time and money. They need to make these decisions in ways that balance the interests of key stakeholders so that sustainable effectiveness is achieved.
- *Be a good follower.* Have the strength and wisdom to know when it is time to be an enthusiastic and competent follower.

What Leaders Who Are Not Managers Should Do

Here are some of the most important things leaders who are not managers should know and do:

- Recognize when leadership moments occur and act accordingly.
- Provide feedback to peers about their performance and how it can be improved.
- Gather and shape information about customers, performance problems, the community, and the business environment that are relevant to their organization's strategy.
- Exert influence without formal power. It is one thing for an individual to get things done when they can command and control people and resources; it is another when someone has to rely on his or her ability to influence others. They need to be able to persuade, convince, and sometimes create mutually beneficial "deals"!
- Be a good follower.

Create a Leadership Capability

The leadership SMOs require is not readily available in the marketplace. It is a different approach, and as a result the number of individuals who are ready to practice it is limited. But even if they were available, hiring them is not enough to create the kind of leadership capabilities an SMO needs. Effective leadership for an SMO requires the right leaders, but it also requires the right organization practices, policies, and culture. Without the whole package, SMOs will not be able to attract, retain, and develop the right leaders, nor will they be able to provide leaders with a setting in which they can be effective. With this point in mind let's look at the things SMOs need to do to develop a leadership capability that supports sustainable effectiveness.

SMO Leadership Principle 1: Establish a Sustainable Leadership Brand

A first step in developing a leadership capability is establishing a leadership brand (that is, a well-understood view of what being a leader means). Having a clear leadership brand can be a powerful factor in helping attract, retain, and motivate the right leaders and employees. A positive leadership brand that permeates the organization can also serve as a touchstone for all current employees, guiding them toward an organization's "true north" with respect to leadership behaviors and skills.

Every organization needs to develop its own leadership brand; no formula exists to indicate what is right. However, there are three essential characteristics we can identify that are critical to strengthening the leadership brand of an SMO and making it effective.

First, the leadership brand must reflect the organization's commitment to being sustainably effective. A leadership brand that does not honor the firm's identity as a sustainably effective organization can create cynicism because what the organization stands for is different from how people are led.

Particularly critical is how members of the organization are treated. There simply is no excuse for treating any employee poorly. Good financial results alone are insufficient. Those results must be achieved in the right way; that is, by trusting people and treating them with respect and dignity.

Second, it must commit leaders to communicating truthfully and openly with their employees about what is going on in the business. Truth telling is a critical feature of SMOs.[10] Managers quickly lose credibility when they give employees inaccurate or misleading information. Sometimes the best answer is, "I don't know"; at other times, it is letting employees know that conditions are worsening and that changes will need to be made. At no time is the best answer a misleading or wrong answer. "I cannot tell you" is the best answer when regulations or other factors mandate periods of nondisclosure.

Third, the leadership brand must apply across the entire organization and at all times; it should not involve what is often called "situational leadership." Some leadership gurus have suggested that the most effective managers consider each work situation and then decide how to behave. They argue that managers should take into account such things as the experience of employees, the time available to make a decision, and the type of work that is to be done. We agree that these should have some influence on how a manager behaves, but we believe that all too often situational leadership results in confusion and alienates people.

Employees don't want to be uncertain about how they will be treated, they want to be able to count on being involved in decisions and informed by their manager. There needs to be a set of givens—including honesty, integrity, providing business information, and helping people understand organizational strategies and decisions—that simply aren't optional.[11] They need to be the foundation of an SMO leadership brand and relevant in all settings and situations.

A brand is a promise, and in an SMO the leadership brand should contain promises about sustainable effectiveness, about truthfulness, and about transparency. These kinds of promises can and should be kept, even as some behaviors change due to the nature of the business situation. Like an organization's identity, its leadership brand must be stable, something that people can count on and trust. Only if it is will the organization develop, attract, and retain the right leaders and followers.

A brand is a promise, and in an SMO the leadership brand should contain promises about sustainable effectiveness, about truthfulness, and about transparency.

SMO Leadership Principle 2: Senior Management Must Support Building the Leadership Capability

It is one thing to argue that shared leadership needs to be an organizational capability in an SMO; it is another to actually make it one. In our experience, senior management support is clearly the building block on which the whole concept of shared leadership needs to rest.

Senior management support is critical because the people at the top need to be teachers as well as advocates of shared leadership. They should know how to provide leadership development experiences and to educate individuals throughout the organization about what it takes to be an effective leader. Nothing will kill a shared leadership culture faster than a senior management group that dismisses the leadership efforts of individuals below them and fails to support the development of leadership skills throughout the organization.

What does it mean for senior management to support leadership development throughout the organization? A wide variety of things. But above all else they need to be sure that the recruitment, selection, and retention processes of the organization put an emphasis on identifying individuals who are comfortable taking leadership roles, possess values consistent with sustainable effectiveness, and are good followers.

It is very difficult—and in fact may be impossible—to get managers throughout an organization to adhere to a leadership brand if its senior managers do not follow it and teach it to others. Both the development of the leadership brand and a consistent leadership style need to start at the very top. Top-level managers in particular need to be excellent communicators and educators who never miss an opportunity to teach everyone in the organization about the company's business and to have a dialogue with employees about how the company is doing. At the very minimum, senior managers must be able to articulate the organization's leadership brand in an "elevator speech."

Senior management also needs to put a major emphasis on leadership development throughout the organization. Admittedly, some different management behaviors are needed at different levels of the organization, but that doesn't mean individuals at all levels of an organization shouldn't be educated in how to influence others and how to provide leadership.

Finally, it's critical that senior executives recognize and reward effective leadership behavior whenever and wherever it occurs in their organization. They need to reward it through formal rewards, such as pay raises, bonuses, and promotions, but they also need to recognize it in informal ways. They need to give praise to the individuals who take on leadership roles and make a significant contribution to the sustainable performance of the organization.

SMO Leadership Principle 3: Develop Managerial and Leadership Skills

Effective leadership in SMOs requires the right approaches to development. We are often asked why there are so few people who are able to combine the managerial and leadership skills that are required to be an effective manager. Clearly there is no simple answer to this question. Despite the many articles and books that have been written on leadership, the reality is that many individuals don't have what it takes to be a successful manager in an SMO. In fact, it may partly be because there are so many articles and books written on leadership that many managers don't know what it takes!

Many of the articles and books on leadership ignore or give only brief consideration to managerial skills. Instead they focus on such leadership skills as inspiring others, giving praise, and storytelling. Further, when all is said and done, there is hardly a dramatic consensus in the leadership literature on what it takes to be a successful leader. The books vary greatly in the types of leadership styles they recommend and claim are successful. They range all the way from presenting highly simplistic views of what constitutes effective leadership (for example, *The One Minute Manager*) to very dense academic tomes that review the massive amount of empirical research on leadership.

While many managers have gone to business school, this does not necessarily mean they have leadership skills and managerial knowledge. All too often they learn more about finance and economics than they do about human behavior and organization design. Thus most organizations must create their own ways to obtain the skilled managers they need. One way is to hire them from the few academy companies (such as P&G, GE, and PepsiCo) that invest in developing managers. But this is an approach that has many limitations, including a small supply and the high cost of recruiting. What should SMOs do? Adopting a limited travel-light approach that combines internal development with very careful hiring from the right companies is usually the best approach.

Every SMO ought to have a clear, well-developed set of leadership competencies that it expects its managers to master. These ought to be more than just general phrases such as "be a good listener" and "educate people about the business." They ought to drill down to another level of specificity so that it is clear which behaviors are part of being a good listener and which parts of the business model should be taught and how they should be taught.

SMOs need to regularly assess whether their managers have the requisite leadership and managerial competencies. This can be done by gathering survey data from observers of managerial behaviors and by testing a manager's content knowledge of leadership behaviors. Fortunately, the growth of management assessment software packages makes it increasingly easy for organizations to gather information about the leadership behaviors of their managers. By using intranet-based systems, such as those at Goldman Sachs, IBM, and Capital One, or those sold by consulting firms, much of the paperwork and forms associated with competency appraisals can now be eliminated.

When an organization assesses someone in a management job, customers, subordinates, peers, bosses, and representatives of the broader stakeholder community should all be asked to offer their views of the manager's leadership performance. This breadth of feedback creates a far more useful appraisal of someone's leadership behaviors and skills than can be derived from a single boss's appraisal. All too often, managers develop the ability to manage upward and as a result get good performance reviews from their bosses, even though their ability to manage downward or laterally is poor.

Leadership development efforts need to start early in someone's career and continue as long as that person is part of the organization. If an organization wants to create a shared leadership capability, it must make development experiences available to a broad range of employees within the organization, not just a select few who have been chosen as candidates for senior management positions.

All members of an SMO need training so that they understand the business and the business strategy. Time after time, surveys of organizations show that many individuals do not understand the business of their organization and its strategy. Encouraging individuals who do not have this knowledge to help lead an organization is not just unwise—it's positively dangerous. There is a very high probability that they will lead the organization in the wrong direction and end up destroying the entire idea of shared leadership.

The research literature on leadership development is quite clear in showing that experience is the best developer of managers and leaders.[12] Development experiences need to involve a challenging task or job as well as conceptual information on how to be an effective leader and what the organization expects of its leaders. Classroom training is important in leadership development, but the right experiences are more powerful.

The research literature on leadership development is quite clear in showing that experience is the best developer of managers and leaders.

Emerging leaders learn the most from taking on challenging job assignments that force them to examine their capabilities and improve their leadership skills. SMOs should identify "crucible" jobs that provide good learning experiences for emerging leaders. For example, to learn about making trade-offs among the demands of customers, employees, and financial markets, emerging leaders should fill a crucible job that contains these performance accountabilities (for example, a general management job). Reflecting can be done with the help of a coach or through an educational experience that focuses on making trade-offs. Overall, the best leadership development efforts are those that combine classroom education, coaching, and strategically timed job changes.

There is one big mistake many companies make in their eagerness to give people a wide range of leadership experiences: they move them from job to job too quickly. This can create managers who lack a deep knowledge of the business. It can also reinforce a quick-fix mentality that leads to risky decisions and a failure to consider the long-term impact of actions.

In many pivotal positions, such as that of division manager, it often takes at least two years to see the impact of a person's managerial and leadership behaviors. The more senior the position, the longer this will be. Usually, senior managers have a good sense of what the right period of time is; they simply must have the discipline to follow that good sense rather than to rush someone's development.

SMO Leadership Principle 4: Commit to Transparency

SMOs should not shroud the features of their leadership development plans and programs in secrecy. Most CCOs keep secret information about their management development plans for individuals. As we already mentioned, most do not even tell individuals what their plans are for them. When we ask organizations why they keep information such as who is being developed secret we get a variety of answers. The most frequent one is a fear that if everyone knows who is on the "fast track" for leadership development, others will be jealous and may lose their motivation. Another common one is that they don't want to make an implied promise that they may not be able to fulfill.

Secrecy may fit well in a world of paternalistic management and top-down moves. But it doesn't make sense in a world in which the need for leadership behaviors is changing, leadership performance is regularly assessed, and shared leadership is the predominant style.

A major advantage of transparency is that it allows individuals to self-manage their careers. As we pointed out earlier, this is an important part of the travel-light employment contract. It goes along with the idea that rapidly changing organizations often can't do a good job of managing individuals' careers and individuals shouldn't count on them doing it.

To take on the responsibility for managing their careers, individuals need to know what opportunities exist and how to take advantage of those opportunities. Job openings should be visible to all candidates, and information should be available about the learning opportunities the jobs offer and, of course, what skills and competencies they require.

Many organizations rate their managers on the level of management that they think he or she is capable of reaching. A key question is whether individuals should be aware of the results of this assessment. In most organizations this like other development information is kept secret. Although doing so may be a bit uncomfortable at times, we think that SMOs should provide just this kind of information to individuals. Having the information can allow them to challenge the perception that others have of them and stimulate a positive dialogue that can lead to a change in either the organization's assessment or the individual's self-assessment.

Admittedly, at times it may lead to the departure of the individual from the organization, but that is not necessarily a bad thing.

Transparent career development systems allow employees to reasonably assess their future in the organization and make informed decisions about how they shape their careers. They can place their bets on whether the situation will change and determine what new skills they will need to change it. It also can help them make a realistic assessment of how likely the organization is to meet their needs.

Travel-light SMOs are not responsible for the careers of their employees and don't guarantee them job security; therefore the ability to access career information is a particularly important feature of their approach to leadership development. Access to it supports development programs that allow most individuals to develop their leadership skills. It also is highly consistent with the model of making every employee a leader, if not a manager.

If leaders can't adapt their managerial and leadership behaviors to fit an SMO's changing strategy and business environments, they clearly will be leaders for only one season. This may not be a severe limitation on the careers of managers whose organizations encounter only one season, but for managers in SMOs, there are likely to be many seasons. They need to be warned that if there is a change of seasons, they may no longer be effective and, therefore, no longer needed by the organization. In other words, they, like other employees, need to know that their continued employment is contingent upon the fit between their skills and the organization's strategy.

Finally, when a major change in an organization is needed, transparency can be a tremendous aid to change management. It can help identify the individuals within the organization who are the best candidates to fill new positions, and it can help individuals sense how they need to change in order to fit the changes that are occurring. If the organization is moving away from the kind of things that they want to do or can do, then transparency can send them an early warning that they need to look elsewhere. Clearly, self-managed departures are much better than organization-mandated departures, for both the individual and the organization.

Conclusion

Sustainable effectiveness requires a rethinking and repositioning of leading, managing, and following. SMOs need to have leaders at all levels and followers at all levels. Creating an SMO that has this type of leadership capability requires a number of organization practices that are not found in CCOs or HIOs. The practices begin with SMOs having a leadership brand that includes truth telling and supporting sustainable effectiveness as well as being a good follower. The most important difference is the large amount of support SMOs need to provide for leadership development. Because effective leadership is such a key determinant of sustainable effectiveness, it must be a top priority. Without it, sustainable effectiveness cannot be achieved.

Assessment Questions

1. What is your leadership brand?

   a. Our reputation among executive search firms and our competitors is that we are a place that develops good leaders.

   b. It is a respected company although it's not known as an "academy company" for leaders.

   c. Having my company's name on my resume is a negative when it comes to getting a management job elsewhere.

   Here is what the answers imply:

   If the leadership brand is not strong, why not? Is it because the organization's ability to attract and develop leaders is poor? If the ability to attract and develop leaders is poor, sustainable effectiveness cannot be achieved.

2. How does the organization react to shared leadership?

   a. The hierarchical order is quite clear, and people not knowing their place is frowned on.

   b. Leaders are very open to input, but leadership roles need to be formally assigned before an individual will take the lead on something.

c. People are used to stepping forward to take the lead on an issue on the basis of their expertise, not their position; others are comfortable being good followers if that is what is required.

Here is what the answers imply:

a. The British Empire did quite well insisting that people know their place, but it is a recipe for poor performance in today's rapidly changing world.

b. Leaders who listen well are a positive, but SMOs need the kind of dynamic flexibility an organization has when it embraces shared leadership.

c. A organization that is comfortable letting people take the lead when their expertise makes them the natural leader for a project is better able to seize temporary competitive advantages.

CHAPTER TWELVE

Transforming to Sustainable Management

The need for a management reset is compelling. Technology, globalization, and workforce changes are pushing for faster, more agile organizations. At the same time, social and ecological forces that once got honorable mention in business strategy discussions are today full-fledged stakeholders demanding attention. Both trends are making profits harder to come by and together are demanding that organizations change the way they think about everything from goals and growth to cultural impact and carbon footprints. The nature and strength of these changes led us to argue for a management reset. As they are currently conceived and operationalized, CCOs and HIOs lack the wherewithal to address both change and multiple stakeholder demands.

The bold focus of this book is on describing a new approach to management. Sustainable management is designed around agility and multiple stakeholders in an attempt to generate economic performance, positive social benefits, and ecological health. It calls for new ways of creating value, organizing, treating people, and leading them. In earlier chapters, we provided ideas on and examples of how an SMO should be designed and operated. Now it is time to address the final critical issue: "How can an organization become an SMO?"

A number of organizations have shown that it is possible to practice sustainable management. Patagonia, The Body Shop, and Ben & Jerry's are good examples of companies that were built from the ground up using the principles we argue lead to sustainable effectiveness. Becoming an SMO undoubtedly is easier for a startup than it is for a successful, or for that matter unsuccessful, HIO or CCO. Startups do not have to deal with entrenched habits, practices, and assumptions. Although becoming an SMO is never easy because of the need to find people who can operate in this mode and adopt many "atypical" practices, it is much easier to do it from scratch than to convert an existing organization to an SMO.

Unilever, Gap Inc., GE, PepsiCo, Cisco Systems, and Procter & Gamble have made (or are making) the transformation to sustainable management. They are challenging long-held assumptions and making important complex changes in their strategies and organization designs. Although there is much we can learn from organizations that are built from their beginnings to be sustainable, this chapter is focused on transforming existing organizations to sustainable ones. Why? Because that is where the challenge is greatest and where the biggest market is. Let's begin by looking at the case of Interface Flooring Systems, which made a transformation to sustainable management. Its experience provides both hope and caution.

The Interface Transformation

Interface Flooring Systems was founded in 1973 by Ray Anderson as a joint venture with Britain's Carpets International to make carpet tiles. Carpet tiles, an alternative to long rolls of carpet, can be replaced piece by piece rather than all at once. Between 1978 and 1983, revenues grew from $11 million to $80 million as the result of the company's close relationships with commercial customers. Interface went public in 1983, and through 2008 grew revenues at an average annual rate of 11.5 percent.

Interface's transformation to sustainable management began in 1994 when Anderson received a memo from a research division task force. The group had been formed in response to questions from customers, architects, and interior designers about what Interface was doing to help the environment. The task force's review of operations was disappointing; the organization wasn't doing much to be environmentally friendly. The memo requested that Anderson speak to the task force on Interface's environmental vision, and he sweated over what he would say since there was no policy other than "comply, comply, comply." At the same time, Anderson received Paul Hawkin's book, *The Ecology of Commerce*.[1] The book's message confronted his sense of responsibility and changed his attitudes about what a business should achieve.

In his speech to the task force, he declared that Interface would become a company that "could grow and prosper without doing harm to the earth." He later said that he didn't want his legacy to be that he dug up the earth, turned petroleum and other materials into polluting products, and dumped them in landfills. At the time, Interface was directly and indirectly involved in an industry that extracted and processed 1.2 billion pounds of material from the earth in order to produce $802 billion of products. Of the 1.2 billion pounds, 800 million pounds was petroleum-based, and two-thirds of the 800 million pounds was burned to convert the remaining third into product. As an industry, carpeting firms were depositing 4.5 billion pounds of material into landfills that would degrade over 20,000 years.

———

[Anderson] later said that he didn't want his legacy to be that he dug up the earth, turned petroleum and other materials into polluting products, and dumped them in landfills.

———

In January 1995, Interface held a "green supply chain" conference with its suppliers to discuss its goals and to gain commitments from its business partners. The eventual sustainability strategy outlined seven goals, including eliminate waste (any measurable input that did not create value); limit toxic emissions from plants; switch to renewable sources of energy; "close the loop," which meant using any waste or discarded carpet as inputs to new products; achieve resource-efficient transportation; and educate customers, suppliers, and even competitors. The seventh goal, to redesign commerce, eventually manifested as the "evergreen service agreement" (ESA). A radical innovation, the ESA attempted to shift Interface's business model from "selling carpet" to "renting flooring systems."

In 1996, Interface held the first "Eco Dream Team" conference of outside environmental experts and organization members to explore the strategy and organizational requirements necessary to achieve its sustainability goals. The conference recommendations led to changes in its products, supply chain, and operations. Implementing the changes required the organization to address a variety of issues.

First, as the new strategy was communicated, organization members expressed a variety of concerns, including what sustainability meant and how the organization was going to change. The depth of misunderstanding was particularly troublesome. After hearing about the sustainability goal, one employee asked, "How many sheep are we planning to have, and where are they going to graze?" In addition, few people in the organization understood how ecologically unfriendly the existing operations were. As a result, Interface made a large commitment to employee training about the environment and operations that led to its being named one of the "Best 100 Companies to Work For" by *Fortune* magazine in 1997.

Second, figuring out *where* to eliminate waste and toxicity or use clean technology was a straightforward process of total quality management that was implemented under the acronym QUEST (quality utilizing employee suggestions and teamwork). However, figuring out *how* to do these things was a giant technical problem. The organization's research group and its engineers had to redesign (or reinvent) almost every process and product, including how to recycle nylon and how to make carpet using less petroleum.

Third, creating the evergreen services agreement required the organization to develop a leasing contract that would make financial sense in the context of existing rules and regulations. The idea of moving funds from capital expense (sale of carpet) to operating expense (lease of carpet) was an easy sell, but getting a lease agreement written that met current tax and accounting standards was a lot more difficult. In particular, the price seemed very high to customers. Few customers actually knew how much they were spending on flooring because the costs of carpet purchase, maintenance, and other services were "hidden" in different accounts.

By 2000, a variety of market and economy changes, including the Y2K threat, the dot.com bust, and other changes that reduced customer budgets, had hurt the industry. In January 2001, Interface held a leaders conference to address a 30 percent workforce reduction and other organization changes in response to the business decline. At the conference, managers affirmed the commitment to sustainability, saying that it was part of the organization's DNA.

In retrospect, Interface's record of sustainable effectiveness is both laudable and spotty. Economically, its stock price and profitability have varied considerably since the transformation, although its annual growth rate is impressive. Socially, it has not been a stable employer, meeting most economic challenges with layoffs. Further, it has not shown evidence of a broader social agenda unless one takes the view that its tremendous accomplishments in environmental matters are social benefits in their own right—a not unreasonable perspective. The highs and lows of its performance during and after the transformation testify to the difficulties of the transformation to an SMO and of trying to achieve all three sustainable effectiveness objectives. The performance variation also makes the point that having a strong sustainability program is not all that is needed to create a sustainably effective organization.

The Interface case is often told with the major focus on Ray Anderson's transformation and leadership. During the transformation, Anderson came to personify the change. He became a spokesperson for sustainability, wrote a book on Interface's journey, and brought a lot of attention to Interface. To be sure, that's a key part of Interface's change, but we think that there is more to this case. We believe it is the organizational changes that did and did not occur that best explain Interface's record of sustainable effectiveness.

There are dilemmas that have to be faced, and there are transition issues that have to be managed in a transformation to sustainable management. We will begin examining them by exploring the challenges and dilemmas associated with the transition to sustainable management. Becoming an SMO requires existing organizations to address the nonsustainable assumptions embedded in their existing management approach before they can begin implementing a transformation. Next, we will explore the process of transformation itself and how an organization can think about orchestrating an SMO implementation.

Dilemmas Associated with Being an SMO

Making the transformation to sustainable management is an enormous task. It requires patience, consistency, stubbornness, resources, knowledge, and skills. Before we actually talk about introducing the changes that are needed, we have to lay the foundation for our discussion by considering the important dilemmas that must be faced.[2] Becoming an SMO is as much about changing mind-sets as it is about changing structures and practices. The Interface case—and our experience with other organizations—suggests three issues that organizations need to address and clarify before the transformation begins. These issues concern strategy, knowledge, and organizational capabilities.

Strategy Dilemmas

Any transformation to an SMO requires a redefinition of the relationship between the organization and its business environment. Understanding and defining this relationship sets the all-important context for organizing, treating people well, and leading them. It requires confronting the organization's assumptions about the nature of value creation, setting appropriate target metrics, and reconciling its strategic intent.

The Nature of Value Creation

The first decision must be agreement by the board and by the top management team regarding the centrality, meaning, and implications of value creation and sustainable effectiveness. CCOs and HIOs are designed to serve a primary stakeholder—owners—and to achieve a primary objective—maximizing shareholder return. SMOs are designed to jointly optimize the three sustainable effectiveness objectives. Most CCOs and HIOs point to values, beliefs, strategies, and goals that support social and environmental ends, but these do not have equal standing with economic objectives, and most of their actions make this clear. In the language of *Good to Great,* this is a cold hard reality that needs to be faced as a part of the initial step in the transformation to sustainable management.[3]

Changing the definition of value creation requires explicit, public support by the board as well as concrete definitive actions and decisions in support of sustainable effectiveness. The first step is to get the board to agree that sustainable effectiveness involves creating value in three areas, not just one. Given the condition of most boards and the difficulties associated with changing them, the best intended transformations to sustainable management may end here because the board is not supportive. Fortunately, more and more boards, such as Northrop Grumman's, are actually leading the change.

Through this lens, Interface did an incomplete job of establishing a strategic commitment to sustainable effectiveness. Although its managers did a fantastic job of adding ecological goals to their value creation definition, they were not explicit about social goals. Given Ray Anderson's percentage of ownership in the corporation, we can safely assume he had a big role in convincing the board and other members of the top management team to come along. Moreover, there is plenty of evidence—in the story of Ray's conversion experience and subsequent events— that Interface was going to broaden its goals. However, the goals broadened mostly along ecological dimensions, not social.

Setting Appropriate Target Metrics

Perhaps the first real test of the board's and the top management team's commitment to sustainable management is the setting of goals against the dimensions of sustainable effectiveness. How equal are the three Ps of people, planet, and profit? In essence, the board and executives must develop perspectives and philosophies about social and environmental concerns that are integrated with economic objectives. A tough balancing act is needed because placing too much emphasis on any one of them at the wrong time can lead to failure. An organization that makes too strong an investment in social sustainability at a time when revenues are down may face serious financial problems. Although some moves can help performance on all three, organizations often don't have this luxury and trade-offs must be made.

As described in Chapter Three, the really difficult conversation often is about growth. Organizations must distinguish between aggressive growth to achieve a competitive advantage and aggressive growth that is associated with performance levels that cannot be sustained and may be harmful.

Perhaps the first real test of the board's and the top management team's commitment to sustainable management is the setting of goals against the dimensions of sustainable effectiveness. How equal are the three Ps of people, planet, and profit?

Align Technologies is the maker of Invisalign orthodontics. Using a series of customized mouthpieces that isolate and rotate teeth, Invisalign achieves the same results as metallic braces without wires. The technology has a smaller carbon footprint, is less expensive, and involves less discomfort for the patient, but challenges the existing skill sets and status of orthodontists. For Align Technologies to be successful, it must move aggressively to establish its position and technology. This is an appropriate situation in which to have an aggressive growth strategy. But Align Technologies must be careful to ensure that a strategic intent that calls for aggressive growth to establish its technology does not become its identity. Expecting the organization to grow at the same rates after it has established its position in the market is not a recipe for sustainable performance, as we saw in the case of Starbucks.

Because they set reasonable growth expectations, the economic targets of an SMO are likely to be lower and less aggressive than those of many organizations today. As a result, when it comes to profitability and financial performance, SMOs may never be the best performers. At any point in time there are likely to be CCOs and HIOs that outperform an SMO. It would be surprising, however, if the same CCO or HIO consistently outperform an SMO. SMOs should consistently perform better than the average organization in their industries. This is much more likely to be sustainable than being the highest performer, which may require commitments and investments that generate short-term results at the expense of longer-term returns.

The transformation to an SMO also requires an organization to be clear about how its history of pursuing profit clouds its thinking on social and cultural issues. McDonald's Corporation, like many other quick-service food companies, saw great growth opportunities in China. McDonald executives noted the growing presence of cars in Beijing and figured opening drive-thru restaurants would be a good idea.

McDonald's found that the drive-thru concept was foreign to the Chinese. If someone actually found the drive-thru lane, they didn't know what to do at the ordering station, didn't know they had to drive up to the next window to pay, and didn't know they needed to drive to the next window to pick up their food. After they picked up their food, they usually drove to a parking space, got out of the car, and went into the restaurant to have their meal.

In response, McDonald's decided to stick to its profitable U.S. drive-thru approach but to change the physical structure of the restaurant and drive-thru lane. The company made it easier for people to find the drive-thru lane and trained the workers to point the car to the next window (including holding the bag of food out of the last window to encourage the drivers to move forward to get their meal!).

Organizations without a clear perspective on social issues are vulnerable to the profit maximization motive. The Chinese do not need to learn to use a drive-thru to be a part of the developed world. In the pursuit of maximizing shareholder returns, McDonald's ended up homogenizing cultures, not celebrating diversity. The growth of drive-thru revenues is not an indicator of success, especially since there were no drive-thru revenues when this all started.

Finally, organizations must have a perspective on ecological health. In the pursuit of profit maximization and economic growth, many manufacturing organizations have tried to lower costs by placing activities in geographic areas with the lowest wage costs. Subsidized by cheap oil prices, large complex supply chains have emerged with tremendous ecological costs. By some estimates, the ocean transportation portion alone of the supply chain between Asia and the United States accounts for between

74 and 86 percent of the carbon pumped into the atmosphere by the supply chain. What if the cost of that carbon and the price of oil was factored into the total cost of the products? Would such a supply chain make sense?

The Interface case highlights the environmental issue. Making, installing, and discarding carpet at great environmental costs was not what Anderson wanted for his legacy. As a result, he had a clear philosophy concerning ecological issues, and the organization worked hard to develop metrics and set clear goals for waste, toxicity, and efficiency. But he also believed that his organization could "grow and prosper without doing harm to the earth." The organization's unsteady performance suggests that the incompatibility of growth and prosperity with ecological health appears to be a dilemma that was not resolved.

In general, the best outcomes for organizations that want to become sustainably effective are a new set of integrated goals. The typical goal-setting process in large, complex organizations involves reconciling inputs from products, functions, and geographies to arrive at economic objectives that everyone can support. The SMO must do this *and* reconcile economic, social, and ecological objectives with additional constituencies.

Figuring out the metrics puzzle of sustainability has occupied many organizations, and we suspect this is an artifact of the CCO mentality. There is a strong belief that being able to measure operations and results is a sign of good management. However, if that perspective is taken to the point of saying "if we cannot measure it, then we can't know if we are improving," it can be a great way to distract attention from the real issue and avoid the pursuit of social and ecological goals. That said, if figuring out how to measure social and ecological outcomes of organizational activity helps move things forward, then the work should be done if only to remove one of the barriers to change.

Reconciling Strategic Intent

With goals established around sustainable effectiveness, the final step in addressing the strategy dilemma is to reconcile the organization's current strategic intent with the new definition of value creation. Recall that strategic intent consists of momentary resource allocations to achieve a particular strategic breadth, aggressiveness, and differentiation. How each of these dimensions supports sustainable effectiveness must be understood.

In the Interface case, the organization was fortunate to have a relatively narrow breadth. Its focus on the commercial segment of the market, on carpet tiles, and on one primary technology made it easy to see how and where its intent affected sustainability. Organizations with broader intents will find assessing their impact much more difficult.

With respect to Interface's aggressiveness, its history, expectation, and stated goals of growth speak to an identity tied to growth. This may have been an important contribution to its long-run struggle to maintain economic and social viability. Instead of more reasonable profit and growth expectations, each downturn became a crisis. To maintain profitability, layoffs occurred and damaged its social sustainability. After 1997, it never again achieved a position on the "Best Places to Work" list.

Finally, Interface's differentiation advantage—its carpet tiles could be easily replaced, saving the customer significant dollars—conferred an ecological advantage for the organization before it even began the sustainability effort. The company's ability to increase this advantage by radically redesigning the product with an ecological lens was facilitated. Thus, Interface's existing strategic intent made it easier to pursue an ecologically oriented transformation.

In general, the outcome of reconciling the strategic intent is a description of how much change in the levels and scope of breadth, aggressiveness, and differentiation will be necessary to support sustainable effectiveness. This too must be done with respect to the philosophies developed in the goal-setting facet of this dilemma. Big changes in breadth, aggressiveness, and differentiation warrant careful study so that the capabilities dilemma discussion can be more productive.

The Knowledge and Awareness Dilemma

Saying you support sustainable effectiveness and redefining your strategy is one thing, but knowing what it takes from an organizational perspective, understanding what it takes from a personal perspective, and doing what it takes from a behavioral perspective are entirely different matters. Almost any move to being an SMO is going to involve a large educational effort. Given the cultural, organizational, social, and psychological barriers to adopting a sustainable approach to management, the educational work should not be judgmental.[4] It is important to bring people along and inspire them, not alienate them. The organization as a whole must become "collectively smart" about sustainable effectiveness.

The educational effort must include material and exercises in systems thinking that introduce and demonstrate how everything is interdependent and connected. The ability to make multi-stakeholder decisions depends on this perspective. The educational effort must also include information about the integrated goals and definition of value creation, the organization's current social activities and environmental footprint, and how changing these may have performance implications in the short run. Finally, any anticipated organizational changes need to be outlined, including how rewards, jobs, and decision-making processes will change, in an effort to create the context for people to do "good" and "effective" work.

An educational effort that focuses on sustainable management will have two important consequences. First, there is likely to be a general increase in anxiety. People are going to want more information than there is available about their jobs and the future of the organization. It will be easy for people to say, "There's something they aren't telling us." Although organizations are often surprised by the lack of resistance to the implementation of sustainability initiatives, managers should listen carefully to questions and concerns that come up. The information provided can be very helpful in designing change processes to accelerate the transformation.

Second, it is inevitable that some people will embrace sustainable management and some will not. Some proportion of the existing workforce will not have the skills and knowledge that are required for them to perform effectively in an SMO and some will. The organization needs to be clear how it will deal with the workforce changes that are required.

For example, HIOs have an employment stability commitment, as do some CCOs, particularly when they are unionized and value tenure. Any changes in employment stability are likely to be seen as an important signal in the shift to sustainability, but any decreases in stability will probably be viewed as a violation of the long-term contract between employees and the organization. The organization could find itself accused of being a poor people organization and not honoring its commitment to social justice.

In general, an important early step in the transition should be the development of a workforce with the skills and knowledge needed to support sustainable effectiveness. People who do not support a triple-bottom-line value set need to be encouraged to leave, and those that remain need to be trained to handle multi-stakeholder decision making. A shift in talent is symbolically and practically important. Symbolically, it sends a clear signal about the centrality of sustainable effectiveness to the future identity of the organization. Practically, future changes will be easier and faster to implement with a workforce that is aligned with the new direction.

Interface did a good job educating its workforce. Part of the change was introduced by its business partners through the research organization, and so there were both internal and external change drivers. Not to be lost is how this process reflects the functioning of an external focus and a maximum surface area structure. Interface was "listening" to its marketplace. Some parts of the organization did show some resistance as Anderson communicated the new strategy.

The feedback about his message provided Anderson and his team with valuable information about what needed to be clarified and changed. They engaged in important training efforts and continued to leverage external pushes for change through stakeholder conferences. In looking back on this part of the change, Anderson said, "Nobody had written the book. There was no how-to book in existence—we were writing it as we went."[5] Given that all organizations are different in some ways, this is likely to be a common feeling among managers and employees during the transformation to sustainable management.

The Capabilities Dilemma

The final dilemma in becoming an SMO is recognizing which existing organization capabilities will and won't support sustainable effectiveness and deciding on the capabilities that need to be developed. Being an SMO requires a set of organizational capabilities that are not present in CCOs and HIOs.

Most organizations will not have enough resources to fund the development of all the capabilities needed, and thus choices have to be made. These choices are important symbolic decisions that will be watched carefully by employees, owners, communities, and NGOs. Understanding the capabilities that need to be developed is one of the key challenges in the transformation to sustainable effectiveness.

Determining which capabilities are needed begins with an understanding of the existing management style and its strengths. Organizations that want to become SMOs need to understand where they are coming from. If an organization is a CCO, the activities and new capabilities needed to become an SMO are different from those needed if it is an HIO. For example, CCOs have reliable operating processes but need to develop a more flexible talent management capability. HIOs have strong employee involvement capabilities but often need to develop more robust strategizing processes, in particular, the ability to look into the future. Both types of organizations need to develop a multi-stakeholder collaboration capability and completely overhaul their management systems with an eye toward social and environmental sustainability.

The multi-stakeholder collaboration capability is the most complex capability to be developed, and it requires changes in both the internal organization and its external alliances and partnerships. At the core of this capability is a revamped decision-making process that considers these multiple perspectives. Fully developed SMOs pursue people, planet, and profit objectives simultaneously; they are able to integrate activities to achieve all three goals. This demands a new set of skills and knowledge in the workplace and a new leadership style.

The building of a multi-stakeholder capability may have to be approached sequentially. Decision making initially may need to acknowledge all three inputs to become aware of the interdependencies and trade-offs that exist, even though economic objectives may remain preeminent. Subsequently, and perhaps after conversations with financial analysts and other stakeholders, decision making can increase the weighting of social and ecological criteria. By sequencing and phasing the priorities in this way, an organization can learn how to integrate them.

Managing the Transformation Process

Managing the transformation to an SMO is a lot like managing many other organization changes. The organization's current configuration of strategy and design features needs to be changed. To become an SMO requires a series of orchestrated changes that lead to a new configuration. But that doesn't mean the process is identical to other changes. The biggest difference is that the transformation to sustainable management requires the development of a new identity.

We have stressed that effective SMOs have an integrated system of practices, policies, and orientations that align to a change-friendly and sustainability-oriented identity. Becoming an SMO likely requires changes in all the areas we have discussed in this book. And just to be clear, we will say it one more time: creating an SMO is not the same as installing a "sustainability program." Creating a recycling program, announcing a policy of double-sided printing, turning lights off, and subsidizing public transportation use are good sustainability activities that can be run as add-ons. They typically do not require multiple management changes or a new identity. HIOs can do them, as can CCOs. Creating an SMO is a matter of resetting how an organization is managed. This makes change particularly difficult because it raises the classic issues of, "Where do we start?" "What's the right sequence of changes?" and "How fast do we have to move?" Before we dive into the details of the change process, let's very briefly look at our answers to these questions.

With respect to where to start, our recommendation is to begin with the acknowledgment that all of the implementation and transformation work needs to be directed toward changing the organization's identity. In particular, it should involve creating an identity that will support both agility and sustainable effectiveness. We have already suggested that the place to start is with choices and commitments regarding three dilemmas. We believe that more than any single organizational change, the organization's mind-sets and definitions of sustainable effectiveness must be addressed before starting. They are the keys to sustaining the transformation, and are central to the ongoing adaptation of the organization.

With respect to the sequence of change, we think the first feature to address is the work system, followed by performance management, structure, and future-focused processes. We choose the work system as the first design feature to address because it represents the most highly leveraged intervention. Work is the primary driver of the organization's carbon footprint; it directly affects a central social issue—the workforce—and is most connected to the creation of economic value.

We think the first feature to address is the work system. . . . It is the primary driver of the organization's carbon footprint; it directly affects a central social issue . . . and is most connected to the creation of economic value.

Finally, with respect to how fast to move, we recommend very fast and suggest that the economic opportunity (not to mention the other benefits) is truly great for early movers. With a change of this magnitude, there is a real risk that change will be so slow that it will never occur and that the commitment to becoming an SMO will waiver. Later we will suggest using several leadership behaviors and organizational practices that have a proven ability to accelerate change.

The Identity Journey

The transformation from a CCO or HIO to an SMO requires a major identity change. It is a big deal, a "re-creation" of the organization's management logic to achieve sustainable effectiveness. This is why we refer to it as a transformation rather than as a transition.

Creating a change-friendly and sustainability-oriented identity is the result or outcome of a change process and the measure of its effectiveness. Organizations cannot change their identities directly. They develop a new identity when they are successful in applying new strategies and organization principles to achieving sustainable effectiveness. Identity tends to be more of a lag variable than a lead variable in change.

The Interface case is a great example of the change in identity that all CCOs and HIOs have to go through. First, identity flows from and is influenced by culture. Initially, neither Interface nor its leaders operated according to values aligned with sustainable effectiveness. While it might be enticing to see Interface's culture change as "CEO-led," the memo Anderson received was from someone below him in the organization and was initiated by stakeholders who wanted to know what Interface was doing in "green" areas. The organization's subsequent efforts—supported by Anderson but created and implemented by a variety of others in the organization over several years—resulted in its adoption of sustainability as a way of life. When the 2001 cost-cutting initiatives spared sustainability, it was because it had become part of Interface's DNA.

Identity also influences and is influenced by image, brand, and reputation. The two early conferences to address sustainability issues, Anderson's speeches, and the media attention given to Interface worked to support the new identity. When pressure arose to cut sustainability as a costly process, it could not. Sustainability had become a part of who the Interface employees thought they were and how everybody else saw them.

This is what we mean when we say an SMO is "identity-driven." It was what Interface was that led to the decision to keep sustainability. But an organization has to get the "right" identity first, and that's no small feat. To begin, the organization needs to know its current identity. The steps in that process were laid out in Chapter Three. They include determining if the firm is successful because it was historically low cost or it was specialized; customizing that label given the firm's history, culture, and industry; and examining whether or not that same orientation explains the way the firm approaches social and ecological outcomes.

For CCOs and HIOs, the key output of this identity discovery process is a list of the organization's values-in-use and the elements of the brand promise and reputation that are agility- and sustainability-friendly. In general, it is best to leverage these strengths as opposed to trying to "fix" the value and reputational elements that are not aligned with sustainable effectiveness. As the organization begins to define specific organization changes, these values should be used to justify and defend the reason for implementation. Because part of Interface's success was built on values associated with serving the customer and keeping its costs down, selling a new carpet tile with better environmental features was an additional customer benefit. But as with any large-scale change, success requires systematic adjustments in the organization's strategies, structures, and processes.

The logical next step is for the organization to specify a desired future design configuration. The future vision of the organization may not resemble what actually gets implemented, but it is still useful to provide organization members, executives, and external stakeholders with a comprehensive picture of where the organization is headed several years out.

The ingredients of this desired future state can be found in the practices and features described in Chapters Three through Eleven. The future state must also reflect the general principles of an SMO and the desired philosophical orientation that is developed while resolving the three dilemmas we began the chapter with. Thinking about these issues can provide the organization with clues about the general approach to change that should be adopted. For example, SMOs are inclusive of multiple stakeholders, transparent, and directed by shared leadership.

How soon can the change process involve multiple stakeholders and how involved can they be? How quickly can information about goals, intentions, and operations be shared with internal organizational members and external stakeholders? How quickly can the change process symbolically and practically reflect this new way of leading? Although a variety of sequences to closing the gap between what is and what needs to be are possible, we think the following sequence makes the most sense.

The Sequence of Change

Having set the general direction of change in support of shifting the organization's identity, the next logical question is, "What is the right sequence?" Given the comprehensiveness of a transformation to create a new identity and in the context of the organization's "ideal state," we think the most effective change process begins by changing the way work gets done. It needs to be complemented by shifts in performance management, structure, and future-focused processes concerning talent and strategy.

Lead with the Work System

Developing a sustainable work system makes sense as a place to start.[6] Changing the way work gets done—so that economic value is added in more socially and environmentally acceptable ways—gets the internal house in order before sustainability goals are proclaimed to the marketplace. In organizations today, given the increasing strength of social and environmental stakeholders, there is a lot of pressure to "do something." Too many organizations have chosen to develop marketing campaigns that proclaim an organization's support of green issues and social concerns without thinking through the implications and without making any changes in how they operate.

The sequencing of initiatives proposed here ensures that the organization's future aspirations are not betrayed by its past and current behaviors. If intentions of sustainable effectiveness are announced too early and with too much fanfare, a great deal of damage to an organization's reputation can occur as a result of marketing greenwash that isn't backed up by behavior. When the organization's hypocrisy is exposed, the ability to change its identity will be set back, perhaps permanently, and it will take a long time to build trust in future corporate sustainability promises.

One very effective early intervention is to hold a series of large-group interventions or decision accelerators (DAs). Just because an organization agrees to redefine value creation, set integrated goals, and explore its strategic intent does not mean that the strategy is set. There is important work to be done in terms of clarifying and establishing those goals with key stakeholders, exploring the implications of strategic intent on capabilities and resources, and refining organization designs. The DA is perfect for this. It has the secondary benefit of initiating future-focused processes, changing the culture by allowing organization members to interact with the business environment, and teaching multi-stakeholder decision-making skills.

The first DA should be concerned with fleshing out the strategies and the organization's future state in collaboration with its stakeholders. The focus should be on how to work together and on the vision, purpose, and goals of the organization. It should be done in a way that gains the support of the stakeholders. It can help teach people to be systemic thinkers and to make decisions when there are multiple constraints and opportunities.

Interface successfully used large-group-intervention-like thinking in its transformation. Soon after Anderson announced the goal of making the organization sustainable, he held a supply chain conference with its stakeholders to discuss the sustainability goals Interface was pursuing. Shortly after that, Interface held its Eco-Dream Team conference to get input from sustainability experts on how to move the organization in a sustainability direction.

The two conferences gave organization members the chance to interact with key stakeholders and hear how their goals aligned with and differed from Interface's. Such awareness is important in thinking about how to make decisions in a multi-stakeholder world. It also allows members to discuss operational issues in the context of the new goals and a new strategy, and builds commitment and momentum for organization change.

In designing the first set of DAs, the board and the executive team need to work closely with internal or external consultants well versed in the large-group-intervention process. A close working relationship is needed to help transfer the skills and knowledge associated with this new way of working to the managers' repertoire.

The initial set of DAs is important not only because of the results and commitments they produce, but as an opportunity to practice and learn new ways of leading and deciding. The DAs should teach organization members and stakeholders how to think about and do innovative work and how to make multi-stakeholder decisions. The outputs of the DAs should be used to define the new workplace and the desired future state of the organization. Where in the organization are reliability, efficiency, and process innovation needed? Where are flexibility and product innovation needed?

Where reliability is needed, HIO practices should be implemented. Where innovation is needed, work that is based on activities not jobs, dominated by shared goals, performed by multiple-stakeholder teams, temporary and iterative, and supported by the physical space should be implemented. Obviously the best place to apply the DA learnings is the core work of the organization.

In a manufacturing firm it is best to use the DA methodology to look at operations, supply and distribution chains, and new product development processes. How can they be modified to involve more employees and stakeholders, lower the organization's carbon footprint throughout a product's life cycle, and support reasonable economic returns? Where can carbon emissions be removed and lowered, and what practices can be put in place to support cultural diversity, employee well-being, and broader social concerns? The results of the DAs should be implemented as soon as possible. The changes and their implementations represent powerful and visible steps in creating alignment with the new definition of value creation and the revised strategic intent. They show that change is possible and that sustainable effectiveness will be the future of the organization.

Create a Reinforcing System

A second set of DAs should be designed by senior managers and aimed at supporting the newly developed work systems in order to create a flexible but reinforcing organizational system. We think addressing performance management practices, structural features, and the futuring process are three highly leveraged points with which to begin a coordinated SMO implementation.

One DA should focus on designing a new performance management system. Each of its components—goal setting, appraisal, and rewards—should be designed for flexibility and to support sustainable effectiveness. In particular, people need to be appraised and rewarded for sustainable behaviors. The new performance management system also should support the emerging work system changes. A system that encourages change, innovation, sustainable performance, and responsible behavior is required.

A second DA should examine the organization's structure. To consistently achieve the integrated goals of sustainable effectiveness, organizations need a design that has a maximum surface area, strong collaboration capabilities, flexible resource allocation systems, and transparent decision-making processes. Having a sense of the way work will be done to create economic value, nurture socially responsible behaviors, and operate in environmentally responsible ways is an important input to the organization structure process. The next step is to implement structural changes to focus attention and resources on the work.

Finally, even as the organization is designing and implementing changes to the work systems, structures, and performance management systems, there is an important process that can be addressed in a third DA. The Interface case supports the conclusion that one must be ready to adapt and adjust to multiple dimensions (not just ecological but also social and economic) and over multiple time horizons. This requires knowledge of emerging and likely future market demands (medium and long term) so that new and required capabilities can be identified and developed. Even at this early stage of the transformation, the organization must prepare for the next set of products or services and momentary advantages. An organization can never stop innovating, and dedicating a third DA to developing a strong future-focused process is an important step.

The heavy use of the DA intervention will have several key benefits. First, it speaks loudly about the way the SMO will operate in the future. DAs are inclusive and transparent, and share leadership. Second, it teaches organization members new skills and knowledge that will serve them well with respect to multistakeholder decision making. Third, it helps the organization build an innovation capability. Finally, it will help the organization implement change quickly because key people know about the change and are committed to implementing it.

Accelerating the Transformation

The organization transformation process we have described is complex and has many moving parts. If done well, it will contribute to the formation of a new identity. It warrants an appropriately sophisticated leadership and change management infrastructure, including program management offices (PMOs), work teams with dedicated facilitation, and coaching. This transformation infrastructure is needed to provide a coordination capability and a center for controlling costs and allocating change resources to their highest and best use.

More important than any of these structures is a deliberate approach to accelerating the change through learning. Many of the elements of this approach have been built into our descriptions of the change process, but it is worth making these points concrete and explicit. Our research at the Center for Effective Organizations supports a two-pronged approach to change acceleration that involves pivotal organizational practices and key leadership behaviors.[7]

Change Acceleration Practices

Organizations can accelerate the change process by using four complementary practices. First, organization change is accelerated when the members of an organization share a common understanding of the meaning of change. This is facilitated by models, language, frameworks, and practices that help people talk about and discuss the relevance of the change to their work. Organizations implementing sustainability strategies often adopt models such as The Natural Step or CERES Principles to help people develop a shared language. However, these models are very focused on ecological outcomes and concerns and as a result need to be modified for sustainable management organizations.

Organization change is accelerated when the members of an organization share a common understanding of the meaning of change. This is facilitated by models, language, frameworks, and practices that help people talk about and discuss the relevance of the change to their work.

Second, shared meaning is facilitated by an overall and systemic view of information. People need to understand how an organization works. With respect to sustainable performance and change, this requires that an organization have clear measures and metrics for its operations as well as a way of thinking about how resources (including cash, labor, and other capital) are acquired and used.

Third, change is greatly accelerated when there is a formal process of learning from experience. In a change as complex as the transformation to sustainable management, an organization has many opportunities to try new processes and practices. To take advantage of these experiences, it must deliberately reflect on its behavior, understand when it is acting in change-friendly or sustainable ways, and use that knowledge in subsequent changes.

Finally, although much of the transformation to sustainable management must be driven from the top, it is important to realize and remember that senior executives cannot control all of the changes that need to be made. Each of the DAs for strategy and organization will identify features that define the values and characteristics of the organization. Those features have to be implemented at a local level. An excellent way to accelerate change is to give the local organizational units—business units, functions, country organizations—the opportunity to implement the changes in ways that make sense to them and are within the boundaries of the design.

Leadership Behaviors That Accelerate Change

Organizations that are able to accelerate the change process use four key leadership behaviors. First, one of the key and stable findings across dozens of studies is the importance of consistently communicating a visioning message that focuses the organization on the transformation. The key word is *consistently*. Creating and discussing the organization's future design configuration is a leadership behavior that helps to meet this need. During a transformation of this magnitude, it is imperative that leaders throughout the organization maintain the message and their commitment to agility and sustainable effectiveness.

Second, in periods of change, when anxiety is elevated, people need to know that everyone in the organization is committed to the new organization and what it stands for. An important and related leadership behavior is the christening of initiatives and the allocation of resources to key transformation tasks. Change is accelerated when organization members see important and scarce resources being devoted to transformation tasks. Effective leaders get ahead of the curve in terms of "giving permission" rather than waiting for people to "ask forgiveness."

The third leadership behavior that contributes to accelerated change is communication that helps people make sense of change. By "connecting the dots"—showing people how certain accomplishments, results, milestones, and other activities are working together to achieve the transformation—leaders help organization members understand that change can happen and is happening.

Finally, leaders need to play a major role in setting the context for the new employment relationship. Sending clear signals in conversations with people about the values and behaviors that will be supported in the new organization—and those values and behaviors that will not be supported—is an important contributor to accelerated change.

Conclusion

We have laid out the key issues and activities associated with becoming a sustainable management organization. By focusing on a set of dilemmas, organizations can provide a compelling logic and rationale for pursuing sustainable effectiveness. Clarifying that the transformation is about forming a new identity and using large-group interventions as a change vehicle can help accelerate the change because it symbolizes the new way of operating. Achieving sustainable effectiveness is a long and rewarding journey. We believe that by following the change process we have described, organizations can take their first or next step toward achieving it.

Notes

Chapter One

1. M. Piore and C. Sabel, *The Second Industrial Divide* (New York: Basic Books, 1984).
2. D. McGregor, *The Human Side of Enterprise* (New York: McGraw-Hill, 1960).
3. M. Beer, *High Commitment, High Performance: How to Build a Resilient Organization for Sustained Advantage* (San Francisco: Jossey-Bass, 2009).
4. J. Elkington, "Towards the Sustainable Corporation: Win-Win-Win Business Strategies for Sustainable Development, *California Management Review,* 1994, *36*(2), 90–100.
5. C. Argyris, *Personality and Organization* (New York: Harper & Row, 1957).
   J. Birkinshaw, *Reinventing Management: Smarter Choices for Getting Work Done* (San Francisco: Jossey-Bass, 2010).
   B. K. Googins, P. H. Mirvis, and S. A. Rochlin, *Beyond Good Company: Next Generation Corporate Citizenship* (New York: Palgrave Macmillan, 2007).
   G. Hamel, *The Future of Management* (Boston: Harvard Business Press, 2007).
   R. M. Kanter, *Supercorp: How Vanguard Companies Create Innovation, Profits, Growth and Social Good* (New York: Crown Business, 2009).
   D. Seidman, *How: Why How We Do Anything Means Everything . . . in Business (and in Life)* (Hoboken, NJ: John Wiley, 2007).
6. Beer, *High Commitment, High Performance.*
   E. E. Lawler, *High-Involvement Management* (San Francisco: Jossey-Bass, 1986).
7. T. Friedman, *The World Is Flat* (New York: Farrar, Straus and Giroux, 2005).

8. G. Brundtland (Ed.), *Our Common Future: The World Commission on Environment and Development* (Oxford: Oxford University Press, 1987).
9. J. O'Toole and E. Lawler, *The New American Workplace* (New York: Palgrave-Macmillan, 2006).
10. Core Writing Team, R. Pachauri, and A. Reisinger (Eds.), *Contribution of Working Groups I, II, and III to the Fourth Assessment Report of the Intergovernmental Panel on Climate Change* (Geneva: IPCC, 2007).

Chapter Two

1. R. D'Aveni, *Hypercompetition: Managing the Dynamics of Strategic Maneuvering* (New York: Free Press, 1994).
2. M. Hatch and S. Majken, "The Dynamics of Organizational Identity," *Human Relations*, 2002, *55*(8), 989–1018.
   Seidman, *How*.
3. M. Beer, *High Commitment, High Performance* (San Francisco: Jossey-Bass, 2009).
4. J. W. Boudreau and P. M. Ramstad, *Beyond HR: The New Science of Human Capital* (Cambridge: Harvard Business School Press, 2007).
5. E. E. Lawler, *Talent: Making People Your Competitive Advantage* (San Francisco: Jossey-Bass, 2008).
6. E. E. Lawler and C. W. Worley, *Built to Change* (San Francisco: Jossey-Bass, 2006).

Chapter Three

1. G. Carroll and M. Hannan, *Organizations in Industry: Strategy, Structure and Selection* (New York: Oxford University Press, 1995).
   D. Hambrick and J. Fredrickson, "Are You Sure You Have a Strategy?" *Academy of Management Executive*, 2001, *15*(4), 48–59.
   E. E. Lawler and C. W. Worley, *Built to Change* (San Francisco: Jossey-Bass, 2006).
   We have also found Mary Jo Hatch's work on identity particularly insightful. For a good overview of her work, consult M. Hatch and S. Majken, "The Dynamics of Organizational Identity," *Human Relations*, 2002, *55*(8), 989–1018.
2. Arthur W. Page Society, *Building Trust: Leading CEOs Speak Out: How They Create It, Strengthen It, and Sustain It* (New York: Arthur W. Page Society, 2004).
3. Kenneth I. Chenault, commencement address, retrieved November 4, 2010 from http://www.youtube.com/watch?v=Misqgyf5rPQ.
4. A. de Geus, *The Living Company* (London: Nicholas Brealey, 1999).
5. B. Nattrass and M. Altomare, *The Natural Step for Business* (Gabriola Island, British Columbia: New Society Publishers, 1999).

6. P. Hawken, A. Lovins, and L. Lovins, *Natural Capitalism: Creating the Next Industrial Revolution* (Boston: Little, Brown, 1999).

Chapter Four

1. D. J. Simons and C. F. Chabris, "Gorillas in Our Midst: Sustained Inattentional Blindness for Dynamic Events," *Perception,* 1999, *28*(9), 1059–1074.
2. Nokia Corp., "Sustainability Performance," retrieved November 4, 2010, from http://www.sustainability-index.com/djsi_pdf/Bios10/Nokia_10.pdf.
3. H. Chesbrough, *Open Business Models: How to Thrive in the New Innovation Landscape* (Boston: Harvard Business School Press, 2006).

   H. Chesbrough, *Open Innovation: The New Imperative for Creating and Profiting from Technology* (Boston: Harvard Business School Press, 2003).
4. Much of the material on Nokia can be found on their website at http://www.nokia.com. For more on Nokia's Open Studio, see the *BusinessWeek* article at http://www.businessweek.com/globalbiz/blog/europeinsight/archives/2008/04/nokia_and_desig.html.
5. The value creation–value capture matrix was adapted from H. Chesbrough and M. Appleyard, "Open Innovation and Strategy," *California Management Review,* 2007, *50*(1), 57–76.
6. N. Karmali, "Aravind Eye Care's Vision for India," *Forbes Asia Magazine,* March 15, 2010; retrieved May 26, 2010, from http://www.forbes.com/global/2010/0315/companies-india-madurai-blindness-nam-familys-vision.html.
7. T. Welbourne, "Extreme Strategizing," *Leader to Leader,* 2009, *52,* 42–48.

Chapter Five

1. J. Gillespie and D. Zweig, *Money for Nothing: How the Failure of Corporate Boards Is Ruining American Business and Costing Us Trillions* (New York: Simon & Schuster, 2010).

   K. A. Merchant and K. Pick, *Blind Spots, Biases, and Other Pathologies in the Boardroom* (New York: Business Expert Press, 2010).
2. J. A. Conger (Ed.), *Boardroom Realities: Building Leaders Across Your Board* (San Francisco: Jossey-Bass, 2009).
3. S. Finkelstein, "What Your Board Needs to Know: Early Warning Signs That Provide Insight to What Is Really Going on in Companies," in J. A. Conger (Ed.), *Boardroom Realities: Building Leaders Across Your Board,* 365–400 (San Francisco: Jossey-Bass, 2009).

4. J. W. Lorsch and E. MacIver, *Pawns or Potentates: The Reality of America's Corporate Boards* (Boston: Harvard Business School Press, 1989).

5. Merchant and Pick, *Blind Spots, Biases, and Other Pathologies in the Boardroom.*

6. J. A. Conger, E. E. Lawler, and D. L. Finegold, *Corporate Boards: New Strategies for Adding Value at the Top* (San Francisco: Jossey-Bass, 2001).

7. Conger, *Boardroom Realities.*

8. J. W. Lorsch, "Leadership: The Key to Effective Boards," in J. A. Conger (Ed.), *Boardroom Realities: Building Leaders Across Your Board,* 25–50 (San Francisco: Jossey-Bass, 2009).

9. J. A. Conger and E. E. Lawler, "Why Your Board Needs a Non-Executive Chair," in J. A. Conger (Ed.), *Boardroom Realities: Building Leaders Across Your Board,* 51–68 (San Francisco: Jossey-Bass, 2009).

10. E. E. Lawler, "Boards as Overseers of Human Capital," *Boards & Directors,* 2009, *22*(3), 56–59.

11. Conger and Lawler, "Why Your Board Needs a Non-Executive Chair."

Chapter Six

1. Data on the Cisco organization were gathered from a number of published sources as well as a round of interviews with executives.
   P. Burrows, "Cisco's Comeback," *Business Week,* November 24, 2003, 116.
   R. Gulati, *Cisco Business Councils: Unifying a Functional Enterprise with an Internal Governance System,* Harvard Business School case 5-409-062, 2009.
   R. Gulati, "The World According to Chambers," *Economist,* 2009, *392*(8646), 59–62.
   R. Gulati, "Cisco CEO John Chamber's Big Management Experiment," *Wall Street Journal,* August 5, 2009.
   HBR Interview, "Cisco Sees the Future—John Chambers Interview," *Harvard Business Review,* November 2008.
   B. Worthen, "Seeking Growth, Cisco Reroutes Decisions," *Wall Street Journal,* August 6, 2009, B1.

2. J. Galbraith, *Competing with Flexible Lateral Structures* (2nd ed.) (Reading, MA: Addison-Wesley, 1993).

3. For a good overview of organization design, see J. Galbraith, *Designing Organizations* (San Francisco: Jossey-Bass, 2001).

4. The idea of a maximum surface area was first introduced in our book *Built to Change* in 2006. E. E. Lawler and C. G. Worley, *Built to Change: How to Achieve Sustained Organizational Effectiveness* (San Francisco: Jossey-Bass, 2006).

5. J. Hope and R. Fraser, *Beyond Budgeting: How Managers Can Break Free from the Annual Performance Trap* (Boston: Harvard Business School Press, 2003).

6. M. Lubatkin, Z. Simsek, Y. Ling, and J. Veiga, "Ambidexterity and Performance in Small-to-Medium-Sized Firms: The Pivotal Role of Top Management Team Behavioral Integration," *Journal of Management,* 2006, *32,* 646–672.

   C. A. O'Reilly III and M. L. Tushman, "The Ambidextrous Organization," *Harvard Business Review,* 2004, *82*(4), 74–81.

   M. L. Tushman and C. A. O'Reilly III, "Ambidextrous Organizations: Managing Evolutionary and Revolutionary Change," *California Management Review,* 1996, *38,* 8–30.

7. The case on Harris Corporation's BCD division was constructed from interviews with Jeff Shuman and Kimberly Ratcliffe.

8. C. K. Prahalad, *Fortune at the Bottom of the Pyramid* (Philadelphia: Wharton School Publishing, 2004).

9. P. Hawken, A. Lovins, and L. Lovins, *Natural Capitalism* (Washington, DC: Earthscan Ltd., 1999).

10. M. Van Alstyne, "The State of Network Organizations: A Survey in Three Frameworks," *Journal of Organizational Computing,* 1997, 7(3), 83–151.

    S. Borgatti and P. Foster, "The Network Paradigm in Organizational Research: A Review and Typology," *Journal of Management,* 2003, *29*(6), 991–1013.

    D. Watts, *Six Degrees* (New York: W. W. Norton, 2003).

11. A. Deutschman, "The Fabric of Creativity," *Fast Company,* 2004, retrieved August 17, 2010, from http://www.fastcompany.com/magazine/89/open_gore.html.

    M. Gladwell, *The Tipping Point* (New York: Little, Brown, 2002).

    The W. L. Gore website at http://www.gore.com.

    G. Hamel, *The Future of Management* (Boston: Harvard Business School Press, 2007).

    M. Kaplan, "You Have No Boss," *Fast Company,* 1997, retrieved August 17, 2010, from http://www.fastcompany.com/magazine/11/noboss.html.

12. Hamel, *The Future of Management.*

Chapter Seven

1. Stu Winby has been a colleague and collaborator with USC's Center for Effective Organizations for over twenty years. This chapter benefitted greatly from our conversations and interviews with him, and we gratefully acknowledge his contributions to our thinking.

2. C. Worley, S. Mohrman, and J. Nevitt, *Large-Group Interventions: An Empirical Study of Their Composition, Process, and Outcomes,* working paper, Center for Effective Organizations, University of Southern California.

3. Adapted from material presented in the following:
V. Reitman, "Toyota Motors Shows Its Mettle After Fire Destroys Parts Plant," *Wall Street Journal,* May 8, 1997, A-1.
D. Watts, *Six Degrees: The Science of a Connected Age* (New York: W. W. Norton, 2003).

4. J. R. Hackman and G. R. Oldham, *Work Redesign* (Reading, MA: Addison-Wesley, 1980).

5. A. Pomeroy, "The Future Is Now," *HRMagazine,* 2007, *52*(9), 46–51; and interviews with Capital One managers.

6. J. Schermerhorn, *Management,* 11th ed (New York: Wiley, 2010).

Chapter Eight

1. E. E. Lawler, *Rewarding Excellence: Pay Strategies for the New Economy* (San Francisco: Jossey-Bass, 2000).
E. E. Lawler, "Reward Practices and Performance Management System Effectiveness," *Organizational Dynamics,* 2003, *32*(4), 396–404.

2. T. Coens and M. Jenkins, "Abolishing Performance Appraisals: Why They Backfire and What to Do Instead," (San Francisco: Berrett-Koehler, 2002).
S. A. Culbert, *Get Rid of the Performance Review: How Companies Can Stop Intimidating, Start Managing—and Focus on What Really Matters* (New York: Business Plus, 2010).

3. Lawler, "Reward Practices and Performance Management System Effectiveness."
E. E. Lawler and M. McDermott, "Current Performance Management Practices," *WorldatWork Journal,* 2003, *12*(2), 49–60.

4. G. P. Latham, *Work Motivation: History, Theory, Research and Practice* (Thousand Oaks, CA: Sage, 2007).

5. Latham, *Work Motivation.*

6. E. E. Lawler, "The Folly of Forced Ranking," *Strategy + Business,* 2002, *28,* 28–32.

7. V. Vara, "Boss Talk (A Special Result): After GE: Intuit's Steve Bennett on Why Some General Electric Alumni Succeed—and Some Don't," *Wall Street Journal,* April 16, 2007, R3.

8. E. E. Lawler, *Talent: Making People Your Competitive Advantage* (San Francisco: Jossey-Bass, 2008).

9. A. Kohn, *Punished by Rewards: The Trouble with Gold Stars, Incentive Plans, A's, Praise, and Other Bribes* (Boston: Houghton Mifflin, 1993). H. H. Meyer, E. Kay, and J.R.P. French, "Split Roles in Performance Appraisal," *Harvard Business Review*, 1965, *43*, 123–129.

10. Lawler, *Rewarding Excellence*.

11. Lawler, "Reward Practices and Performance Management System Effectiveness."

Chapter Nine

1. G. Hofstede, *Culture's Consequences* (Thousand Oaks, CA: Sage, 2001).

2. D. H. Pink, *Drive: The Surprising Truth About What Motivates Us* (New York: Riverhead Books, 2009).

3. E. E. Lawler, *Rewarding Excellence: Pay Strategies for the New Economy* (San Francisco: Jossey-Bass, 2000).

4. T. Erickson, *Plugged In: The Generation Y Guide to Thriving at Work* (Cambridge, MA: Harvard Business School Press, 2008).

5. E. E. Lawler, *Motivation in Work Organizations* (San Francisco: Jossey-Bass, 1994).

6. G. P. Latham, *Work Motivation: History, Theory, Research and Practice* (Thousand Oaks, CA: Sage, 2007).

7. J. R. Hackman and G. R. Oldham, "Development of the Job Diagnostic Survey," *Journal of Applied Psychology*, 1975, *60*, 159–170.

8. E. E. Lawler, *Talent: Making People Your Competitive Advantage* (San Francisco: Jossey-Bass, 2008).

9. J. R. Hackman and G. R. Oldham, *Work Redesign* (Reading, MA: Addison-Wesley, 1980).

10. J. R. Hackman and E. E. Lawler, "Employee Reactions to Job Characteristics," *Journal of Applied Psychology*, 1971, *55*, 259–286.

11. Lawler, *Rewarding Excellence*.

12. Lawler, *Rewarding Excellence*.

13. J. W. Boudreau and P. M. Ramstad, *Beyond HR: The New Science of Human Capital* (Cambridge, MA: Harvard Business School Press, 2007).

14. S. M. Cantrell and D. Smith, *Workforce of One: Revolutionizing Talent Management Through Customization* (Boston: Harvard Business Press, 2010).
E. E. Lawler and D. Finegold, "Individualizing the Organization: Past, Present, and Future," *Organizational Dynamics*, 2000, *29*(1), 1–15.
E. E. Lawler, "For a More Effective Organization—Match the Job to the Man," *Organizational Dynamics*, 1974, *3*(1), 19–29.

15. Lawler, *Rewarding Excellence*.

Chapter Ten

1. E. E. Lawler, *High-Involvement Management* (San Francisco: Jossey-Bass, 1986).
   E. E. Lawler, *From the Ground Up: Six Principles for Creating the New Logic Corporation* (San Francisco: Jossey-Bass, 1996).
2. P. Capelli, *Talent on Demand* (Boston: Harvard Business Press, 2008).
   E. E. Lawler and C. G. Worley, *Built to Change: How to Achieve Sustained Organizational Effectiveness* (San Francisco: Jossey-Bass, 2006).
   E. E. Lawler, *Talent: Making People Your Competitive Advantage* (San Francisco: Jossey-Bass, 2008).
3. J. W. Boudreau and P. M. Ramstad, *Beyond HR: The New Science of Human Capital* (Boston: Harvard Business School Press, 2007).
4. Boudreau and Ramstad, *Beyond HR*.
   J. W. Boudreau, *Retooling HR: Using Proven Business Tools to Make Better Decisions About Talent* (Boston: Harvard Business School Press, 2010).
5. S. R. Barley and G. Kunda, "Itinerant Professionals: Technical Contractors in a Knowledge Economy," in E. E. Lawler and J. O'Toole (Eds.), *America at Work: Choices and Challenges*, 173–191 (New York: Palgrave Macmillan, 2006).
6. S. M. Cantrell and D. Smith, *Workforce of One: Revolutionizing Talent Management Through Customization* (Boston: Harvard Business School Press, 2010).
7. Lawler and Worley, *Built to Change*.
8. J. P. Wanous, *Organizational Entry* (Reading, MA: Addison-Wesley, 1980).
9. S. A. Mohrman and E. E. Lawler, *Doing Research That Is Useful for Theory and Practice* (San Francisco: Berrett-Koehler, 2011).
10. E. E. Lawler and J. W. Boudreau, *Achieving Excellence in Human Resources Management: An Assessment of Human Resource Functions* (Palo Alto, CA: Stanford University Press, 2009).
11. Lawler and Boudreau, *Achieving Excellence in Human Resources Management*.

Chapter Eleven

1. W. Bennis and B. Nanus, *Leaders: The Strategies for Taking Charge* (New York: Harper & Row, 1985).
2. J. Lynn Lunsford, "Boss Talk: Piloting Boeing's New Course; CEO Jim McNerney Reshapes Aerospace Giant After Scandal; Tying Executive Pay to Ethics," *Wall Street Journal* (Eastern edition), June 13, 2006, B1.

3. E. E. Lawler, *From the Ground Up: Six Principles for Creating the New Logic Corporation* (San Francisco: Jossey-Bass, 1996).
4. H. Mintzberg, *29 Days of Managing*, 2009, retrieved August 18, 2010, from http://www.pearsoned.co.uk/highereducation/resources/mintzbergmanaging.
5. McKinsey Quarterly, "McKinsey Conversations with Global Leaders: Paul Polman of Unilever," October 2009, available at http://www.mckinseyquarterly.com/Strategy/Strategic_Thinking/McKinsey_conversations_with_global_leaders_Paul_Polman_of_Unilever_2456.
6. S. J. Palmisano, P. Hemp, and T. A. Stewart, "Leading Change When Business Is Good: An Interview with Samuel J. Palmisano," *Harvard Business Review,* December 2004.
7. General Electric Company, *Go Big: 2005 Annual Report,* n.p.
8. P. Gumbel, "Chrysler's Sergio Marchionne: The Turnaround Artista," *Time,* June 18, 2009, available at http://www.time.com/time/magazine/article/0,9171,1905416,00.html.
9. Jeff Immelt, "Reviewing American Leadership," speech to the United States Military Academy at West Point, December 9, 2009, available at http://files.gereports.com/wp-content/uploads/2009/12/90304-2-JRI-Speech-Reprint1-557.qxd_8.5x11.pdf.
10. M. Beer, *High Commitment, High Performance* (San Francisco: Jossey-Bass, 2009).
   W. Bennis, D. Goleman, J. O'Toole, and P. W. Biederman, *Transparency; How Leaders Create a Culture of Candor* (San Francisco: Jossey-Bass, 2008).
11. J. O'Toole and D. Mayer (Eds.), *Good Business: Exercising Effective and Ethical Leadership* (New York: Routledge, 2010).
12. J. A. Conger and B. Benjamin, *Building Leaders: How Successful Companies Develop the Next Generation* (San Francisco: Jossey-Bass, 1999).
   M. McCall, M. Lombardo, and A. Morrison, *The Lessons of Experience: How Successful Executives Develop on the Job* (Lexington, MA: Lexington, 1988).

Chapter Twelve

1. P. Hawkin, *The Ecology of Commerce* (New York: HarperBusiness, 1994).
2. S. Mohrman and T. Cummings, *Self-Designing Organizations* (Reading, MA: Addison-Wesley, 1990).
3. J. Collins, *Good to Great* (New York: HarperBusiness, 2001).
4. A. Hoffman, "Climate Change as a Cultural and Behavioral Issue: Addressing Barriers and Implementing Solutions," *Organizational Dynamics,* 2010, *39*(4).

5. B. Posner, "One CEO's Trip from Dismissive to Convinced," *Sloan Management Review,* 2009, *51*(1), 46–51. Quote appears on 48.
6. P. Docherty, M. Kira, and A. B. Shani, "Organizational Development for Social Sustainability in Work Systems," in R. Woodman, R. Passmore, and A. B. Shani (Eds.), *Research in Organizational Change and Development: Vol. 17* (pp. 77–144) (Amsterdam: JAI Press, 2009).
7. R. Tenkasi, S. Mohrman, and A. Mohrman, "Accelerated Learning During Organizational Transition," in S. Mohrman, J. Galbraith, E. Lawler, and Associates (Eds.), *Tomorrow's Organization,* 330–361 (San Francisco: Jossey-Bass, 1998).

Acknowledgments

For encouraging both of us to think about sustainability, we want to acknowledge our colleague, Susan Albers Mohrman, for her passion, zeal, enthusiasm, and dedication to useful research. We also want to thank Ursula Barlow, Arienne McCracken, and Lois Rosby from the CEO staff for their help with our writing activities. They never complained about helping with yet another draft!

Chris would like everyone to know how lucky he is to have his family—Debbie, Sarah, Hannah, Sam, and Max, the wonder dog—and to thank them for supporting him in all the things he does.

Ed would like to thank his wife, Patty, for her decades of support as he has wandered from book to book and for bringing her puppy, Fanny, into his life.

As he did with our earlier book, *Built to Change*, David Creelman made a big contribution to the writing of this book. He contributed examples, insights, editing, and ideas. Thank you, David.

The Authors

Edward E. Lawler III is Distinguished Professor of Business and Director of the Center for Effective Organizations in the Marshall School of Business at the University of Southern California. He joined USC in 1978 and, during 1979, founded and became director of the University's Center for Effective Organizations. He has consulted with over one hundred organizations on employee involvement, organizational change, and compensation, and has been honored as a top contributor to the fields of organizational development, organizational behavior, corporate governance, and human resource management. The author of over 350 articles and forty-three books, Lawler has placed articles in leading academic journals as well as in *Fortune, Harvard Business Review,* and leading newspapers, including *USA Today* and the *Financial Times.* His most recent books include *Rewarding Excellence* (2000); *Corporate Boards: New Strategies for Adding Value at the Top* (2001); *Organizing for High Performance* (2001); *Treat People Right* (2003); *Human Resources Business Process Outsourcing* (2004); *Built to Change* (2006); *America at Work* (2006); *The New American Workplace* (2006); *Talent: Making People Your Competitive Advantage* (2008); and *Achieving Excellence in HR Management: An Assessment of Human Resource Organizations* (2009). For more information, visit http://www.edwardlawler.com and http://ceo.usc.edu.

    Christopher G. Worley is a Senior Research Scientist at the Center for Effective Organizations at the Marshall School of Business at the University of Southern California. He is a recognized leader in the field of organization development. Prior to coming to CEO, he was director of the Master of Science in Organization Development (MSOD) program at Pepperdine University and remains a primary faculty member in that program. He was awarded the Luckman

317

Distinguished Teaching Fellowship in 1997. Prior to Pepperdine University, Dr. Worley taught undergraduate and graduate courses at the University of San Diego, University of Southern California, and Colorado State University. Dr. Worley has co-authored over thirty books, chapters, and articles. His most recent books, co-authored with Ed Lawler, are *Management Reset* and *Built to Change*. He also authored *Integrated Strategic Change: How OD Builds Competitive Advantage* in Addison-Wesley's OD Series, and with Tom Cummings has co-authored five editions of *Organization Development and Change*, the leading textbook on organization development. His articles on strategic change and strategic organization design have appeared in the *Journal of Applied Behavioral Science, Journal of Organization Behavior, Sloan Management Review,* and *Organizational Dynamics.*

David Creelman is CEO of Creelman Research, providing writing, research, and commentary on human capital management. He works with a variety of academics, think tanks, consultancies, and HR vendors in Canada, the United States, Japan, Europe, and the Middle East.

He has a particular research interest in what sort of attention investors and boards give to human capital intangibles or, more to the point, what attention they should be giving to the subject.

In 1999, as chief of content and research, David helped launch HR.com. Working for Deb McGrath, he was the first employee and is proud to see that HR.com remains a successful "dot.com" to this day. Prior to this venture David did management consulting in Malaysia and Canada, primarily with the Hay Group. He also taught a course in rewards for the executive MBA program at the University of Malaya.

Before his consulting days David worked in the United Kingdom in the finance industry and before that in Toronto in the oil industry. He has a Bachelor of Science degree in Chemistry and Biochemistry and an MBA degree from the University of Western Ontario. His science background is complemented by a keen interest in the humanities.

Index